PROBLEMS OF THEORETICAL PHONOLOGY

JANUA LINGUARUM

STUDIA MEMORIAE
NICOLAI VAN WIJK DEDICATA

edenda curat

C. H. VAN SCHOONEVELD

INDIANA UNIVERSITY

SERIES MINOR

41

1968
MOUTON
THE HAGUE · PARIS

PROBLEMS OF THEORETICAL PHONOLOGY

by

S. K. ŠAUMJAN

1968
MOUTON
THE HAGUE · PARIS

Original title: Problemy teoretičeskoj fonologii
published by
Izdatel'stvo Akademii Nauk SSSR (Moscow, 1962)

Translation by Anthony L. Vaňek, revised by the author and P. M. Waszink

LIBRARY OF CONGRESS CATALOG CARD NUMBER: 68-17897

Printed in The Netherlands by Mouton & Co., Printers, The Hague

PREFACE

The task of the following investigation is a systematic explication of basic phonological concepts within the framework of theoretical phonology. The results of this explication lead the author to the formulation of a new phonological theory which he terms the two-level theory of phonology.

In order to clarify the general character of this investigation we deem it necessary to say a few words about the subject of theoretical phonology, and about the essence of concept explication.

Theoretical phonology is quite often confused with general phonology; in effect, they are two different disciplines. The subject matter of theoretical phonology is the nature of phonological reality which is studied with the help of the corresponding conceptual apparatus, while general phonology is concerned with the typology of concrete phonological systems. The different subject matters use correspondingly different methods. The basic tool of theoretical phonology is the hypothetico-deductive method which enables us to disclose the immanent laws of phonological reality. In so far as general phonology is concerned, its basic method is generalization, which reduces concrete phonological systems to a limited number of basic types of phonological systems. Since it discloses the immanent laws of phonological reality, theoretical phonology functions as a foundation of general phonology, as well as a foundation of phonemic descriptions of concrete languages, upon which general phonology rests.

Theoretical phonology should be differentiated not only from general phonology, but also from descriptive phonology which has been developed in the United States. In contrast to theoretical phonology whose main task is the elaboration of a conceptual apparatus that characterizes the nature of phonological reality, descriptive phonology concentrates on the actual technique of phonological description. Descriptive phonology is not a theory of phonological reality but a methodical discipline which systematizes technical methods used in the description of concrete phonological systems. Not without reason does the well-known work of K. L. Pike, devoted to a systematic presentation of descriptive phonology, contain the characteristic subtitle: "A Technique for Reducing Languages to Writing". [1] It is obvious that descriptive phonology is closely connected with theoretical phonology since the technique of description of concrete phonological systems must rely on a conceptual apparatus which characterizes the nature of phonological reality; this fact should, however, in no way outweigh the basic difference between theoretical phonology and descriptive phonology in regard to the problems which fall within their respective domains.

All that has been said so far about descriptive phonology applies in an equal degree to descriptive linguistics in general, descriptive phonology being a component part of this system. As E. Coseriu rightly writes, "American structuralism is only a *method of investigation*, just as European structuralism constitutes an a priori conception (hypothesis) which determines the method of investigation."[2]

In contemporary logic of science the term "explication" describes a critical analysis of established concepts, as a result of which the established concepts undergo a split-up and are replaced by new, more exact and revealing concepts. R. Carnap calls such new concepts explicata, the old concepts explicanda.[3]

The importance of a critical analysis of concepts can hardly be overstressed. The history of science demonstrates that a critical analysis of basic, apparently selfevident, concepts has more than once led to fruitful progress in any field of knowledge, and at

[1] K. L. Pike, *Phonemics: a Technique for Reducing Languages to Writing* (Ann Arbor, 1947).

[2] E. Coseriu, *Forma y sustancia en los sonidos del languaje* (Montevideo 1954), p. 146.

[3] Cf. R. Carnap, *Einführung in die symbolische Logik* (Vienna, 1954), p. 2.

times has effected even the rise of totally new fields of knowledge. In this connection it is interesting to introduce the words of A. Einstein and L. Infeld regarding the origin of differential calculus: "The rigorous analysis of such words as 'very near', 'very short' is far from simple. Indeed, it was this analysis which led Newton and Leibnitz to the discovery of differential calculus."[4]

In subjecting the system of basic concepts of contemporary theoretical phonology to a critical analysis we will regard each of these concepts as an explicandum for which we will seek the corresponding explicatum.

Since the time of the publication of N. S. Trubetzkoy's *Grundzüge der Phonologie* there appeared a number of excellent works which elaborated and deepened the knowledge of basic phonological concepts. In the light of what has already been accomplished in the sphere of investigation of basic phonological concepts it would seem that within this sphere no important new results of fundamental methodological significance are likely to be attained. It is our belief, however, that in contemporary phonology there exists the possibility of disclosing, by means of the application of the hypothetico-deductive method, inherent antinomies whose overcoming should lead to a radical review of the established phonological concepts and to a formulation of a new phonological theory which differentiates strictly the two abstraction levels: (1) the level of phonological observation and (2) the level of phonological constructs. It is this kind of phonological theory that we propose to investigate.

The two-level theory of phonology, as formulated by us, is in full agreement with the concept of the structure of science in contemporary logic of science. Contemporary logic of science differentiates in every field of science two main abstraction levels: (1) the level of observation and (2) the level of constructs. Constructs are concepts which deal with unobservable entities that are postulated for the explanation of facts given through direct observation. Constructs relate to the level of observation through the so called rules of correspondence.

[4] A. Einstein and L. Infeld, *Evolution of Physics* (Cambridge, 1947), p. 25.

The theory of constructs corresponds to the "black box" theory in cybernetics. The term "black box" describes a system inaccessible to direct observation which has to be discerned through an analysis of directly observed data.

When we say that the two-level theory of phonology is in full accord with the conception of the structure of science as formulated by the logic of science and by cybernetics, we do not intend to profess that we have arrived at the two-level theory of phonology so to say "from above", i.e. through an a priori subjection of phonology to the logical scheme of the structure of science. It is necessary to stress most emphatically that the demarcation of the two abstraction levels in phonology can, and should, be clarified from the standpoint of the contemporary logic of science, but that its existence is contingent not on logic but rather on linguistic data. The demarcation is not dictated by general logical considerations but by the necessity to overcome fundamental linguistic antinomies, fundamental linguistic difficulties which arise during the analysis of linguistic data.

Our investigation attempts to disclose the basic methodological consequences that arise from a consistent demarcation of the two abstraction levels in phonology. This consistent demarcation has inevitably resulted in a clash with the entire system of accepted views in the domain of crucial problems which are encountered in theoretical phonology. Criticism of these views should not be taken in any way as an attempt to minimize the historical merits of the prominent linguists who have erected the edifice of contemporary theoretical phonology. On the contrary, we want to stress the great debt we owe to a number of authors whose views we have not wholly been able to share.

Adhering strictly to the proposed program of investigation we have considered it expedient to present what is customarily called the history of the problem, only as far as it was necessary for to a complete explanation of the basic principles of the two level theory of phonology. A systematic critical review of the work done by our predecessors lies beyond the limits of this program of investigation and could constitute a separate publication.

It is selfevident that we do not profess to present a conclusive solution to the investigated problems. We will be satisfied if our work will focus attention on the essential ideas which have been bypassed by theoretical phonology until the present time and which might evoke discussion that will further the progress of this science.

Since theoretical phonology constitutes a part of theoretical structural linguistics we hope that this work will make clear the need to extend the demarcation of the two abstraction levels to the entire field of structural linguistics. The demarcation of the two levels of abstraction extended to other spheres of theoretical structural linguistics should yield results which will parallel in their essence those attained in theoretical phonology.

Presenting his book to the judgment of his readers the author would like to express his gratitude to all who have aided him in his work.

The manuscript of the book was discussed by the author at various times with the corresponding member of the Academy of Sciences of the USSR R. I. Avanesov, O. S. Akhmanova, Ju. D. Apresjan, K. I. Babickij, A. B. Dolgopol'skij, N. I. Žinkin, V. V. Ivanov, I. I. Revzin, P. A. Soboleva, and V. N. Toporov. The preparation of the manuscript for publication and the proof reading was aided by I. V. Al'tman and Z. M. Gerasimova. The indices were prepared by I. V. Al'tman. To all the participants the author extends his deepest thanks.

The author thanks the management of Institute of the Russian Language of the Academy of Sciences of the USSR for creating of propitious working conditions, and the Editorial-publishing Council and the Publishing house of the Academy of Sciences of the USSR for the publication of the book within an extremely short period of time.

I had help with the revision of the English translation of my book from Mr. P. M. Waszink. The proofs of the English translation were also read by Professor C. H. van Schooneveld, Professor D. Abercrombie and J. Miller, who made useful suggestions. I am most grateful to all of them.

TABLE OF CONTENTS

I

THE TWO-LEVEL THEORY OF PHONOLOGY

1. THE PROBLEM

"Often it is only after immense intellectual effort, which may have continued over centuries, that humanity at last succeeds in achieving knowledge of a concept in its pure form, in stripping off the irrelevant accretions which veil it from the eyes of the mind."[1] These words of the great German logician apply to phonology no less than to any other branch of knowledge. More than a half century has passed since the concept of phoneme has been introduced into the science of language, but even at the present time the problem of the definition of the phoneme cannot be considered to have been fully resolved.

Wherein lies the essence of the problem which concerns the definition of the phoneme?

Every definition of a concept is arbitrary, since every scholar can define any concept in a way which is to his advantage. From this point of view the definitions of concepts are not concerned with the essence of the matter, and arguments concerning such definitions can hold only terminological interest. Although the definitions of concepts are in themselves arbitrary, we can regard any definition of a concept as a statement which possesses an explanatory function. In this case the definition of the concept answers the question: "What is the nature of x?": for example, "what is the nature of light?", "what is the nature of meaning?", "what is the nature of truth?", etc. Since the definitions of concepts which are based

[1] G. Frege, *Die Grundlagen der Arithmetik* (Breslau, 1884), p. vii.

on the formula "what is the nature of x?" require on the part of the scholar a deep penetration into some sphere of reality, and are at the same time formulated not in the form of single, isolated statements but in the form of an entire system of statements, such definitions can be called theories as well; for example, the "definition of light" can be called the "theory of light", the "definition of meaning", the "theory of meaning", the "definition of truth", the "theory of truth". The aforementioned words of G. Frege do not apply to all definitions of concepts, but only to definitions of concepts based on the formula "what is the nature of x?" because this type of concept definition in particular presents fundamental problems which are rooted in the process of human knowledge. The history of science shows that the strife for progress in any field of knowledge often takes on the form of a conflict of pro and con definitions of concepts based on the formula "what is the nature of x?"[2] Conflicts of this type have existed in connection with the concept of the phoneme over the past fifty years. The question is, then, which definition of the phoneme based on the formula "what is the nature of x?", i.e. which phoneme theory, reflects most closely the linguistic reality.

If we disregard the psychological theory of the phoneme (J. Baudouin de Courtenay, E. Sapir) and the physical theory of the phoneme (L. V. Ščerba, D. Jones), which are now only of a historical significance then at the present developmental stage of phonology there exist in principle the following three theories: (1) the relational-physical theory of the phoneme, (2) the theory of micro- and macrophonemes, and (3) the glossematic theory of the phoneme.

As will be pointed out, every one of these theories harbors some fundamental difficulty which can be overcome only through the formulation of a new theory that distinguishes two levels of abstraction: the level of observation and the level of constructs. It

[2] Cf. I. M. Copi, *Introduction to Logic* (New York, 1954), pp. 99-100; C. G. Hempel, "Fundamentals of Concept Formation in Empirical Sciences", *International Encyclopedia of Unified Science*, II, 7 (Chicago, 1952), pp. 6-14.

is precisely this kind of theory of the phoneme that we will attempt to formulate in the following chapter.

Since the concept of phoneme relates closely to the concept of distinctive feature and cannot be conceived apart from the latter, we will undertake alongside the analysis of the concept of phoneme also the analysis of the concept of distinctive feature. Thus, our task will be the formulation of a two-level theory of phonology.

Since the formulation of the two-level theory of phonology stemmed from the need to overcome the fundamental difficulties inherent in the relational-physical theory of the phoneme, we consider it expedient to adopt the following procedure: first of all we will sum up the relational-physical theory of the phoneme and point out the occurrence of the inherent fundamental difficulties; subsequently, we will single out the analogical difficulties related to the concept of distinctive feature: furthermore, we will show the direct link between the necessity to surmount these difficulties and the formulation of the two-level theory of phonology; finally, we will compare the two-level theory of phonology with the theory of micro- and macrophonemes and the glossematic theory of the phoneme, and show why these theories are not satisfactory.

2. RELATIONAL-PHYSICAL THEORY OF THE PHONEME

The relational-physical theory of the phoneme occupies a dominant position in contemporary phonology. This theory was set forth by various authors, but it was most fully and clearly presented by N. S. Trubeckoj.[3] Since we are interested only in the basic essentials of the relational-physical theory of the phoneme, it is not necessary to digress into the individual phrasing of this theory by various authors and to delve into the enumeration of the merits and demerits of these phrasings. It is sufficient to concentrate on the relational-physical theory as it has been presented by N. S. Trubec-

[3] N. S. Troubetzkoy [N. S. Trubeckoj], *Principes de phonologie* (Paris, 1949), pp. 33-46.

koj, since references to other authors cannot make any significant contributions to the criticism of the basic essence of this theory.

N. S. Trubeckoj derives the concept of phoneme from an analysis of the concept of sound opposition and of the concept of phonological unit.

Sound oppositions are either phonological or non-phonological; phonological oppositions are, moreover, subdivided into direct and indirect oppositions.

N. S. Trubeckoj defines the distinction between phonological and non-phonological oppositions as follows: "Sound oppositions which have the ability to differentiate between the meanings of two words of a given language are called *phonological* (or *phonologically distinctive*, or also *distinctive*) oppositions. On the other hand, such sound oppositions which lack this characteristic, can be termed *phonologically irrelevant* or *non-distinctive*."[4] For instance, in German the vowel opposition *o/i* constitutes a distinctive opposition, while the opposition of the labial *r* and the uvular *r* should be regarded as a non-distinctive opposition since in German there exist no two words which differ mutually only in regard to this sound opposition.

The difference between the direct distinctive opposition and the indirect distinctive opposition becomes clear in connection with the subdivision of sounds into mutually interchangeable and mutually exclusive. The former are those sounds which are encountered in a given language in identical sound environment; the latter are sounds whose presence in identical sound environment is precluded. Mutually interchangeable sounds can form both distinctive and non-distinctive oppositions. For instance, the sounds *r* and *l* in German are mutually interchangeable and constitute a distinctive opposition (e.g. *Rand* 'edge' — *Land* 'country'). By the same token, while in Japanese the sounds *r* and *l* are likewise mutually interchangeable, they do not constitute a distinctive opposition. On the other hand the mutually exclusive sounds do not, as a rule, form distinctive oppositions; however, in the case when such

[4] N. S. Trubeckoj, *op. cit.*, p. 33.

mutually exclusive sounds lack even a single common characteristic which would distinguish them from all other sounds within the same system, they do constitute distinctive oppositions. For instance, in German the so called *ich*-Laut and *ach*-Laut do not form a distinctive opposition because they are mutually exclusive sounds whose common features (voicelessness, dorsality, fricativeness) are not repeated in any other sound of the German sound system.

The mutually exclusive sounds *h* and *ŋ* (*h* is encountered only preceding vowels with the exception of the unstressed *e* and *i*; *ŋ*, on the other hand, only preceding the unstressed vowels *e* and *i*, preceding consonants and in terminal position) form a distinctive opposition, since their sole common characteristic — consonancy — is not limited to them and, consequently, does not warrant their isolation from the remaining consonants of the German language. Specifically those distinctive oppositions which comprise mutually exclusive sounds are called by N. S. Trubeckoj indirect distinctive oppositions as opposed to those distinctive oppositions which comprise mutually interchangeable sounds and which he calls direct distinctive oppositions.

Hence, sound oppositions are subdivided into distinctive (direct and indirect) and non-distinctive. From the concept of distinctive opposition N. S. Trubeckoj turns to the concept of phonological unit.

Every member of a distinctive opposition is a phonological unit.

From this definition it follows that phonological units can vary in size; they can be larger and smaller. For example, in the case of the word pairs *stol* 'table' and *krug* 'circle' in Russian, *Mann* 'man' and *Weib* 'woman' in German, the counterposed words differ in their entirety; in the case of word pairs *ručka* 'pen' and *ranec* 'satched' in Russian or *tausend* 'thousand' and *Tischler* 'carpenter' in German, the difference is limited to the sound segments, which follow the (identical) initial consonants.

The method of the subdivision of the large phonological units into smaller ones is examined by N. S. Trubeckoj on the example of the phonological units [mɛ:] and [by:] in the German words *Mähne* 'mane' and *Bühne* 'stage'. From the oppositions of *Mähne* 'mane' — *gähne* 'I yawn' and *Mähne* 'mane' — *mahne* 'I admonish' it follows that the phonological unit [mɛ:] splits into smaller phonological units [m] and [ɛ:], and from the oppositions *Bühne* 'stage' — *Sühne* 'confession' and *Bühne* 'stage' — *Bohne* 'bean' it follows that the phonological unit [by:] splits into [b] and [y:]. The resulting phonological units [m], [b], [ɛ:], [y:] cannot be further subdivided into smaller consecutive phonological units.

From the concept of phonological unit N. S. Trubeckoj turns to the concept of phoneme: "Phonological units which from the standpoint of the given language cannot be subdivided into smaller consecutive phonological units are called *phonemes*".[5]

Having defined the concept of phoneme, N. S. Trubeckoj focuses his attention on the analysis of the relationship between phoneme and sound event.

One and the same sound can be simultaneously a member of a distinctive and a non-distinctive opposition. For instance, in German the opposition of *ach*-Laut — *ich*-Laut is a non-distinctive opposition, while the opposition of each of these sounds to the sound *k* constitutes distinctive opposition (e.g. *stechen* 'to stab' — *stecken* 'to push in'; *roch* 'smelled' — *Rock* 'coat'). In accordance with the simultaneous presence of one and the same sound in both distinctive and non-distinctive oppositions, its acoustic-articulatory features split up into phonologically relevant and irrelevant. Thus, in the above example in German the aperture between the blade of the tongue and the palate is phonologically relevant while the localization of this aperture in regard to the area of the palate is phonologically irrelevant. Phonological oppositions between sounds are contingent only on the phonologically relevant features of the sounds. Since every phoneme must constitute, without fail, a member of a distinctive opposition, the phoneme cannot be identified with a concrete sound, but only with a bundle of phonologically relevant features of such a sound. In this connection N. S. Trubeckoj supplements the aforementioned definition of the phoneme with the following definition: "*Phoneme — is the sum*

[5] N. S. Trubeckoj, *op. cit.*, p. 37.

total of the phonologically relevant features of a given sound formation".[6]

Every phoneme is realized through various sounds. For instance, in German the phoneme *g* is realized through a number of concrete sounds which include: (1) labial velar *g* (e.g. *gut* 'good', *Glut* 'glow'), (2) narrow-labial palatal *g* (e.g. *Güte* 'quality', *Glück* 'luck'), (3) non-labial velar *g* (e.g. *ganz* 'whole', *Wage* 'scales', *tragen* 'carry'), (4) non-labial strongly palatal *g* (e.g. *Gift* 'poison', *Gier* 'greed'), (5) moderately palatal *g* (e.g. *gelb* 'yellow', *liege* 'I lie') etc. Referring to this type of phenomenon N. S. Trubeckoj introduces the term "phonetic variant". "All these different sounds," he writes, "which realize one and the same phoneme, are designated as *variants* (or phonetic variants) of the corresponding phoneme".[7]

Such is the system of definitions which form the basis of N. S. Trubeckoj's theory of the phoneme. We call this theory relational-physical, since the concept of distinctive opposition on which N. S. Trubeckoj bases his definitions of the concepts of phonological unit and phoneme expresses also a variation of sound opposition, i.e. in other words, a definite relationship between sounds and hence the phoneme, being a member of a phonological opposition, possesses simultaneously both a relational and physical nature.

As has been previously mentioned, various authors present the relational-physical theory of the phoneme in different ways, but the essence of the theory remains unchanged. The likelihood of various phrasings of the relational-physical theory of the phoneme was pointed out already by Trubeckoj who stressed, however, that all such phrasings would lead to one and the same end. In this context he wrote: "The phoneme can only ... be defined on the basis of its function in the language. Whether we define it as the minimal distinctive unit (L. Bloomfield) or as the sound sign of the word envelope (K. Bühler), the outcome is the same: namely, that any

[6] N. S. Trubeckoj, *op. cit.*, p. 40. N. S. Trubeckoj refers here to the analogous definition of the phoneme which was given earlier by R. Jakobson in the Czech encyclopedia *Ottův slovník naučný*, Dodatky, II, 1, p. 608, under the heading "fonéma".

[7] N. S. Trubeckoj, *op. cit.*, p. 41.

language assumes the presence of "phonologically" distinctive oppositions and that the phoneme is considered to be member of such an opposition which cannot be further subdivided into smaller distinctive "phonological" units. This clear and unequivocal definition cannot be altered in any way. Any modification of this definition would only lead to a complication which can be avoided."[8]

The relational-physical theory is so clear and unequivocal that it seems unshakable; it firmly dominates modern phonology. However, as we propose to show in the following sections of this chapter, one encounters in it certain basic difficulties whose surmounting requires the formulation of a basically new theory of the phoneme.

3. PHONEME AND THE PROBLEM OF MEANING IN PHONOLOGY

First of all it is necessary to point out the fundamental difficulties inherent in the relational-physical theory of the phoneme which relate to the question: should one introduce semantic criteria into the definition of the phoneme?

This question has to be brought up at the very beginning since it concerns every theory of the phoneme. Having clarified this question we will be able to introduce into the aforementioned definition of phoneme of N. S. Trubeckoj the necessary clarity which will enable us to concentrate in subsequent discussion fully on the essence of the relational-physical theory of the phoneme and on our two-level theory of the phoneme, as contrasted with the former, without being distracted in consideration of the essentials.

We will commence with the term "distinctive". In the aforementioned definition of phonological opposition N. S. Trubeckoj uses the expression "distinctive opposition" synonymously with the expression "phonological opposition". The equalization of the terms "distinctive" and "phonological" can lead to the erroneous idea of a direct connection between the sounds of a language and the meaning of words. In reality we speak, however, not about a

[8] N. S. Trubeckoj, *op. cit.*, p. 44.

distinctive, but only about a differential function of the sounds of a language, referring to the function of differentiation of the signifiants (i.e. the sound envelopes) of the words. In so far as the signifiés of the words, i.e. the meaning of words, is concerned, the sounds of a language possess no direct connection with the signifiants. Thus, in the words *lom* 'crow' — *tom* 'tome' the sounds /l/ and /t/ in themselves have no meaning and are not directly connected with the meanings of the given words, but merely signalize differentiation of the signifiants /lom/ — /tom/. In any linguistic unit the meaning is contained not in the separate speech sounds but rather in the entire sound complex which contains the signifiant of the given linguistic unit. For instance, in the word *lom* the meaning is not inherent in the separate speech sounds /l/, /o/, /m/, but in the entire sound complex /lom/, i.e. in the signifiant of that word. The signifiant /lom/, being the carrier of a definite meaning (or, in accord with the terminology adopted by us, signifié) represents in itself qualitatively another level in contrast to the sounds /l/, /o/, /m/, into which it can be separated. Although it is true that in the case of some linguistic units is the separate sounds and not the sound complexes that act as signifiants it does not necessarily follow that separate speech sounds in themselves can possess meaning. For example, the speech sound /i/ acts as the signifiant of the Russian word *i*. However, it would be erroneous to think on the basis of this case, that the speech sound /i/ in the Russian word *i* is in itself a carrier of meaning. The speech sound /i/ in the Russian word *i* does not possess any meaning in itself. The meaning is inherent in the signifiant /i/ which, although it coincides with the sound /i/, represents at the same time a qualitative phenomenon of another order than does the speech sound /i/ taken by itself.[9]

In respect to the above exposition it becomes necessary to define more precisely the aforementioned definition of phonological and non-phonological oppositions, as stated by N. S. Trubeckoj. This definition can be reformulated as follows: *phonological oppositions*

[9] Cf. S. K. Šaumjan, "Sistema glasnyx fonem sovremennogo pol'skogo literaturnogo jazyka", *Učenye zapiski Instituta slavjanovedenija*, III, 1951, p. 394.; O. S. Akhmanova, *Fonologija* (Moscow, 1954), p. 12.

— are those sound oppositions which can differentiate between the signifiants of two words of a given language. Non-phonological oppositions are those sound oppositions which do not possess this ability.

If we accept this more exact definition of the phonological and non-phonological oppositions, we must, consequently, deal with the following question: what criteria constitute the basis for considering the given signifiants as different signifiants?

At a first glance the answer to this question does not pose any difficulty. Let us take, for instance words which we have already used, *lom-tom*. Although the separate sounds of these words are not connected directly with their meaning, the signifiants /lom/ and /tom/ possess such a direct relationship. Therefore, in respect to the fact that /lom/ and /tom/ are different signifiants one can infer that these signifiants possess correspondingly different meanings. It is not necessary to embark upon an analysis of the meanings of the words *lom* and *tom*; it is sufficient to simply state that these meanings are not identical, but different. Thus, we arrive at the following answer to the above posed question: in order to define the different signifiants it is essential to establish that these signifiants possess correspondingly different meanings. Hence the conclusion is that phonology cannot evade semantic data. Although such semantic data are kept at a minimum, since one does not deal with a specific analysis of the meaning of words but with a simple statement about the identity or difference between meanings, it is still apparent that phonology cannot exclude semantic criteria, even if they are merely minimal.

If we examine the problem with greater thoroughness our conclusion about the necessary inclusion of semantic criteria into phonology encounters, however, a serious difficulty. Let us examine, for instance, the Russian lexical doublets *škaf* and *škap*, 'cupboard', *okolotok* and *okolodok*, 'neighborhood', *kalif* and *xalif*, 'caliph'.[10] Here we encounter the phonological oppositions /f/-/p/, /t/-/d/, and /k/ – /x/, whose purpose is to differentiate between corresponding signifiants which possess absolutely identical meanings. Hence, one

[10] Other examples of lexical doublets in Russian are given in: O. S. Akhmanova, *Očerki po obščej i russkoj leksikologii* (Moscow, 1957), p. 197.

can conclude that different signifiants do not necessarily correspond to different meanings and that the semantic criterion of differentiation between signifiants can lead to false conclusions. Indeed, if we proceed on the basis of semantic criteria, we are bound to consider the signifiants /škaf/ and /škap/ as identical in respect to the identity of the meanings of the words *škaf* and *škap*; such a conclusion would, however, contradict the above defined phonological opposition, according to which phonological oppositions are sound oppositions which can differentiate between different signifiants. Therefore, if we consider /škaf/ and /škap/ to be identical signifiants we have to admit with logical inevitability that in Russian the phonological opposition /f/ – /p/ does not differentiate between significations and, as a result, that /f/ and /p/ are not different phonemes of the Russian language.

In every language there exist lexical doublets; this fact in itself induces us to refute any reference to meaning and to look for non-semantic criteria as factors in the definition of the identity or difference of signifiants. Yet this does not constitute the main difficulty connected with the introduction of semantic criteria into phonology. The main difficulty arises in connection with the definition of the identity or difference of meanings. In this respect, we shall allow that in a given language there exist no lexical doublets and, consequently, we shall be free, in defining the identity or difference of signifiants, to refer to the identity or difference of the semantic meanings. However, at this point there arises the question of the exact definition of the identity or difference of meanings. If we want to remain on a strictly linguistic ground we have to admit that identity and difference of meaning can be defined only on the basis of the difference between signifiants. From the linguistic point of view the meanings of the words *lom* and *tom* differ not because "crow" and "volume" are different objects but because these meanings possess corresponding different signifiants /lom/ and /tom/. The meanings of the words *myt'* 'wash' and *stirat'* 'launder' differ in Russian not because washing and laundering are different actions, but because these meanings possess different corresponding signifiants /mit'/ and /st'irát'/. In English the meanings of "myt'" and "stirat'" do not differ from the linguistic point of view since in that language to both meanings corresponds one single signifiant in the English word *to wash*. In "Languages and Logic", Benjamin L. Whorf indicates that as far as English is concerned the sentences *I pull the branch aside* and *I have an extra toe on my foot* do not have anything in common in regard to their semantic contents. But if we take into consideration the Amerindian language Shawnee then almost all the semantic elements of both English sentences seem identical since in that language the given semantic elements possess corresponding identical signifiants.[11] Hence, it can be concluded that the identity or difference of meanings can be determined only on the basis of the identity or difference of signifiants. If this is true, then the criterion of the identity or difference of meanings and its relation to the definition of the identity or difference of signifiants brings us to a vicious circle; and exactly this circumstance harbors the main difficulty connected with the application of semantic criteria to phonology.

As a result of the above facts we arrive at the conclusion that phonology is, apparently, forced to eliminate semantic criteria in the consideration of the definition of the identity or difference of signifiants. By the same token it appears that it is advantageous to replace the semantic criteria with criteria of linguistic behaviour of the speakers. Linguistic behavior includes specific linguistic reaction of the speaker during the process of mastery and usage of both his native and of a foreign language. Linguistic behavior should be regarded as the so called protocol base, i.e. the sum of primary raw data which serve as material for theoretical construction. Within this scope fall observations and experiments dealing with the language of children and adults. The speaker whose language serves as an object of observation and experimentation is called an informant. The standard procedure for the definition of identities or differences of signifiants should be the presentation of various types of tests to the adult informant for whom the given language is native.[12]

[11] Cf. Benjamin L. Whorf, "Languages and Logic" (1941).

[12] Of works dealing with treat the non-semantic methods of analysis in

As long as we depend on the linguistic behavior of the speakers we can be accused of introducing into phonology a psychological criterion of knowledge which, like any other psychological criterion, should not be permitted to enter into the science of language. Such an accusation of psychologism cannot be, however, considered well grounded. Our approach to linguistic behavior is actually directly opposite to the approach to linguistic behaviour which is based on the psychological concept of the phoneme. For the linguist who adheres to the psychological concept of phoneme any reference to the linguistic behavior of the speakers constitutes a means to explain phonological data, while for us, on the contrary, the given linguistic behavior of the speakers constitutes initial data which we seek to explain through the use of phonological data. For the linguist who adheres to the psychological point of view the linguistic behavior data are primary, while for us, on the contrary, the linguistic behavior data consequences of inherent linguistic regularity which need to be disclosed through strict linguistic analysis.

In the case of protocol data which are subject to theoretical explanation we accept those identities or differences between the signifiant segments which can be fixed on the basis of the intuitive deposition of the informant. For the identification of such types of differences we introduce the term "contrast". Contrast is the difference between signifiant segments fixed on the basis of the deposition on the part of the informant.[13]

Referring to the concept of contrast we can regard Trubeckoj's definitions of the concepts of phonological opposition, phonological unit, and phoneme, as hypotheses whose function is to explain theoretically the protocol data requisite for the contrasting and non-

---

phonology the most noteworthy are C. F. Hockett, *A Manual of Phonology* (= *Indiana University Publications in Anthropology and Linguistics*, Memoir 1) (Baltimore, 1955); Z. S. Harris, *Methods in Structural Linguistics* (Chicago, 1951); M. Halle, "The Strategy of Phonemics", *Word*, X, 2-3 (1954); N. Chomsky, *Syntactic Structures* (The Hague, 1962).

[13] The meaning which we assign to the term "contrast" does not have anything in common with its use by several authors in connection with the labeling of syntagmatic relationship (cf. for instance A. Martinet, *Éléments de linguistique générale* (Paris, 1960), p. 33).

contrasting of the signifiant segments which are established on the basis of the intuitive deposition on the part of the informant.

The method of interpreting concept definitions as hypotheses or laws whose function is to explain theoretically the protocol data is employed widely in all abstract empirical sciences. Characterizing this method by the example of the definition of the concept of life in biology, C. Hempel writes: "[The given definition] would then have the character of an empirical law, and its validation would require reference to empirical evidence concerning the characteristics of living beings. In this case, the real definition represents what we shall call an *empirical analysis* of the property of being a living organism."[14]

The interpretation of the definitions of phonological opposition, phonological unit, and phoneme as hypotheses permits us to determine, through empirical analysis of the sound aspect of language, whether these hypotheses are justified and whether they disclose the essence of the examined linguistic phenomena.

4. THE HYPOTHETICO-DEDUCTIVE METHOD

We will regard the definitions of phonological opposition, phonological unit, and phoneme as hypotheses whose function is to explain theoretically the protocol data for the contrasting and non-contrasting of the signifiant segments which are established on the basis of the intuitive deposition on the part of the informant.

Such approach requires the adoption of a special method which is usually called the hypothetico-deductive method. This method which serves as the methodological pivot of physics and other abstract theoretical sciences, is described in detail in the modern literature of the logic of science.[15] We will dwell only on some of the

[14] C. G. Hempel, *op. cit.*, p. 8.

[15] A good description of the hypothetico-deductive method can be found, for example, in the following books: R. B. Braithwaite, *Scientific Explanation: A Study of the Function of Theory, Probability and Law in Science* (Cambridge, 1953); S. Toulmin, *The Philosophy of Science* (London, 1953).

essential aspects of this method which are of paramount importance with respect to our further discussion.

The hypothetico-deductive method consists of a cyclical procedure which commences with facts and concludes with facts; it comprizes four distinct phases:

(1) establishment of relevant data;

(2) advancement of the hypotheses for the explanation of the given data;

(3) deduction from the hypotheses, of the predicted facts which are beyond the limits of the facts for whose explanation were advanced the hypotheses;

(4) verification of the facts predicted by the hypotheses, and determination of the probability of the hypotheses.

The hypothetico-deductive method differs basically from the inductive method which is employed in such scientific disciplines as, for instance, descriptive botany or descriptive zoology. Let us examine the difference between both methods.

In contrast to the inductive method which in principle requires a simple accumulation of the greatest possible number of data the hypothetico-deductive method requires a strict selection of data, relative to their contribution to the resolution of the given theoretical problem. Let us see what the English logician, S. Toulmin, writes in this respect: "In natural history, accordingly, the sheer accumulation of observations can have a value which in physics it could never have. This is one of the things which the sophisticated scientist holds against natural history: it is 'mere bug-hunting' — a matter of collection, rather than insight.

Now there is something important in this way of putting the difference, which is reflected in the sorts of thing that could be accepted as observations in physics and natural history respectively. As one cannot start doing physics just anywhere, so also there are very definite limits to what will count in physics as an observation. Gilbert White was able to make valuable contributions to natural history by keeping a diary of the things he noticed as he went around the Hampshire countryside, for in natural history all facts about fauna are logically on a par. But, as Popper has pointed out, one could not hope to contribute to physics in this way. However full a note-book one kept of the phenomena one came across in the ordinary course of one's life, it would in all probability be of no value to physicists at all. In physics, it is no use even beginning to look at things until you know exactly what you are looking for: observation has to be strictly controlled by reference to some particular theoretical problem."[16]

Why does the collection of facts in the case of the inductive method lead to a simple accumulation of the greatest possible number of facts while the hypothetico-deductive method requires a strict selection of facts? The reason for this is the fact that the inductive method considers all facts to be equal in the logical sense while the hypothetico-deductive method recognizes a strict logical hierarchy of data. Simple accumulation of facts is necessary only in the case when all facts are considered to be equal in the logical sense. In connection with this Toulmin writes: "... one would hesitate to assert, say, that all ravens were black if one had seen only a half a dozen of the species, whereas to establish the form of a regularity in physics only a few careful observations are needed".[17]

The application of the hypothetico-deductive method does not lead to the discovery of new facts; rather it effects the reevaluation of already known facts in a new light. Pointing out this circumstance on the example of the analysis of light in physics, Toulmin writes that the transition from the everyday to the physicist's concept of light involves not so much "the discovery of new facts as the adoption of a new approach".[18]

Consequently it should be especially stressed that any success resulting from the adoption of the hypothetico-deductive method in empirical sciences is based on this opportunity to reevaluate the known facts in a new light. Let us see, for instance, what A. Einstein and L. Infeld write in their *Evolution of Physics*: "To raise new questions, new possibilities, to regard old problems from a new angle, requires creative imagination and marks real advance in

[16] S. Toulmin, *op. cit.*, pp. 53-54.
[17] S. Toulmin, *op. cit.*, p. 110.
[18] S. Toulmin, *op. cit.*, p. 64.

science. The principle of inertia, the law of conservation of energy were gained only by new and original thoughts about already well-known experiments and phenomena. Many instances of this kind will be found in the following pages of this book, where the importance of seeing known facts in a new light will be stressed and new theories described."[19]

The inductive method does not extend beyond the level of a classification of directly observed facts and phenomena while the hypothetico-deductive method permits the advancement of hypotheses on the basis of direct observation.

In order to deepen the interrelation among elements which are hidden from direct observation we use a special method of investigation which is usually called a mental experiment. A mental experiment is a deductive process which consists of the deduction of specific consequences from statements acknowledged to be true which, although not confirmedly empirical facts, appear to be fundamentally possible.

The mental experiment represents in itself an effective means of verifying the justifiability of the hypothesis which was developed for the explanation of a given group of facts. If the execution of the mental experiment contradicts other consequences derived from the developed hypothesis, the hypothesis is unfounded.

As we will see from further discussion, the mental experiment is of basic significance in the resolution of the basic problems of phonology.

5. ANTINOMY OF TRANSPOSITION

Having introduced the hypothetico-deductive method we will embark upon an analysis of the definitions of phonemic opposition, phonemic unit, and phoneme, regarding them as hypotheses for the explanation of protocol data. We will see that the consequences of these hypotheses will lead us unavoidably to antinomies.

[19] A. Einstein and L. Infeld, *op. cit.*, pp. 95-96.

After reevaluation, we have obtained the following system of definitions within the relational-physical theory of the phoneme:

(1) Phonological oppositions are those sound oppositions which can differentiate between the signifiants of two words of a given language. Non-distinctive oppositions are those sound oppositions which do not possess this ability.

(2) A phonological unit is any member of a phonological opposition.

(3) A phoneme is a phonological unit which from the standpoint of the given language cannot be further segmented into smaller consecutive phonological units.

This system of definitions must explain the peculiarity of the linguistic behavior of speakers, consisting in their intuitive restriction of the sound variety of language, and its limitation to a strictly defined number of invariants. In every language the number of concrete sounds is practically limitless but the speakers disregard many differences. For example, in the Russian words *tut*, 'here', *tom*, 'volume', *tam*, 'there', we find in the first word /t_1/ with a velar coloring, in the second word /t_2/ with a less pronounced velar coloring, and in the third word /t_3/ with a minimal velar coloring; the speakers, however, do not consider these differences essential and transform the sound variety into invariants.

The problem of the restriction of sound variety is a specific case of the general problem of variety restriction which occupies the central position in every science. The basic significance of this general problem is contained in the fact that any law of nature is in principle a restriction of variety. Let us see what W. E. Ashby writes in this connection: "Further, as every law of nature implies the existence of an invariant, it follows that *every law of nature is a constraint*. Thus, the Newtonian law says that, of the vectors of planetary positions and velocities which might occur, e.g. written on paper (the larger set), only a smaller set will actually occur in the heavens; and the law specifies what values the elements will have. From our point of view, what is important is that the law *excludes* many positions and velocities, predicting that they will never be found to occur. *Science looks for laws; it is therefore much con-*

cerned with looking for constraints." (italics in the last clause are ours — S. Š.)[20] The fundamental significance of the problem of variety restriction in language was pointed out in different terms by F. de Saussure. The following thesis of F. de Saussure constitutes the cornerstone of modern structural linguistics: "The linguistic mechanism is geared to differences and identities, the former being only the counterpart of the latter. Everywhere then, the problem of identities appears ...".[21]

The above system of definitions should be regarded as a system of hypotheses whose function is to explain the principle of the invariance of sounds in any language. In order to clarify more thoroughly this system of hypotheses which constitutes the cornerstone of modern phonology, we will compare it with an alternate hypothesis which had been developed at one time by E. Zwirner. According to his hypotheses phonological invariants represent nothing more than norms for the forming of sounds. According to this hypothesis phonemes can be distinguished in any concrete language through a statistical investigation of sound variations and a calculation of the average values of the separate sounds.[22] At a superficial glance this hypothesis seems attractive but in practice it is incapable of explaining why speakers of one language and speakers of another language are aware of the difference between their languages in respect to the corresponding sound differences. We will assume, for instance, that Russian speakers equalize the vowel ε in the word *cex* 'shop' and the vowel *e* in the word *cel'*, 'goal' into one phoneme since the formation of these vowels can be governed by a single norm. In regard to this one may ask why French speakers regard the vowels ε in the word *taie* [tε] 'pillowcase', and *e* in the word *thé* [te] 'tea', as different phonemes. The concept of the norm and the statistical method cannot contribute anything to the explanation of similar facts. If we accept the Saussurian contrast of langue and parole it is possible to assert that the concept of norm applies not to the level of langue but to the level of parole. Since the phoneme

[20] W. R. Ashby, *An Introduction to Cybernetics* (London, 1956), pp. 130-131.
[21] F. de Saussure, *Cours de linguistique générale* (Paris, 1962), p. 151.
[22] Cf. E. Zwirner and K. Zwirner, *Grundfragen der Phonometrie* (Berlin, 1936).

is related to the langue the concept of norm cannot suitably explain the method of reduction of sounds to phoneme. In so far as parole is concerned, the calculation of average significances of separate sounds for the definition of the norm of their formation is of basic importance. Starting from the concept of norm we arrive at the concept of sound type which is essential for the study of parole. Consequently, it should be strongly stressed that the concept of sound type has nothing in common with the concept of phoneme. Criticizing the application of the concept of norm to langue in the Saussurian sense, N. S. Trubeckoj justly pointed out: "Of course, the exact calculation of the average normal pronunciation of any sound in a definite position is certainly very desirable, and the application of the biological-statistic methods, as they were contrived by E. Zwirner, should be certainly greeted as a great step forward. But it is a mistake to think that thereby all the tasks of the science of language have been resolved. The phonological tasks are thereby not affected since language lies completely outside 'size and number'".[23]

Thus we arrive at the conclusion that if we consider the definition of the phoneme based on the relational-physical theory of the phoneme, and the definition of the phoneme as a norm of sound formation developed on the basis of statistical analysis, as two alterernative hypotheses, we should concentrate on the first hypothesis. However, as we will see below, a consistent application of the hypothetico-deductive method will lead us to the discovery of certain fundamental difficulties even in the first hypothesis, forcing us to renounce it as well and to develop in its place a new hypothesis.

We will focus our attention on the above introduced system of hypotheses:

(1) Phonological oppositions are those sound oppositions which can differentiate between the signifiants of two words of a given language. Non-phonological oppositions are those sound oppositions which do not possess this ability.

(2) A phonological unit is any member of a phonological opposition.

[23] N. S. Trubeckoj, *op. cit.*, p. 9.

(3) A phoneme is a phonological unit which from the standpoint of a given language cannot be further segmented into smaller consecutive phonological units.

From this system of hypotheses there evolve inevitably the two following statements:

Statement 1: Phonemes are elements whose function is to differentiate between signifiants.

Statement 2: Phonemes are acoustic elements.

Let us examine the conclusions which can be drawn from these statements.

If it is true that the function of phonemes is to differentiate between signifiants then it follows that there exists an inherent possibility of transposing the acoustic substance into other forms of physical substance — graphic, chromatic, tactile. Any system of distinctive features and phonemes can be presented not only as acoustic properties but as graphic, chromatic or tactile symbols as well.

In order to prove the existence of an inherent possibility of transposing acoustic substance into other forms of physical substance we will execute the following mental experiment. We will transpose phonemes into circles of identical dimension but different color, let us say in Russian the vowel *a* into a blue circle, the vowel *o* into a brown circle, the consonant *s* into a green circle, the consonant *n* into a red circle, and the consonant *m* into a yellow circle. The words *son* 'sleep', *nos* 'nose', *san* 'dignity', *som* 'sheat fish', *sam* 'self', *nas* 'us', *nam* 'to us', can then be represented as chains consisting of combinations of the different color circles, as is shown in the following table:

Words	*Circles*
son	green – brown – red
nos	red – brown – green
san	green – blue – red
som	green – brown – yellow
sam	green – blue – yellow
nas	red – blue – green

Hence, from statement 1 it follows that phonemes can be transposed from acoustic substance into other forms of physical substance.

Let us turn now to statement 2. If it is true that phonemes are acoustic elements it follows that they cannot be transposed into other forms of physical substance since in that case they would cease to be themselves, i.e. acoustic elements.

Here we encounter an evident antimony: both statement 1 and statement 2 are valid in respect to modern phonology; yet statement 1 implies that phonemes can be transposed into other forms of physical substance while statement 2 implies a direct contradiction, i.e. that phonemes cannot be transposed into other forms of physical substance.

This contradiction constitutes an inherent theoretical difficulty which maybe termed the antinomy of transposition.

The antinomy of transposition may evoke to the following objection. According to statements 1 and 2, a phoneme is, by definition, at the same time an element whose function is to differentiate between signifiants, and an acoustic element. Although this definition is adequate for natural languages the property of the differentiation between signifiants and the property of being an acoustic element are equally essential for the phoneme, and the bond between these two properties must be considered indispensable within the limits of natural languages. Therefore, we are not justified in deducing from statement 1 that the phoneme can be transposed from acoustic substance into other forms of physical substance.

This objection can be answered as follows. If we regard definitions as convenient compressed descriptions of directly observed data then, since in natural languages phonemes are always sound elements, we are not justified in separating the functional properties of the phoneme from its acoustic properties. But the subject matter of science comprises not only empirical data, not only what *is* but also that which in principle *can be*; hence, if a mental experiment arrives at what can be, we disclose the essence of the studied subject. We regard the definition of the phoneme not as a convenient compressed description of an empirical fact but as a hypothesis, i.e. speaking in the words of H. Reichenbach, as a nomological statement. "In a general nomological statement the range of the all-operator is given by all possible argument-objects and is not restricted to all real argument-objects."[24] The antinomy of transposition develops specifically at the level of the interpretation of the relational-physical definition of the phoneme as a nomological statement. At this level there exists the question whether the communicative function of natural language would be violated if its acoustic substance were transposed into other forms of physical substance. Obviously, no such violation would occur. We are, therefore, justified in transposing phonemes, by means of mental experiment, from acoustic substances into other forms of physical substance. The results of the mental experiment contradict, however, the interpretation of the acoustic properties as the essential properties of the phoneme, since if the acoustic properties are essential properties of the phoneme the phoneme cannot be transposed from an acoustical substance into any other form of physical substance.

Before seeking a way to surmount the antinomy of transposition we will turn our attention to two fundamental theoretical difficulties which are related to the system of hypotheses under consideration.

6. ANTINOMY OF THE PARADIGMATIC IDENTIFICATION OF PHONEMES

Every language differentiates two basic types of relations: paradigmatic and syntagmatic. Paradigmatic relations are relations of linguistic units which undergo a mutual alternation within the same position. Syntagmatic relations are linear relations between linguistic units within the speech flow.

L. Hjelmslev defines paradigmatic relations as the relations of "either-or", i.e. disjunctive in the logical sense, and syntagmatic relations as relations of "both and", i.e. conjunctive in the logical

[24] H. Reichenbach, *Elements of Symbolic Logic* (New York, 1947), p. 401.

sense.[25] This characterization of both types of relations requires a more precise definition. If in logical operations the terms "true" and "false" are replaced by the terms "existent" and "non-existent", then the syntagmatic relations can be regarded as analogous to the logical operation of conjunction. This is evident from the truth table of the logical operation of conjunction:

p	q	p ∧ q
T	T	T
T	F	F
F	T	F
F	F	F

If we interpret the symbols of the components of the compound logical statement, *p* and *q*, as linguistic units, the connective ∧ as a syntagmatic relations, the "true" symbol *T* and the "false" symbol *F* as the terms "existent" and "non-existent", then we see from the above table that a syntagmatic relations between two linguistic units is possible only in the case when both of them coexist in the speech flow. As far as the paradigmatic relations are concerned, they cannot be viewed as analogies of the logical operation of disjuction. In modern formal logic the truth table for the operation of disjunction has the following appearance:

[25] L. Hjelmslev, *Prolegomena to a Theory of Language*, trans. by F. J. Whitfield (= *Indiana University Publications in Anthropology and Linguistics*, Memoir 7) (Baltimore, 1953).

p	q	$p \vee q$
T	T	T
T	F	T
F	T	T
F	F	F

This truth table indicates that the connective "or", represented by the symbol $\vee$ has in modern formal logic a so-called inclusive meaning, i.e. the statements connected by this connective are not necessarily mutually exclusive, but can coexist side by side.[26] The specific character of the paradigmatic relations, however, precludes the coexistence of the members of the relations; they must be mutually exclusive. Therefore the paradigmatic relation-can be analogous only to the so called exclusive disjunction which is in the works of some mathematicians designated by the symbol $\underline{\vee}$.[27] Exclusive disjunction can be represented by means of the following truth table:

p	q	$p \underline{\vee} q$
T	T	F
T	F	T
F	T	T
F	F	F

[26] The difference between the exclusive "or" and the inclusive "or" can be seen from the following examples: (1) exclusive "or": "In the evening I will return home or I will stay overnight with a friend"; (2) inclusive "or": "At this meeting you can meet mathematicians or linguists whom you have met before."

[27] Cf. J. G. Kemeny, J. L. Snell, G. L. Thompson, *Introduction to Finite Mathematics* (Englewood Cliffs (N.J.), 1956), pp. 5-6.

This truth table shows that there exists a full analogy between paradigmatic relations and the operation of exclusive disjunction.

In accordance with the differentiation between paradigmatic and syntagmatic relations we may distinguish between the paradigmatic and syntagmatic language axes. Any linguistic unit can be considered to be a vector which possesses two components: paradigmatic and syntagmatic.[28]

Having explained the exact meaning of the paradigmatic and syntagmatic relations within a language we can now clearly formulate the problems of the paradigmatic identification of phonemes. Identification of phonemes on a paradigmatic axis consists of the isolation of phonemes in various positions in the speech flow, and determination of their mutual identity or difference.

Since the solution of the given problem is based on the relational-physical theory of the phoneme we must return to the two statements introduced in the preceeding section.

Statement 1. Phonemes are elements whose function is to differentiate between signifiants.

Statement 2. Phonemes are acoustic elements.

In regard to our problem it is possible to infer on the basis of statement 1, in a purely deductive way, the following consequence: *If in the speech flow in position* P_1 *we encounter a class of phonemes* K_1, *then in position* P_2 *there exists a class of phonemes* K_2, *which corresponds to the class of phonemes* K_1 *in such a way that the phonemes which differ in respect to their phonation are in identical correspondence while those phonemes which are identical in respect to their phonation are in non-identical correspondence.* Thus, if one assigns to position P_1 the class of phonemes A, B, C and to position P_2 the class of phonemes B, C, D, the correspondence between the phonemes of the two classes can be represented in the following table:

[28] Generally a vector is defined as "a compound object having a definite number of components" (W. R. Ashby, *op. cit.*, p. 31); cf. J. G. Kemeny, J. L. Snell, G. L. Thompson, *op. cit.*, pp. 178-179.

$$\begin{array}{cc} P_1 & P_2 \\ A \leftrightarrow & B \\ B \leftrightarrow & C \\ C \leftrightarrow & D \end{array}$$

It is certainly possible to construct the following mental experiment: we will assume that position P_1 can be assigned the phonemes *q*, *k*, *k*', while position P_2 can be assigned the corresponding phonemes *k*, *k*', *ħ*; this case can be represented in a tabular manner thus:

$$\begin{array}{cc} P_1 & P_2 \\ q \leftrightarrow & k \\ k \leftrightarrow & k' \\ k' \leftrightarrow & \hbar \end{array}$$

Since the given consequence derives necessarily from statement 1 it is easy to accept the following reasoning: if, in accordance to statement 1, phonemes possess a function of differentiation between signifiants, then phonemes which occur in different positions can be altered in respect to their phonation as sharply as desired as long as they do not get confused with one another.

Thus the correctness of the examined consequence of statement 1 is not subject to any doubt. But if the correctness of this consequence is acknowledged there arise the following contradictions: on the one hand, in accordance with statement 2, phonemes are acoustic elements while, on the other hand, it appears that phonemes which differ in their phonation, i.e. different acoustic elements, can be identical and, conversely, phonemes which are equal in their phonation, i.e. equal acoustic elements, can be non-identical; hence in our example those phonemes which differ in phonation (*q* and *k*, *k* and *k*', *k* and *ħ*) are identical while those phonemes which are equal in their phonation (*k* in position P_1 and *k* in position P_2, *k*' in position P_1 and *k*' in position P_2) are non-identical.

Hence, there exists an irreconcilable contradiction between the acoustic nature of phonemes and their function of differentors between signifiants. This contradiction is called the antinomy of the paradigmatic identification of phonemes.

7. ANTINOMY OF THE SYNTAGMATIC IDENTIFICATION OF PHONEMES

Recent research in the field of spectrographic analysis of speech sounds has proven that there exists a natural segmentation of the speech flow into sounds.[29] Physical segmentation of the speech flow into separate sounds, i.e. into separate acoustic segments, is an objectively ascertained phonetic fact. The phonologist's task is, taking this phonetic fact as a starting point, to discover the chain of phonemes on the syntagmatic axis of the language.

Since the resolution of the problem of the syntagmatic identification of phonemes is contingent on the relational-physical theory of the phoneme we must once again return to the two aforementioned statements.

We will begin with statement 1. If, in accordance with this statement, phonemes are elements whose function is to differentiate between signifiants then, as far as our problem is concerned, it follows that any group of acoustic segments viewed along the syntagmatic axis can be regarded as a single phoneme. Let us take, for instance, the chain of acoustic segments:

$$A\ B\ C\ D$$

Theoretically, this chain of acoustic segments can be regarded as one phoneme, two phonemes, three phonemes or four phonemes.

(1) One phoneme: $[ABCD]$

(2) Two phonemes: $[A]+[BCD]$
or: $[AB]+[CD]$
or: $[ABC]+[D]$

(3) Three phonemes: $[A]+[B]+[CD]$
or: $[AB]+[C]+[D]$
or: $[A]+[BC]+[D]$

(4) Four phonemes: $[\mathrm{A}]+[B]+[C]+[D]$

[29] Cf. G. Fant, *Acoustic Theory of Speech Production* (The Hague, 1960), pp. 21-24.

It is in effect possible to construct the following mental experiment: we will assume that in a given language we never encounter the acoustic segment *s* but do encounter the following acoustic segments:

ta	da	pa	ba	ka	ga
to	do	po	bo	ko	go
tu	du	pu	bu	ku	gu
te	de	pe	be	ke	ge
ti	di	pi	bi	ki	gi
at	ad	ap	ab	ak	ag
ot	od	op	ob	ok	og
ut	ud	up	ub	uk	ug
et	ed	ep	eb	ek	eg
it	id	ip	ib	ik	ig

We assume that the given acoustic segments represent bi-phonemic chains. Consequently, while leaving the phonological system of the given language unchanged, we can precede the acoustic segment *t* with the acoustic segment *s*. In this case the resulting acoustic segment *st* which becomes a component of the chains *sta*, *sto*, *stu*, *ste*, *sti*, *ast*, *ost*, *ust*, *est*, *ist*, should be regarded as one phoneme since now both its components *s* and *t* are mutually inseparable: *s* is predicted by the sound *t* and, conversely, *t* is predicted by the sound *s*. Thus we establish a functional identity between the segments *t* and *st* in the situation in question.

Let us turn now to statement 2. If, in accordance with this

statement, phonemes are acoustic elements, then it follows that a single phoneme cannot be composed of different acoustic elements. Since the acoustic segments *s* and *t* are inherently different acoustic elements they cannot be component parts of a single phoneme. In this regard it becomes interesting to introduce the following statement of N. S. Trubeckoj: "... such a sound complex as *st* cannot, under any circumstances, be regarded as mono-phonemic since one encounters here a progressive 'growth' of an occlusion which then 'subsides' (i.e. breaks up). Similarly, the combination *ks* cannot be regarded as mono-phonemic since it presupposes two different articulatory movements".[30]

Since the relational-physical theory of the phoneme regards phonemes as acoustic elements, N. S. Trubeckoj was right to reject the contingency that such groups of acoustic segments as *st* and *ks* should be regarded as mono-phonemic. By the same token, while he regarded similar groups necessarily as bi-phonemic, N. S. Trubeckoj was not aware of other consequences which arose from the system of definitions which he had developed. Had he been aware of these consequences he would have been compelled to acknowledge the following.

From the acknowledgement of the functional role of the phoneme (statement 1) it follows that different acoustic segments in general, and the acoustic segments $s+t$ or $k+s$ in particular, *can* constitute a single phoneme.

From the acknowledgement of the acoustic nature of the phoneme (statement 2) it follows that different acoustic segments in general, and the acoustic segments $s+t$ or $k+s$ in particular, *can never* constitute a single phoneme.

This is the third fundamental contradiction inherent in the relational-physical theory of the phoneme. This contradiction will be termed the antinomy of the syntagmatic identification of phonemes.

8. ELEMENTARY CONCEPTS AND CONSTRUCTS

A consistent application of the hypothetico-deductive method to the

[30] N. S. Trubeckoj, *op. cit.*, p. 60.

analysis of the relational-physical theory of the phoneme has disclosed three fundamental theoretical difficulties: the antinomy of transposition, the antinomy of the paradigmatic identification of phonemes and the antinomy of the syntagmatic identification of phonemes.

In order to find a way to eliminate these difficulties we must now venture outside the framework of linguistics and investigate the general logical problem of the formation of concepts in abstract theoretical sciences.

The problem of the formation of concepts is contingent upon the application of the hypothetico-deductive method.

The entire sphere of the application of the hypothetico-deductive method can be subdivided into two main areas.

The hypothetico-deductive method can be, and is, applied to the reconstruction of data connected with the history of mankind, history of the fauna and flora, history of the Earth, history of the solar system and history of the Universe. The hypothetico-deductive method is applied also to the reconstruction of such kinds of data in social sciences, biology, geology, astronomy, and other sciences. All historical data which have been established on the basis of the hypothetico-deductive method are characterized by the fact that although at the present time we are unable to observe these facts we can, in principle, observe them. They could be observed by us in principle if we would transport ourselves into the corresponding era. Let us take, for instance, the theory about the origin of the population of Polynesia. The resemblance between the ancient legends of the native population of South America and the ancient legends of the Polynesians induced a group of ethnographers to postulate that the forebears of the present day Polynesians were the inhabitants of South America. An alternative hypothesis presented the supposition that the islands of the Pacific Ocean had been populated from the shores of South-east Asia. The first hypothesis seemed rather unlikely since it was difficult to believe that primitive people could have, more than a thousand years ago, undertaken an open sea journey lasting several months. The hypothesis concerned with the population of Polynesia from the shores of South America surmised that in a given geographical area it is indeed possible to realize a several months' sea voyage using primitive means, such as a large sea raft. In order to test this deductive conclusion developed from the foregoing hypothesis a group of ethnographers completed such a voyage at the risk of their lives; their voyage lasted more than three months. According to the ancient legend of the native population of Polynesia the great god Kon-Tiki navigated their forebears to the islands from a far-off land on exactly such a raft. Thus, the hypothesis stood the test.[31] If the given hypothesis is to be acknowledged as true then in a distant past a lengthy sea voyage of primitive people on rafts took place from the shores of South America to Polynesia. Although this voyage is outside of the possibility of modern man's observation, in principle it appears to be an object which is within the reach of observation.

The matter stands differently when the hypothetico-deductive method is applied to abstract theoretical sciences. In this area one distinguishes two main abstraction levels: (1) the level of observation and (2) the level of constructs. The level of observation encompasses the so called elementary concepts (for example: "white", "heavy", "elastic", "heavier", "more elastic"), i.e. concepts denoting observable qualities and relations. Constructs are concepts of unobservable objects of science (for example: "electron" or "proton" in physics, "gene" in biology). Constructs are related to elementary concepts by means of the so called correspondence rules.[32] The application of the hypothetico-deductive method in abstract theoretical sciences is contingent upon the introduction of the hypotheses which deal with unobservable objects, i.e. hypotheses which operate with constructs.

[31] Cf. T. Heyerdahl, *Kon-Tiki, across the Pacific by Raft*, trans. by F. H. Lyon (Chicago, 1950).

[32] Cf. for instance R. Carnap, "The Methodological Character of Theoretical Concepts", *Minnesota Studies in the Philosophy of Science*, I (Minneapolis, 1956); C. G. Hempel, "The Theoretician's Dilemma: a Study in the Logic of Theory Construction", *Minnesota Studies in the Philosophy of Science*, II (Minneapolis, 1958); A. Pap, *Semantics and Necessary Truth* (New Haven, 1958).

The demarcation of the two abstraction levels in the modern logic of science has been lately corroborated by the results achieved in cybernetics. In cybernetics to the demarcation of the two abstractions levels corresponds the theory of the "Black Box".[33] From the point of view of cybernetics any object of cognition can be regarded as the so called Black Box. The concept of Black Box has been taken over from electrical engineering where it is often necessary to deduce the contents of a sealed device which has input and output terminals. By subjecting the input terminals to different influences and by observing the results of these influences on the output terminals the engineer makes conclusions as to the contents of the device. All similar objects, whose contents are inaccessible to direct observation are called Black Boxes. If one regards the object of cognition as an epistemological[34] Black Box, then its input will be the operations to which the experimenter subjects the object while its output will be the observations of the results of these operations. The object of cognition and the experimenter together form a system with feedback. Every science is based on the so called protocol, i.e. the recording of the states of the input (operations on the object under consideration) and the output (results of the operations on the object under consideration) of the epistemological Black Box. Information gained from the protocol serves as a starting point for the disclosure of the nature of elements which are inaccessible to direct observation, and of the inherent relationship between those elements. The problems of theoretical investigation are inherent in the need to transform the information gained from protocol into information about the directly unobservable nature of the object under consideration. Information of the former kind can be termed elementary information while information of the latter kind is labeled information about constructs. Thus, the living nerve of the process of cognition is undoubtedly the transformation of elementary information into information about constructs. Information about constructs is

[33] W. R. Ashby, *op. cit.*, Chapter VI.

[34] The term "epistemological" (from ἐπιστήμη 'knowledge') signifies "that which concerns epistemology" (i.e. logical theory of knowledge).

represented through formal models, but both these concepts are in no way mutually reciprocal: although information about constructs must always be represented through formal models it is not conversely true that every formal model contains information about constructs; there exist formal models which are analogies of directly observed facts and phenomena as well.

As we will see below, the demarcation of the two abstraction levels, the level of observation and the level of constructs, is no less significant for phonology than for physics or other abstract theoretical sciences.

9. PHONEME AS A CONSTRUCT

Thus, our problem consists of the necessity to find a way to eliminate the fundamental theoretical difficulties of the relational-physical theory of the phoneme, which have been disclosed in the foregoing sections.

We believe that in phonology the elimination of the above examined antinomies is possible only by means of a demarcation of the two abstraction levels, the level of observation and the level of constructs.

Referring to the two-level abstraction theory of modern logic of science we will pose the following question: why can phonemes be transposed from one form of physical substance into another, let us say from acoustic substance into graphic or tactile?

From the standpoint of the two-level abstraction theory we can regard phonemes as ideal diacritical elements which are not perceived through direct observation but are embodied in some physical substratum. Thus phonemes must be conceived as elements which have no inherent physical substance. From this point of view phonemes and sounds relate to different abstraction levels: phonemes are hypothetical units which relate to the level of constructs, while sounds are directly observable elements which function as substrata of phonemes.

Since the property of being a phoneme is not directly observable, as are the physical properties of sounds, but is attributed to sounds as a hypothetical element, there arises the necessity to postulate the presence of a particular hypothetical relationship between sounds and phonemes which will be termed the relationship of embodiment.

The term "embodiment" has been borrowed from cybernetics where it is generally used in reference to real machines embodying transformations which are abstract analogies of the real machines.[35]

If we regard phonemes as constructs and sounds as substrata of phonemes which are directly observable, then the above discussed antinomy of transposition is eliminated since now nothing prevents the transposition of phonemes from one form of physical substance into another.

If we regard phonemes as constructs we also eliminate the antinomy of the paradigmatic identification of phonemes. Returning to the previously discussed mental experiment we can now speak not about the identity of phonemes *q* and *k*, *k* and *k*', *k*' and ħ, but about the fact that each of these pairs represents directly observable sounds which act as substrata of identical phonemes.

Similarly, we can also eliminate the antinomy of syntagmatic identification of phonemes. The aforementioned combinations of sounds *st* and *ks* can now be regarded in respect to one language as substrata of two different phonemes and in respect to another language as the substrata of a single phoneme. This theoretical example will be supplemented by the following concrete example: in German one and the same sound segment *tš* acts as a substratum of two phonemes, *t* and *š*, while in Spanish it acts as a substratum of a single phoneme, *č*. We raise the question: why does *tš* in German act as a substratum of two phonemes while in Spanish the same *tš* acts as a substratum of a single phoneme? The fact that both of these segments are not fully identical and that in Spanish *tš* is considerably more fussed than in German has no bearing on the answer to the question. The point lies not at all in the fact that in Spanish *tš* is more fused than in German but in the fact that in Spanish the sound *š* is used only in connection with the sound

[35] W. R. Ashby, *op. cit.*, p. 29.

t while in German the sound *š* is independent; in other words, in Spanish the sound *t* is predicted by the sound *š* while in German this is not the case. If we denote the relationship of embodiment by the symbol *I*, then in our example of the sound segment *tš* in Spanish and in German the relationship between sounds and phonemes can be expressed in the language of symbolic logic by the following formulae (in order to differentiate the transcription of phonemes and of sounds which are in relation of embodiment to phonemes we have placed the transcription symbols denoting the phonemes into quotation marks):

For Spanish:

$$I\,(t\check{s},\ \text{“}\check{c}\text{”})$$

This formula should be read as follows: sound segment *tš* is in relation of embodiment to phoneme "*č*".

For German:

$$I\,(t,\ \text{“}t\text{”})$$

(i.e. sound *t* is in relation of embodiment to phoneme "*t*").

$$I\,(\check{s},\ \text{“}\check{s}\text{”})$$

(i.e. sound *š* is in relation of embodiment to phoneme "*š*").

At this point it is necessary to turn our attention to the following important circumstance: sounds which are in relation of embodiment to phonemes are not simply physical elements but relational physical elements, and therefore we will assign to them a special term — "phonemic substrata". Hence, if we regard in Spanish as well as in German the sound segment *tš* from a purely physical standpoint we will encounter two sounds: *t* and *š*; if we, however, regard this same sound segment from the standpoint of the relation of embodiment we encounter three phonemic substrata: *tš* (in Spanish), and *t* and *š* (in German). Thus it is necessary to stricly differentiate the following three concepts: concept of sound, concept of phonemic substratum and concept of phoneme. Sounds are physical elements, phonemic substrata are relational physical elements and phonemes are purely relational elements, i.e. constructs.

The above discussion leads to the conclusion that it is essential to replace the relational-physical theory of the phoneme with a theory of the phoneme as a construct.

In our theory phoneme is regarded as a primary, undefinable concept. By the same token we also introduce the concepts of paradigmatic oppositions and syntagmatic oppositions as primary, undefinable concepts. Both these oppositions we also rank among constructs.

Phonemes are subject to the following rule: every phoneme must be in opposition to at least one phoneme on the paradigmatic axis and to at least one phoneme on the syntagmatic axis.

At the level of observation phonemes are embodied in sounds, and oppositions are embodied in contrasts which are established through an analysis of the informant's deposition.

A definition of the phoneme as a construct can be expressed in the language of symbolic logic thus:

$$P =_{Df} (x)\,(\exists y)\,[S(x)\,.\,S(y)\,.\,C(x, y) \supset I(x, P)],$$

where P denotes the phoneme, S the sound segment, C relationship of contrast established on the basis of the informant's deposition, and I relationship of embodiment. Before the square brackets there occur the symbols of quantifiers which are generally accepted in modern symbolic logic: the symbol (x) which stands for "given any x" is a universal quantifier; the symbol $(\exists y)$ which stands for "there exists at least one y such that" is an existential quantifier.

This formula which is the correspondence rule between the construct "phoneme" and the level of observation should be read as follows: if x is a sound segment and is in relation of contrast to at least one sound segment y, then x is in relation of embodiment to the phoneme P.

10. THE TWO-LEVEL SYSTEM OF PHONEMES AND PHONEMOIDS

Above we have introduced N. S. Trubeckoj's definition of the term "variants of the phoneme" as sounds which realize one and the same phoneme. In order to stress the physical nature of variants of the phoneme he uses the epithet "phonetic" equating the term "variants of the phoneme" and the term "phonetic variants of the phoneme". Thus N. S. Trubeckoj, in regarding phonemes as relational-physical units, limits them in effect to the designation of a definite class of sounds. In modern phonological literature the term "variant of the phoneme" has been replaced by the widely used term "allophone". The term "allophone" is defined by H. Gleason thus: "Any sound or subclass of sounds which is in complementary distribution with another so that the two together constitute a single phoneme is called an *allophone* of that phoneme. A phoneme is, therefore, a class of allophones."[36] Elsewhere H. Gleason writes simply: "Phoneme is a class of sounds".[37]

If we acknowledge phoneme as a construct, one may ask whether we can continue to regard it as a class of allophones as well?

Before answering this question we must determine if allophones are related to the level of observation or to the level of constructs. This is an easy task since we have already stated that allophones are defined as definite speech sounds. If allophones are speech sounds they must consequently be obtained through direct observation and must relate to the level of observation, in contrast to the concept "phoneme" which belongs to the level of constructs.

Since phoneme and allophone relate to different abstraction levels the answer to the question whether a phoneme can be regarded as a class of allophones should be transferred to a general methodological plane; the answer to this question depends on whether modern logic of science permits us, in principle, to regard constructs as classes of directly observable elements.

Let us ask: will it be permissible, from the point of view of modern logic of science, to regard the phoneme, which is related to the level of constructs, as a class of allophones which, as we have just established, relate to a basically different abstraction level, the level of observation?

[36] H. A. Gleason, *An Introduction to Descriptive Linguistics*, rev. ed. (New York, 1961), p. 263.
[37] H. A. Gleason, *op. cit.*, p. 258.

This question must be answered negatively since contemporary logic of science requires the class and its members to be homogeneous and to relate to the same main abstraction level. If the given class is a construct then the members of the class must be constructs as well. Let us take, for example, a construct such as the mathematical pendulum in physics. The members of the class of "mathematical pendulum" are not directly observable and are, therefore, constructs. Between physical pendulums which can be directly observed and mathematical pendulums there can exist neither a relation of class membership nor a relation of class inclusion since each of the pendulums belongs to a basically different abstraction level.

The absence of the relation of class membership and the relation of class inclusion between directly observed elements and scientific constructs can be expressed in other words as a lack of a deductive bond between the level of constructs and the level of observation. There exists an interesting analogy advanced by S. Toulmin which deals with the relation between theoretical terminology and geographical map. Speaking about the absence of a deductive bond between the level of constructs and the level of observation, S. Toulmin indicates that statements at the level of constructs and statements at the level of observation fail to be logically homogeneous; this phenomenon is analogous to the heterogeneous evidence of geographical map and geographical statements.[38]

Thus, in the light of modern logic we must admit that phonemes and allophones cannot relate to each other as a class and members of that class. What, we may ask then, is the actual logical relation between the phoneme and its allophones?

For the answer to this question we have to return to the formula of the definition of phoneme which was introduced in the preceding section; this formula facilitates the grasp of the process of transition from the concept of sound to the concept of phoneme.

Let us apply the formula of the definition of phoneme to a concrete example.

We will take the Russian words *palka* 'stick', *tačka* 'wheelbarrow',

[38] Cf. S. Toulmin, *op. cit.*, pp. 106-107.

trjapka 'rag', *Ljal'ka* (a proper name), and will focus our attention on the vowels of the initial stressed syllables of these words. We encounter four different positions P_1 (between plain consonants), P_2 (following a plain and preceding a sharp consonant), P_3 (following a sharp and preceding a plain consonant), P_4 (between sharp consonants) which contain four corresponding individual vowel sounds a_1, a_2, a_3, a_4; these sounds differ in regard to their articulation: vowel a_4 has a maximal palatal (sharp) coloring, vowel a_3 has a palatal coloring in the initial phase of its duration, vowel a_2 has a palatal coloring in the final phase of its duration, and vowel a_1 has an absence of palatal coloring. Likewise, it would be possible to discover in additional positions the individual sounds a_5, a_6, etc. (for instance, R. I. Avanesov points out that it is necessary to differentiate at least the following eight positions for vowels under stress: (1) in initial position preceding a plain consonant [*at*], (2) between plain consonants [*tat*], (3) in terminal position following a plain consonant [*ta*], (4) in initial position preceding a sharp consonant [*at'*], (5) following a plain and preceding a sharp consonant [*tat'*], (6) following a sharp and preceding a plain consonant [*t'at*], (7) in terminal position following a sharp consonant [*t'a*], (8) between sharp consonants [*t'at'*])[39] but for our purposes we will limit ourselves to the above specified positions.

If in the word *palka* the individual sound a_1 is replaced by the individual sound o_1, we obtain *polka* 'shelf'. There must, therefore, exist at least one individual sound to which the sound a_1 is in relation of contrast; hence we can conclude that the individual sound a_1 is a substratum of the individual phoneme "a_1". The transition from the individual sound a_1 to the individual phoneme "a_1" can be represented in accordance with the formula for the definition of phoneme as follows:

$$(\exists y)\,[S(a_1)\,.\,S(y)\,.\,C(a_1, y) \mathrel{\acute{\supset}} I(a_1, \text{“}a_1\text{”})]$$

(the accent mark above the implication sign is taken over from H. Reichenbach as a designation of an internal, so called connective

[39] Cf. R. I. Avanesov, *Fonetika sovremennogo russkogo literaturnogo jazyka* (Moscow, 1956), p. 95.

bond between the antecedent and the consequent, in order to avoid the paradox of material implication).[40]

Substituting in the word *tačka* o_2 for a_2, in the word *trjapka* o_3 for a_3, and in the word *Ljal'ka* o_4 for a_4 we obtain the words *točka, trjopka, Ljol'ka.* Hence we should regard the individual sounds a_2, a_3, and a_4 as substrata of the individual phonemes "a_2", "a_3" and "a_4". This can be represented by the following formulae:

$$(\exists y)\,[S(a_2)\,.\,S(y)\,.\,C(a_2, y)\;\overset{\frown}{\supset}\;I(a_2, \text{“}a_2\text{”})]$$
$$(\exists y)\,[S(a_3)\,.\,S(y)\,.\,C(a_3, y)\;\overset{\frown}{\supset}\;I(a_3, \text{“}a_3\text{”})]$$
$$(\exists y)\,[S(a_4)\,.\,S(y)\,.\,C(a_4, y)\;\overset{\frown}{\supset}\;I(a_4, \text{“}a_4\text{”})]$$

These formulae denote that the transition from the concept of sound to the concept of phoneme proceeds from the individual sounds to the individual phonemes by means of individual phonemic substrata.

Now, we may inquire, how, does the transition from individual phonemes to classes of individual phonemes take place?

This transition from individual phonemes to classes of individual phonemes will be investigated by way of a further analysis of sound contrasts in the already examined four positions.

Investigating in Russian the contrast of vowel sounds in positions P_1, P_2, P_3, and P_4 we obtain four sets of substrata of individual phonemes as can be illustrated by the following table:

P_1	P_2	P_3	P_4
a_1	a_2	a_3	a_4
o_1	o_2	o_3	o_4
u_1	u_2	u_3	u_4
i_1	i_2	i_3	i_4
e_1	e_2	e_3	e_4

[40] Cf. H. Reichenbach, *op. cit.*, pp. 27-34, 40-43.

The set of vowels in position P_1 is designated by the symbol M_1, in position P_2 by the symbol M_2, in position P_3 by the symbol M_3 and in position P_4 by the symbol M_4.

Analyzing the properties of the sets M_1, M_2, M_3 and M_4 we can postulate that among these sets there exists a definite relation of equivalence.[41] This relationship we will term the one-one positional transformation.

Before we define the one-one positional transformation we have to explain the exact meaning of the concept of transformation and of several other concepts connected with it. In defining these concepts we will rely on the work of W. R. Ashby.[42]

We will commence with the concept of transition. Every change takes place under the influence of some factor. The element which is acted on is called the operand; the acting factor is called the operator; the element into which the operand changes is called the transform. The change of the operand into the transform is called the transition.

Science is interested not in single transitions but in those transitions in which a single operator acts simultaneously on several operands, giving thus rise to a definite set of homogeneous transitions. "Such a set of transitions, on a set of operands, is a transformation."[43]

Transformations where, the number of operands and transforms being the same, each operand has one and only one corresponding transform and, vice versa, each transform has one and only one

[41] In set theory we find the following definition of the equivalence of sets: set M is considered equivalent to the set N, symbolically expressed as $M \sim N$, if the elements of the set N can be placed into a one-one correspondence with the elements of the set M, i.e. if it is possible for every element m of the set M to have a corresponding element n in the set N in such a way that on the basis of this correspondence each element of the set M has one and only one corresponding element of the set N. The definition of equivalence has the following properties:

1) $M \sim M$ (reflexivity)
2) if $M \sim N$, then $N \sim M$ (symmetry)
3) if $M \sim N$ and $N \sim P$, then $M \sim P$ (transitivity).

[42] W. R. Ashby, *op. cit.*

[43] W. R. Ashby, *op. cit.*, p. 10.

operand, are called one-one transformations. As on example of a one-one transformation we can take the change of the set of numbers 1, 2, 3, 4 into the set 4, 5, 6, 7, by means of an addition of the number 3:

$$\Big\downarrow \begin{matrix} 1 & 2 & 3 & 4 \\ 4 & 5 & 6 & 7 \end{matrix}$$

Let us return to our example of the four sets of individual sounds M_1, M_2, M_3, M_4. We can regard these sets as a definite number of conditions which arise from a definite number of positional transformations. Taking any one of these sets, let us say the set M_1, as representing a set of operands, we can regard the sets M_2, M_3, M_4 as sets of transforms, while the positions P_2, P_3, P_4 should then be regarded as operators.

On the basis of the work of R. I. Avanesov the characteristics of the operators P_2, P_3, P_4 are represented as follows:[44] in position P_2 (i.e. following plain and preceding sharp consonants) vowels undergo articulatory shift forward and upward in the final phase of their articulation; in position P_3 (i.e. following sharp and preceding plain consonants) vowels undergo articulatory shift forward and upward in the initial phase of their articulation; in position P_4 (i.e. between sharp consonants) the back vowels undergo articulatory shift forward and upward and the front vowels undergo articulatory shift upward during the entire duration of their articulation.

Let us now consider the individual sound sets M_1 and M_2 and compare the elements of these sets among themselves. Comparing, for instance, the vowel a_1 with the vowel a_2 it becomes evident that the differences between these vowels are, on the whole, conditioned by the action of the operator P_2; if we compare the vowel a_1 with any other vowel, let us say with the vowel o_2, then the difference between these vowels appears to be only partially, not wholly, conditioned by the action of the operator P_2. If we arrange the vowels of the set M_1 and the vowels of the set M_2 systematically in respect to the full conditioning of their mutual differences on the

[44] R. I. Avanesov, *op. cit.*, pp. 95-96.

part of the operator P_2 then, taking the vowels of the set M_1 as operands and the vowels of the set M_2 as transforms, we can postulate the relation of a one-one positional transformation between both sets, as illustrated in the following table:

M_1		M_2
a_1	$\leftrightarrow$	a_2
o_1	$\leftrightarrow$	o_2
u_1	$\leftrightarrow$	u_2
i_1	$\leftrightarrow$	i_2
e_1	$\leftrightarrow$	e_2

If we designate the action of the operator P_2 (i.e. the articulatory shift upward and forward during the final phase of articulation) by the symbol P'_2 and the vowel, as the operand, by the symbol Op, then the given transformation can be expressed by the formula:

$$Op \rightarrow Op + P'_2$$

This positional transformation should be regarded as a one-one transformation since in the case of an identical number of vowels which act both as operands and as transforms in the sets M_1 and M_2, each vowel of the set M_1 is corresppnded by one and only one vowel of the set M_2 and, conversely, each vowel of the set M_2 is corresponded by one and only one vowel of the set M_1.

Since between the vowels of the sets M_1 and M_2 there exists a one-one relation of positional transformation, the sets M_1 andM_2 should be regarded as mutually equivalent.

Having designated the actions of the operators P_2 and P_3 by the symbols P'_2 and P'_3 we can, by analogy, postulate between the sets M_1 and M_3, and the sets M_1 and M_4 a relation of a one-one positional transformation as well, as can be illustrated by the following formulae:

$$Op \rightarrow Op + P'_3$$
$$Op \rightarrow Op + P'_4$$

From the above shown equivalences of the sets ($M_1 \sim M_2$, $M_1 \sim M_3$, $M_1 \sim M_4$) one can derive, in accordance with the principle of transitivity, the remaining equivalences ($M_2 \sim M_3$, $M_2 \sim M_4$, $M_3 \sim M_4$).

Having established the equivalence of the sets of the individual sounds M_1, M_2, M_3, M_4, we have thereby established a class of equivalent sets of the individual sounds M.

Let us concentrate now on the relationship between the individual sounds a_1, a_2, a_3, a_4. We discover that the relation between these individual sounds is contingent upon the possibility of a union of these sounds into ordered pairs, i.e. a mutual union of any two given sounds into a pair.[45]

Since the individual sounds a_1, a_2, a_3, a_4 serve as substrata of individual phonemes "a_1", "a_2", "a_3", "a_4", then, bearing in mind that the relation between the individual sounds a_1, a_2, a_3, a_4 is a connected relation, we can postulate the relation of identity between the individual phonemes "a_1", "a_2", "a_3", "a_4". In this manner we create a class of identical individual phonemes which we will designate by the symbol "a". It is self-evident that this class encompasses not only the individual phonemes "a_1", "a_2", "a_3", "a_4", but individual phonemes "a_5", "a_6", "a_7", "a_8", etc., as well since the number of positions in the speech flow is not limited to those four which we have concentrated upon for the purpose of convenience, but is, indeed, theoretically unlimited.

Following an analogical argumentative course we can postulate likewise classes of identical individual phonemes "*o*", "*u*", "*i*", "*e*", as well as classes of any identical individual consonantal phonemes.

It is necessary, however, to take into account an accompanying serious obstacle. When we postulate the relation of identity between individual phonemes, let us say between the individual phonemes "a_1", "a_2", "a_3", "a_4", etc., this relation of identity is not contingent upon the fact that the relation between the substrata of these individual phonemes, i.e. between the individual sounds a_1, a_2, a_3, a_4, etc., is connective. Even the fact that individual sounds

[45] In symbolic logic a connected or (in the terminology of H. Reichenbach) interconnective relation denotes any two-place relation "characterized by the property that the relation holds for any two different elements of its field in one direction or in the other". (H. Reichenbach, *op. cit.*, p. 116.)

can unite into mutual pairs does not account for the inevitable mutual identity of the given individual sounds, as well as of the individual phonemes which they embody. Although the connective relation between the individual sounds a_1, a_2, a_3, a_4, etc. is a requisite condition, it is not sufficient for the postulation of a relation of identity between the individual phonemes "a_1", "a_2", "a_3", "a_4". We can postulate the relation of identity between these individual phonemes only because the physical difference between their substrata, i.e. between the individual sounds a_1, a_2, a_3, a_4, etc., is stipulated on the whole only by positional conditions, and can be removed by means of a mental experiment. Hence, since the relation of identity between the individual phonemes is contingent on a mental experiment which eliminates positional differences between individual sounds that act as substrata of individual phonemes, the relation of identity between individual phonemes, similarly as individual phonemes themselves, belongs to the level of constructs.

We have traced the transition from individual phonemes to classes of individual phonemes. In order to be able to differentiate between the term "phoneme" as a designation of the individual phoneme and the term "phoneme" denoting a class of individual phonemes it will be expedient to introduce the terms "concrete phoneme" for the former and "abstract phoneme" for the latter. The above discussion indicates that allophones are nothing else but individual sounds which act as substrata of individual phonemes. In order to differentiate between an individual sound which acts as a substratum of an individual phoneme and a class of individual sounds which act as a substratum of identical individual phonemes it will be expedient to introduce the terms "concrete phonemoid" for the designation of the former and the term "abstract phonemoid" for the designation of the latter.

Thus, while answering the question, posed at the beginning of the present section, about the immanent relation between the phoneme and its allophones, we have found it necessary to formulate a two-level conceptual system of phonemes and phonemoids which corresponds to the demarcation of two abstraction levels in phonology, the level of observation and the level of constructs. At the level of observation we deal with concrete and abstract phonemoids, but at the level of constructs we deal with concrete and abstract phonemes.

The two-level system of phonemes and phonemoids can be illustrated by the following scheme:

Level of constructs	*Concrete phonemes* cf.: "a_1", "a_2", "a_3", "a_4", "a_5", "a_6", "a_7", "a_8", ...	*Abstract phoneme* cf.: "*a*".
Level of observation	*Concrete phonemoids* cf.: a_1, a_2, a_3, a_4, a_5, a_6, a_7, a_8, ...	*Abstract phonemoids* cf.: *a*.

We are already aware that between phonemoids which act as substrata of identical concrete phonemes there exists a definite physical difference which is, on the whole, traceable to the influence of varied positional conditions. We may ask, however: what differences occur between identical concrete phonemes which belong to one and the same class? If we follow A. Tarski and call those elements which agree in form but differ only in regard to their position in space equiform elements,[46] then those phonemes which belong to one and the same class should be regarded as equiform. Concrete phonemes represent ideal diacritical elements which are not subject to positional changes but which differ from each other only in regard to their location on the syntagmatic axis of the language.

11. DISTINCTIVE FEATURES AS CONSTRUCTS

In the second section of this chapter, the relational-physical definition of phoneme as the shortest phonological unit has been

[46] A. Tarski, *Introduction to Logic and to the Methodology of Deductive Sciences*, rev. ed. (New York, 1946), p. 112.

complemented by an alternate definition of phoneme as an aggregate of definite distinctive features.

If we accept the second definition of the phoneme as a base, then the distinctive feature can be regarded as a primary, undefinable concept, and phoneme can be defined, in respect to this concept, as a bundle of distinctive features.

At this point we have to subject the concept of distinctive feature to a critical analysis using the hypothetico-deductive method, just as we have previously done in the case of the relational-physical concept of the phoneme, since the concept of distinctive feature plays as fundamental a role in modern phonology as the concept of phoneme with which it is insolubly connected.

In modern phonology distinctive feature is generally treated as a relational-physical concept. But the relational-physical interpretation of distinctive features is confronted with the very same theoretical difficulties as the relational-physical interpretation of the phoneme.

In so far as distinctive features are concerned, modern phonology accepts as equally valid the two following statements:

Statement 1. Distinctive features are diacritical elements whose function is to differentiate between signifiants of linguistic units.

Statement 2. Distinctive features are acoustic elements.

Let us consider the consequences of these statements.

If it is true that distinctive features possess a diacritical function, i.e. that they differentiate between signifiants of linguistic units, then there must exist an inherent fundamental possibility of transposing acoustic substance into other forms of physical substance: graphic, chromatic, tactile. Any system of distinctive features and phonemes can be presented not only as acoustic properties but as graphic, chromatic or tactile symbols as well.

In order to substantiate the fundamental possibility of transposing acoustic properties into other forms of physical substance we will execute the following mental experiment. Let us transpose distinctive features into squares of identical dimensions but different color: vocality into a dark blue square, non-vocality into a light blue square, consonantness into a dark brown square, non-consonantness into a light brown square, compactness into a dark green square, non-compactness into a light green square, diffuseness into a dark red square, non-diffuseness into a light red square, graveness into a dark yellow square, acuteness into a light yellow square, etc. Consequently every phoneme can be expressed as a combination of different color squares. If we, for instance, take the system of Russian vowel phonemes as described by M. Halle,[47] the phoneme *a* can be expressed as a combination of dark blue, light brown, dark green and light red squares; the phoneme *i* as a combination of dark blue, light brown, dark red and light yellow squares; the phoneme *e* as a combination of dark blue, light brown, light green, light red and light yellow squares: the phoneme *o* as a combination of dark blue, light brown, light green, light red and dark yellow squares; the phoneme *u* as a combination of dark blue, light brown, dark red, and dark yellow squares.

Hence, statement 1 upholds the inherent possibility of transposing distinctive features from acoustic into other forms of physical substance.

Let us now turn to statement 2. If distinctive features are, indeed, acoustic elements then they obviously cannot be transposed into other forms of physical substance since in that case they would cease to be themselves, i.e. acoustic elements.

Here we encounter a clear antinomy: both statement 1 and statement 2 are regarded as valid, although statement 1 stipulates, that distinctive features can be transposed into other forms of physical substance while statement 2 stipulates the reverse, namely, that distinctive features cannot be transposed into other forms of physical substance.

We see thus that in the case of distinctive features there arises the same antinomy of transposition which we have already encountered in connection with the analysis of the relational-physical concept of phoneme.

If we regard distinctive features as relational-physical elements

[47] M. Halle, *The Sound Pattern of Russian: A Linguistic and Acoustical Investigation* (The Hague, 1959), p. 45.

then, as in the case of the analysis of the relational-physical concept of phoneme, we encounter as well the antinomy of paradigmatic identification. Let us take an example from Greenlandic.[48]

In Greenlandic the vowel phonemes *i* and *æ* are opposed to each other with respect to the distinctive feature of diffuseness and compactness (*i* is a diffuse vowel, while *æ* a compact one); in the pre-uvular position the vowel phoneme *i* changes into *a* and the vowel phoneme *æ* into ɑ; this can be illustrated by the following table:

in usual positions	in pre-uvular positions
i	*a*
æ	ɑ

In these oppositions the acoustic properties clash with the distinctive features. It can be seen that different acoustic properties appear to be identical while, *vice versa*, the same acoustic properties turn out to be different. Thus, the diffuseness of *i* and the compactness of *a* prove to be identical as distinctive features, and the same acoustic properties, the compactness in *æ* and the compactness in ɑ, turn out to be different.

If distinctive features are acoustic properties, one may ask how different acoustic properties can constitute the same distinctive features and, conversely, how the same acoustic properties can constitute different distinctive features? If distinctive features are in fact acoustic properties, then identity and difference of distinctive features should derive from the physical nature of acoustic properties and should not contradict their physical nature.

Thus we see that if distinctive features are regarded as acoustic properties, a contradiction arises between their semiotic, relational nature on the one hand, and their acoustic nature on the other.

The question arises: how can we eliminate the above examined antinomy which relates to the interpretation of distinctive features as relational-physical elements?

Obviously, in this case we have to rely, once again, on the dif-

[48] Cf. E. Fischer-Jørgensen, "What Can the New Techniques of Acoustic Phonetics Contribute to Linguistics?", *Proceedings of the VIII International Congress of Linguists* (Oslo, 1958), p. 474.

ferentiation of two abstraction levels, the level of observation and the level of constructs.

In order to explain the real nature of distinctive features it is useful to consider a concrete example, borrowed from an article by R. Jakobson on the Gilyak language.[49] In Proto-Gilyak the contrast of *k* and *x* in weak (non-initial) position corresponds to the contrast of tense *k'* and lax *k* in strong (initial) position. If we designate the strong position by the symbol P_1 and the weak position by the symbol P_2, then this correspondence can be represented as follows:

$$\begin{array}{ccc} P_1 & & P_2 \\ k' & \leftrightarrow & k \\ k & \leftrightarrow & x \end{array}$$

As R. Jakobson correctly points out the distinctive feature of *k* in position P_1 is non-tenseness while the distinctive feature of *k* in position P_2 is tenseness. This statement causes us to inquire whether non-tenseness and tenseness, as distinctive features of *k* in position P_1 and *k* in position P_2, respectively, can be obtained through direct observation.

This inquiry has to be answered negatively. We can observe tenseness and non-tenseness directly only as acoustic properties; at the level of direct observation both the former *k* and the latter *k* have one and the same acoustic property, namely non-tenseness. By the same token, we can also observe directly various relations between acoustic properties; thus, in the case of the former *k* non-tenseness is an independent acoustic property, while in the case of the latter *k* it is a dependent acoustic property. Distinctive features of tenseness and non-tenseness are not directly observable but are ascribed to the acoustic properties with the aim to clarify their contrasting.

Like phonemes, distinctive features are not obtained through direct observation but are postulated by us as hypothetical elements, i.e. theoretical constructs which act as abbreviated denotations of

[49] R. Jakobson, "Notes on Gilyak", *Bulletin of the Institute of History and Philology* (Academia Sinica), XXIX (1957), pp. 255-281.

the observed relations of contrast between acoustic properties, and which simultaneously possess an explanatory function. Hence we ought to postulate a relation of embodiment between acoustic properties and distinctive features, which we ascribe to those properties. If we designate non-tenseness, as an acoustic property, by the symbol *L*, non-tenseness, as a distinctive feature, by the symbol "*L*", and tenseness, as a distinctive feature, by the symbol "*T*", then the relation between acoustic properties and distinctive features in the case of *k* in position P_1 and *k* in position P_2 can be expressed by the following formulae:

$$\text{For } k \text{ in } P_1: I\,(L, \text{“}L\text{”})$$

(the acoustic property of non-tenseness is in relation of embodiment to the distinctive feature of non-tenseness).

$$\text{For } k \text{ in } P_2: I\,(L, \text{“}T\text{”})$$

(the acoustic property of non-tenseness is in relation of embodiment to the distinctive feature of tenseness).

The definition of distinctive feature as a construct may be expressed in terms of symbolic logic as follows:

$$D =_{Df} (x)\,(\exists y)\,[A(x)\,.\,A(y)\,.\,C(x, y) \supset I(x, D)],$$

where *D* is the distinctive feature, *A* the acoustic property, *C* the relation of contrast and *I* the relation of embodiment.

This formula which represents the correspondence rule between the construct "distinctive feature" and the level of observation, should be read: if *x* is an acoustic property and is in relation of contrast to at least one acoustic property *y*, then *x* is in relation of embodiment to the distinctive feature *D*.

We will now return to the table of Gilyak vowels and apply the above formula to the analysis of the contrast between the acoustic properties of these vowels. First of all, we will replace, in the given table, the individual sounds with corresponding individual acoustic properties. Thus we obtain:

$$\begin{array}{ccc} P_1 & & P_2 \\ T_1 & \leftrightarrow & L_2 \\ L_1 & \leftrightarrow & Cn_2 \end{array}$$

where T represents tenseness, L, non-tenseness, and Cn, fricativeness. The numerical indices indicate that we deal with individual acoustic properties, which correspond to the concrete positions P_1 and P_2.

Let us now concentrate on the acoustic property T_1. Since T_1 is counterposed to L_1, there must exist at least one acoustic property to which T_1 is in relation of contrast. Hence we can conclude that the individual acoustic property T_1 must be a substratum of an individual distinctive feature which we will designate by the symbol "T_1". The transition from the individual acoustic property T_1 to the individual distinctive feature "T_1" can be expressed, in accordance with the formula for the definition of distinctive feature, thus:

$$(\exists y)\,[A\,(T_1)\,.\,A(y)\,.\,C\,(T_1, y)\ \supset I\,(T_1, \text{“}T_1\text{”})]$$

By analogy, the transition from the individual acoustic property L_2 to the individual distinctive feature, designated by the symbol "T_2", can be expressed correspondingly as:

$$(\exists y)\,[A\,(L_2)\,.\,A(y)\,.\,C(L_2, y) \supset I\,(L_2, \text{“}T_2\text{”})]$$

These formulae show clearly that the transition from the concept of acoustic property to the concept of distinctive feature passes through three distinct individual phases: individual acoustic property, individual substratum of distinctive feature, and individual distinctive features per se.

If we examine the above formulae we will see clearly the full analogy between these formulae and the formulae of the transition from individual sounds to individual phonemes which was discussed in the preceding section. There exists also a full analogy between these two transitions and the transition from individual distinctive features to classes of distinctive features. Thus, if we apply the reasoning discussed in the preceding section in connection with the transition from individual phonemes to classes of phonemes to our table which shows contrapositions of individual acoustic properties, we will easily perceive that individual distinctive features (let us say the above discussed individual distinctive features "T_1" and "T_2"), belong to one and the same class since their substrata are paired elements which belong to the system of equivalent sets of acoustic properties that are in relation of one-one transformation.

Thus, logical analysis of the concept of distinctive feature leads us to the conclusion that there exists a full parallel between the relation of sounds and phonemes, and the relation of acoustic properties of sounds and distinctive features.

At the level of observation we differentiate between individual substrata of distinctive features and classes of the individual substrata of distinctive features. In order to denote the former we consider it expedient to introduce the term "concrete differentoids", and to denote the latter by the term "abstract differentoids".

At the level of constructs we differentiate individual distinctive features and classes of individual distinctive features. The former can be, for expediency, given the term "concrete differentors" and the latter the term "abstract differentors".

This two level conceptual system can be illustrated by the following scheme:

Level of constructs	*Concrete differentors* cf.: "T_1", "T_2", "T_3", "T_4", "T_5", "T_6", ...	*Abstract differentor* cf.: "T"
Level of observation	*Concrete differentoids* cf.: T_1, T_2, T_3, T_4, T_5, T_6, ...	*Abstract differentoid* cf.: T

12. COMMENTS ON THE THEORY OF MICRO- AND MACROPHONEMES AND THE GLOSSEMATIC CONCEPT OF THE PHONEME

Let us compare the above discussed two level theory of the phoneme and distinctive features with W. Twaddell's theory of micro- and macrophonemes and L. Hjelmslev's glossematic conception of the phoneme. This comparison should be valuable for a thorough understanding of the fundamental significance of an explicit demarcation of the level of observation and the level of constructs in phonology, and in structural linguistics in general.

Within the scope of the present work we do not intend to engage in a detailed explanation of the theory of micro- and macrophonemes or of the glossematic conception of the phoneme (for that the reader can turn to the corresponding works of W. Twaddell and L. Hjelmslev);[50] we will limit our discussion merely to the most important questions. We ought to stress, however, the immense merit of W. Twaddell and L. Hjelmslev who, by developing the logical corollaries of F. de Saussure's brilliant disclosure that language is based on a system of linguistic values, made an important contribution to the eradication of the scientific notion of phoneme as an element of physical reality given through direct observation.

We will turn our attention first to the theory of micro- and macrophonemes.

If we compare certain utterances it is possible to disclose concrete sound complexes which, while differing from each other in pronunciation, appear to be identical as to their meaning. Disregarding objective differences, it is possible to abstract the common feature which is inherent in every one of these sound complexes. This abstraction is termed by W. Twaddell a "form". (For example, if we compare the utterances "*The* LAMP *stands on the table*"; "*What a beautiful* LAMP!"; "Where is your old LAMP?", it is possible to abstract the form LAMP, which is common to all the concrete words LAMP occuring in these utterances.) With the exception of homonyms, forms differ from each other in respect to their phonation. Sound differences between forms are called phonological differences while the forms themselves are termed phonologically different forms. If two forms are phonologically different then there must exist consistently recurring significant differences between the two sets of phonological events from which these forms have been abstracted. (For example, if we take a set of phonetic events $lamp_1$, $lamp_2$, $lamp_3$, $lamp_4$, etc., which differ from each

[50] W. F. Twaddell, "On Defining the Phoneme", *Language Monograph*, No. 16 (Baltimore, 1935) (reprinted in M. Joos, ed., *Readings in Linguistics*, (Washington, 1957), pp. 55-84); L. Hjelmslev, *op. cit.*

other either because of the idiolects of the speakers or because of different phonetic conditions within the speech flow, and the set of phonetic events $limp_1$, $limp_2$, $limp_3$, $limp_4$, which are different in respect to the same factors, we can abstract from these two sets of phonetic events, in the first place, two phonologically different forms *lamp* and *limp* and, in the second place, the phonological difference between *æ* and *i*.) Phonological differences are either minimal or maximal. A group of forms which are minimally phonologically different constitutes an ordered class of forms. (For example the English words *pill* – *till* – *kill* – *bill* constitute an ordered class of forms.) The relations among the members of such a class are minimal phonological oppositions. Members of such minimal oppositions are called microphonemes (in the given example *p* – *t* – *k* – *b* represent microphonemes in respect to which members of the ordered class of forms, characterized by the common complex *-ill*, differ from each other). Two or more classes of forms are called similarly ordered if their microphonemes can be placed into a one-one correspondence. For instance, the classes of forms *pill* – *till* – *kill* – *bill* and *nap* – *gnat* – *knack* – *nab* are similarly ordered since, although the microphonemes of both classes are not pronounced identically (in initial position the character of *p* – *t* – *k* – *b* is explosive, while in final position it is non-explosive; in addition, the initial *p* – *t* – *k* are aspirated while the final *p* – *t* – *k* lack aspiration) these microphonemes can nevertheless be placed into a one-one correspondence. A sum of micro-phonemes which occupy a similar position in similarly ordered classes of forms is called a *macrophoneme*. Let us consider the characteristics of the concept of macrophoneme. W. Twaddell points out that the macrophoneme functions as a terminological convenience for the description of relations among the elements of a language, among its forms.

It is not difficult to see that the term "form", with which Twaddell operates, corresponds to our abstractions derived from the aggregation of concrete phonetic events. For instance, when in section 10 of the present chapter we had analyzed the contraposition of the individual sounds a_1 and o_1 in the words *palka* and *polka*, we have actually regarded the words *palka* and *polka* as abstract sums of concrete phonetic events $palka_1$, $palka_2$, $palka_3$, $palka_4$, ... and $polka_1$, $polka_2$, $polka_3$, $polka_4$ ... which represented concrete conditions of the given individual words *palka* and *polka*; correspondingly, the individual sounds a_1 and o_1 themselves were regarded as abstract sums of concrete phonetic events $a_{1(1)}$, $a_{1(2)}$, $a_{1(3)}$, $a_{1(4)}$, ... and $o_{1(1)}$, $o_{1(2)}$, $o_{1(3)}$, $o_{1(4)}$, ... which represented concrete conditions of the individual sounds.

The term "microphoneme" corresponds to our term "concrete phonemoid", while the term "macro-phoneme" corresponds to our term "abstract phoneme".

W. Twaddell does not use the term "construct" but when he characterizes the phoneme as an abstract fictitious unit, his definition corresponds generally to what we understand under the term "construct" (although the term "fiction" and several other terms used by W. Twaddell must be regarded by us as unacceptable since they can lead to various misunderstandings on the epistemological plane.)

Although we acknowledge the importance of the theory of micro- and macrophonemes, since its concept of phoneme can be interpreted as a theoretical construct, we are aware, at the same time, that this theory harbors the following fundamental contradiction. On the one hand, W. Twaddell characterizes the macrophoneme (as a synonym of the term "macrophoneme" W. Twaddell uses also the term "phoneme") as a construct, but on the other hand, he defines this concept as a sum of microphonemes occupying a similar position in similarly ordered classes of forms. Since the term "microphoneme" corresponds to our term "concrete phonemoid" and since, as we have shown in section 10, concrete phonemoids do not belong to constructs, it follows that for W. Twaddell the construct "macrophoneme" represents a class of elements which, apparently, are not constructs. This fundamental contradiction is the result of an inherent lack, on the part of the theory of micro- and macrophonemes, of an explicit demarcation of the two abstraction levels, the level of observation and the level of constructs. From the standpoint of this demarcation it is not possible for the macro and microphonemes to coexist as a class and members of that class. Hence, there arises the need to replace this pair of concepts with a two-level system of concepts, akin to that which we propose to formulate in our investigation.

Let us now transfer our attention to the glossematic conception of the phoneme.

L. Hjelmslev did not engage exclusively in the study of phonological theory; he investigated the concept of phoneme within the framework of his general theory of language which he called the glossematic theory.

Following F. de Saussure's theory, L. Hjelmslev differentiates two planes in language — the content plane (signifié, in the terminology of F. de Saussure) and the expression plane (signifiant); in addition, at each of these planes he differentiates form and substance. The object of linguistic theory ought to be a study of the pure form of language, i.e. the pure form of content and the pure form of expression which are in no way dependent on the substance of content and the substance of expression. In describing the pure form of language L. Hjelmslev uses also the term "linguistic scheme". The linguistic scheme constitutes an immanent framework of language which is not dependent on sounds and symbols since the real units of language are not sounds and symbols but elements of pure relationship which are manifested in sounds and symbols. The phoneme is nothing more than a unit of the expression plane which, being an element of pure relationship, is manifested in sounds but does not comprise any physical substance. Since the term "phoneme" has been etymologically connected with the concept of sound L. Hjelmslev prefers the term "taxeme of expression", in order to liberate the concept of phoneme from any association with the concept of sound.[51]

L. Hjelmslev does not make use of the term "construct"; the glossematic concept of language, the glossematic concept of linguistic units and, in particular, the glossematic concept of the phoneme, however, should be unquestionably attributed to constructs.

[51] L. Hjelmslev, "Metod strukturnogo analiza v lingvistike", *Acta Linguistica*, VI, pp. 2-3 (Copenhagen, 1950-51).

Although the fundamental statement of the glossematic concept of the phoneme, according to which the phoneme comprises no inherent physical substance but appears to be an element of pure relation, manifested in sounds, constitutes an important achievement of linguistic science and should be regarded as the cornerstone of modern phonology, the glossematic concept of the phoneme harbors a serious difficulty which arises from Hjelmslev's unexpected conclusion.

According to L. Hjelmslev, phonemes can be studied only through distributive analysis since they do not comprise any inherent physical substance but are elements of pure relations. Consequently, the subject of phonology is narrowed down to such an extent that the investigation of distinctive features is expelled from within its scope, since it somehow relates to the physical substance of language.

We have already attempted to show that distinctive features ought to be regarded as constructs no less than the phonemes themselves. Therefore it seems that Hjelmslev's conclusion which eliminates distinctive features from within the scope of phonology, is unjustified.

It is our belief that L. Hjelmslev came to his conclusion as a result of the glossematic theory's lack of an explicit demarcation of the two abstraction levels, the level of observation and the level of constructs. The core of the problem lies in the fact that if we fail to separate these two abstraction levels it is, obviously, easy to confuse distinctive features with their substrata which actually do belong to the physical substance of language. Furthermore if these two abstraction levels were not distinguished, distributional analysis could be wrongly regarded as an operation dealing with pure form. By the same token it is necessary that we differentiate two types of distributional relations: distributional relations between phonemic substrata at the level of observation and a distributional relations between phonemes themselves at the level of constructs. Since only the distributional relations between phonemic substrata are directly observable it is clear that the distributional relations between phonemes can be ascertained only by means of an analysis of the distributional relations between phonemic substrata, i.e. by means of an analysis of the physical substance of language. Hence it becomes evident that even if the subject of phonology is reduced to the study of distributional relations between phonemes, the linguist will be unable to free himself from the investigation of physical substance since direct observation yields nothing save physical elements, and relations between physical elements.

The problem of form and substance in phonology as well as in general structural linguistics amounts to nothing more than the problem of the correspondence between the level of observation and the level of constructs. Therefore, the linguist should not merely ignore the physical substance; his task should lie, instead, in the demarcation of the two abstraction levels, and in the investigation of the transitions from the elements of physical substance to the constructs, i.e. among others, to phonemes and distinctive features.

13. PROSODIC FEATURES

So far we have discussed the two-level theory of the phoneme and of distinctive features. Our task will be now to apply the principle of the demarcation of the two abstraction levels to the entire scope of phonology. As an initial step in this direction, we will concentrate in this section on prosodic features.

In order to clarify the original semiotic nature of prosodic features we will introduce first of all the definition of prosodic features and their classification in modern phonology.

A definition of prosodic features characteristic of modern phonology can be found in one of the works of A. Martinet: "Prosodic elements affect and characterize units of speech flow, whose duration usually differs from the duration of phonemes. Often these units are larger than phonemes; by way of an example we can take a syllable or a syllabic crest which frequently contains a diphthong consisting of two phonemes. They can however be smaller than the phoneme, as well as for example in the case when the syllabic crest (which can consist of one phoneme) splits up into two consecutive morae."[52]

In essence prosodic features are subdivided into two groups: accentual and non-accentual.[53]

Accent, or stress, should be defined as the setting off of one syllable within a bisyllabic or a polysyllabic word. The basic function of stress is the so-called culminative (crest forming) function which consists of the fact that the accents signalize the number of independent words within the given speech flow. Since every self-contained word possesses usually only one stress it follows that the number of stresses in any given speech flow determines the number of self-contained words, as well.

In respect to the place it occupies in the word, stress can be either bound or free. A stress is called a bound stress if in the given language it always falls in one and the same place (in Czech, for instance, the stress falls always on the first syllable, in Turkish always on the last syllable), or if its place is determined strictly by the phonemic structure of the word (in Latin, for instance, where the stress can fall either on the penult or the antepenult, its place is determined by the phonemic structure of the penult). A stress is called a free stress if it can occupy various places independently of the phonemic structure of the word; consequently, it possesses, aside from culminative function, also the function of word differentiation (for instance, in Russian where the stress is free, the words *píli* and *pilí* differ phonologically only in respect to their place of stress).

According to the manner of the setting off of the stressed syllable, we differentiate the following types of stress:

(a) strong, or dynamic, stress (the stressed syllable is set off by greater tenseness of its articulation);

(b) quantitative stress (the stressed syllable is set off by increased lengthening of the articulation of the vowel);

[52] A. Martinet, *Economie des changements phonétiques* (Berne, 1955), pp. 153-154.

[53] A. Martinet, *Phonology as Functional Phonetics* (London, 1949), pp. 12-14.

(c) tonal, or musical, stress (the stressed syllable is set off by a change in the tone pitch).

Dynamic stress, which is innate in Russian, is rather widespread among the various languages of the world.

Quantitative stress is seldom encountered; it is found, for instance in modern Greek.

Tonal stress, which is used by various languages of the world, can have several variations. In Lithuanian there exists an opposition of a rising and a falling intonation. In Swedish and Norwegian there exists an opposition of a simple and a complex stress; a simple stress consists of a falling or rising pitch (the direction of the tone movement is immaterial since it changes in respect to dialectic changes), while a complex stress consists of a falling-rising pitch.

Prosodic features which in one and the same word are relevant to more than one syllable are called non-accentual. For example in the African language Lonkundo there exists a contrast between the words *lòkòlò* 'palm fruit' and *lòkóló* 'invocation' (the symbol ` represents a low register tone, the symbol ′ a high register tone).[54] Non-accentual prosodic features do not possess a culminative function; their only purpose is word differentiation.

In order to simplify the description of prosodic features it is useful to introduce the concept of mora. Mora is the minimal segment of the speech flow which can be a carrier of a prosodic feature. In respect to the concept of mora, a long vowel phoneme which, let us say, has a rising pitch, can be regarded as a succession of two morae, the first of which is a carrier of a sharp tone of low register and the second a carrier of a sharp tone of high register. On the other hand, if the long vowel has a falling pitch it can be regarded as a succession of two morae, the first of which is a carrier of a sharp tone of high register and the second a carrier of a sharp tone of low register. For instance, if we take the Lithuanian word *nósis* 'nose' (with a falling intonation) and the word *tãkas* 'footprint, track' (with a rising intonation), we can regard each of these words as possessing three morae; in the word *nósis* the first mora is set off, in the word *tãkas* the second. A simplification of the description can

[54] N. S. Trubeckoj, *op. cit.*, p. 216.

be attained by the reduction of the twofold characteristic of intonation (quality of intonation and place of intonation) to a single characteristic (place of intonation) because the application of the concept of the mora makes the quality of intonation phonologically redundant.

The above discussion presents, in short, the classification of prosodic elements in modern phonology. It is unnecessary to go into further details since the above summarization is fully sufficient to our inquiry into the semiotic nature of prosodic features.

As can be seen from the aforementioned, contemporary phonology regards prosodic features as relational acoustic elements. As relational elements, prosodic features possess either the function of crest formation (culminative function) or the function of word differentiation. As acoustic elements, prosodic features possess certain acoustic quality: this can be either higher intensity, longer duration, or, finally, a certain pitch of the set-off syllable. Thus in so far as prosodic features are concerned modern phonology accepts as equally valid the two following statements, analogous to the two statements which have been introduced in the preceding sections in connection with the phoneme and with distinctive features.

Statement 1. Prosodic features are relational elements which possess either a culminative function or a function of word differentiation.

Statement 2. Prosodic features are acoustic features.

In adopting the above statements, we must adopt all their consequences as well.

In accordance with Statement 1, prosodic features can be transposed from acoustic substance into other forms of physical substance, let us say, into chromatic, graphic, or tactile. If in the words *píli* and *pilí* we transpose the phoneme *p* into a blue circle, the phoneme *l* into a yellow circle, the phoneme *i* into a red circle, and indicate higher and lower tonal intensity, characteristic of the stressed and unstressed syllable, by a darker or lighter color hue, then the stressed phoneme *i* can be transposed into a dark red circle and the unstressed phoneme *i* into a light-red circle. In those languages where various types of tones serve as prosodic features, the difference between tones can be transposed into an entire range of dark and light hues of any given color.

Statement 2, however, poses a direct contradiction, namely that prosodic features cannot be transposed from acoustic into other forms of physical substance.

Thus, as in the analysis of the phoneme and of distinctive features, we encounter here an antinomy of transposition.

One should, however, consider likewise the fact that in the case of prosodic features this antinomy arises even if we do not attempt to transpose prosodic features from acoustic into other forms of physical substance. As has already been indicated, the reason for this lies in the fact that modern phonology connects prosodic features with intensity, duration or a certain tone pitch of a syllable, i.e. not with any acoustic substance but with concrete aspects of acoustic substance. However, if prosodic features are relational elements which need only to possess definite functions, then why should prosodic features be connected only with the concrete aspects of acoustic substances? Such an inconsistency was pointed out already by A. Martinet who formulated the following mental experiment in order to prove that other aspects of acoustic substance can also constitute prosodic features. He imagined a language which would allow only syllables of the type *mã* or *ba*, i.e. fully nasalized or fully non-nasalized syllables. If we assume at the same time that in this language every word could have only one nasalized syllable it becomes apparent that the function of nasality would be basically identical to the function of stress in such languages, as, let us say, Russian, English, or German.[55] This mental experiment which represents a logical consequence of the theorem postulating the relational, functional nature of prosodic features, contradicts the statement which posits that prosodic features are limited in regard to their physical nature to the intensity, duration and pitch of a syllable. Thus, even from the purely acoustic standpoint there arises an antinomy of transposition: the statement of the functional nature of prosodic features postulates

[55] A. Martinet, *Phonology as Functional Phonetics*, p. 11.

that prosodic features can be transposed into any form of acoustic substance while such a transposition is prohibited by the just outlined limitation imposed upon prosodic features by modern phonology. In seeking to overcome this antinomy we can remove this limitation by substituting it with a general statement which postulates that prosodic features are acoustic elements. But having made this substitution we encounter a new antinomy. Indeed, if we allow that any form of acoustic substance, let us say, nasal articulation of syllabic elements, can serve as a prosodic feature, we encounter a situation where such fundamentally heterogeneous acoustic features as intensity and nasality of vowel phonemes appear to be identical. This introduces the antinomy of identity which derives from a contradiction between the consequences of the statement of the functional nature of prosodic features and the statement which postulates their acoustic nature: the former theorem indicates that it is possible for those prosodic features which are heterogeneous in acoustic relationships to become identical, while the latter statement is directly contraposed to the former, considering such identity to be impossible.

Thus, the relational-physical theory of prosodic features encounters fundamental antinomies analogous to those which were encountered by the relational-physical theory of the phoneme and of distinctive features. In order to overcome these antinomies we are compelled to split the concept of prosodic feature into two corresponding concepts: the concept of prosodic feature as a construct and the concept of the substratum of prosodic feature. To the former concept we will assign the term "prosodeme" and to the latter the term "prosodemoid".[56] In correspondence with the demarcation of the two abstraction levels, the level of observation and the level of constructs, phonology should distinguish two types of prosodic features as well: prosodemoids, at the former level, and

[56] The meaning which we ascribe to the term "prosodeme" has nothing in common with the use of this term in contemporary phonological literature. It is well known that the term "prosodeme" was used by N. S. Trubeckoj and other authors as a general designation of the concept of the syllable and the mora (cf. N. S. Trubeckoj, *op. cit.*, pp. 212-213.)

prosodemes at the latter. Prosodemes are in relation of embodiment to prosodemoids; in other words, prosodemoids embody prosodemes, while prosodemes are embodied in prosodemoids.

By the same token one should differentiate between concrete prosodemoids and prosodemes, on the one hand, and abstract prosodemoids and prosodemes on the other. This can be shown through an example of the Russian words *stólik* 'small table', *kóška* 'cat', *kníga* 'book', and similar words in which stress is placed on the initial syllable; individual stresses encountered are A_1, A_2, A_3, ..., A_n. These individual stresses represent concrete prosodemoids which serve as substrata of concrete prosodemes "A_1", "A_2", "A_3", ..., "A_n" (quotation marks here distinguish prosodemes from prosodemoids). Since concrete prosodemes "A_1", "A_2", "A_3", ..., "A_n" are identical in respect to their placement within the word, they unite into a class which is designated as the abstract prosodeme "A". Correspondingly, concrete prosodemoids A_1, A_2, A_3, ..., A_n, as the substrata of corresponding concrete prosodemes, unite into a class which is designated as the abstract prosodemoid A.

Thus we have arrived at a two-level system of prosodic features which can be illustrated by the following table:

Level of constructs	*Concrete prosodemes* cf.: "A_1", "A_2", "A_3", ..., "A_n"	*Abstract prosodeme* cf.: "A"
Level of observation	*Concrete prosodemoids* cf.: A_1, A_2, A_3, ..., A_n	*Abstract prosodemoids* cf.: A

Having established the two level system of prosodemes and prosodemoids, we will now concentrate on a further clarification of the relation between the concept of prosodic feature and the prosodeme.

We have shown above that the concepts of prosodeme and prosodemoid resulted from the split-up of the concept of prosodic feature in adherence to the demarcation of the two abstraction levels, the level of observation and the level of constructs. Having split the concept of prosodic feature into the concept of prosodeme and the concept of prosodemoid we have liberated the prosodic feature from physical substance which had obstructed its original semiotic nature. But this is insufficient. We must necessarily ask whether it would not be possible to liberate the prosodic feature also from its function of word differentiation, as immaterial to its semiotic nature and, consequently, to limit prosodeme only to its culminative function.

In attempting to answer this inquiry we will, first of all, focus our attention on non-accentual prosodic features, returning to the aforementioned example from the African language Lonkundo. In this language the words *lòkòlò* and *lòkóló* differ only in respect to the contrast of the sharp tones of low and high register. We may ask, however: how do such tones differ from the differentors of the phoneme? If differentors are constructs, then nothing prevents us from embodying these constructs in tonal or other forms of acoustic substance which are, as a rule, connected with the concept of prosodic features. Therefore, we are justified in interpreting the tones in the above cited words simply as differentors of the corresponding vowel phonemes; substrata of these differentors are then those features which represent the acoustic substance of a low or high register. The same can be said in regard to other non-acoustic prosodic features: they all differ in regard to their culminative function, but in respect to the function of word differentiation they do not differ from the differentors of the phoneme. Hence, non-accentual prosodic features are, in fact, pseudo-prosodic features which should be regarded as ordinary phonemic differentors.

We will concentrate now on acoustic prosodic features, comparing the words *dúšu* 'soul', and *dušú* 'suffocate'. Should the presence and absence of stress in these words be regarded as a feature of the vowel phonemes? In order to facilitate the answer to this question we will compare the placement of stresses by means of a successive segmentation of the words into phonemes. This comparison can be illustrated by the diagram:

d	*ú*	*š*	*u*
d	*u*	*š*	*ú*

It is obvious that the stressed *ú* and the unstressed *u* do not occur in one and the same position, since the difference between *ú* and *u* is accompanied by differences in the remaining segments of the contraposed words and is, consequently, not isolated, Similarly, other cases of a similar kind of contraposition will show equal results: the differences between stressed and unstressed vowels will always be accompanied by differences in the remaining segments of the words and, hence, will not be isolated. We can conclude that stress cannot serve as a sign of any one separate vowel phoneme, but that it forms a superstructure over the entire word. Thus, in our example, the word *dúšu* should be interpreted as a chain of phonemes (d+*u*+*š*+*u*) plus a stress on the first syllable, while the word *dušú* should be interpreted as a chain of phonemes (d+*u*+*š*+*u*) plus a stress on the second syllable.

The interpretation of stress as a phonological element which supercedes the limits of word segmentation into phonemes and forms a superstructure over the word, namely over the signifiant of the word, is fully justified since it is adequately clarified by the observed factors. This interpretation cannot, however, successfully liberate the prosodic feature from its function of word differentiation, as essential to its semiotic nature, since stress, even as a superstructure over the signifiant of the word, can, along with the fulfillment of its culminative function, differentiate between words as well; stress has a function of word differentiation in the already shown contraposition of words *dúšu* and *dušú* which differ precisely as to its placement. There arises the question whether one could not find, aside from the interpretation of stress as a superstructure over the signifiant of the word, an additional interpretation, equally justified from the standpoint of an adequate explanation of observed factors, which would facilitate the liberation of the prosodic feature from its function of word differentiation, as non-essential to its semiotic nature.

In order to be able to resolve this question we will introduce the concept of zero as a construct; this concept will enable us to advance the hypothesis that contraposed words of the above shown type *dúšu* and *dušú* differ not in respect to the placement of the stress but in respect to the distribution of zeros within the chain of phonemes. Introducing the concept of zero, we can reformulate the contraposition *dúšu* – *dušú* as follows:

Ø	Ø	*d*	*ú*	*š*	*u*
d	*u*	*š*	*ú*	Ø	Ø

In this diagram the stress of the first word and the stress of the second word coincide as to their placement: they are located in the fourth position from the beginning of both chains. In effect, both words differ now not in respect to the placement of the stress but in respect to the placement of two hypothetical zero phonemes positions at the beginning of the first word and at the end of the second word.

If we regard this diagram as a hypothesis we reduce the observed differences in the placement of the stress to differences within the phonemic chains which contain hypothetical zero phoneme positions. Such interpretation liberates the prosodic feature from its function of word differentiation and limits it thus to a single specific inherent function, the culminative function.

Above we have split the concept of prosodic feature into the concepts of prosodeme and prosodemoid; now we have completed the next step, having established that it is unnecessary to ascribe to the prosodeme a function of word differentiation in addition to its culminative function. The culminative function can be, hence, regarded as the sole function of the prosodeme.

14. THE CONCEPT OF PROSODEME AND THE CONCEPT OF CULMINATOR

In the preceding section we have established that the culminative function is the sole function of the prosodeme. Let us now scrutinize in more detail the nature of this function.

It has already been pointed out that the culminative function of prosodemes implies the signalization of the number of self-contained words in a given speech flow. But there exist languages in which the stress does not fall on separate words.

For instance, French is quite interesting in this respect; L. V. Ščerba compares the function of stress in French with the function of stress in Russian: "in Russian the speech flow is separated into words due to the fact that every word possesses verbal stress: *my čitáem knígu naúčnogo soderžánija* 'we are reading a scientific book'; this sentence possesses five stresses and five words. It is, of course, true that in Russian there exist some unstressed words, the so-called enclitics, and especially proclitics; yet this does not change the basic fact, since the number of such unstressed words is small; and since such words possess, as a rule, the character of moveable prefixes and suffixes; moreover the word which is affected by enclitics always preserves stress in its usual place. Therefore we talk in Russian about the 'verbal stress'. No analogy to this exists in French: there stress relates not to individual words but to a group of words, which represent a complete meaningful unit. The stress falls on the penult of the final word of the group unless the penult contains the so called *e* muet (the only apparent exception to this is the pronoun *le* which can stand in the terminal position of such a group but remains under stress: *donne-le!*). The remaining words of the group remain unstressed, as can be seen from these examples: *un grand mouchoir de soie* 'a large silk handkerchief'; *je viendrai vous voir* 'I will come to see you'; *quelques minutes après* 'a few minutes later'; *en lisant le journal* 'while reading the newspaper'; *aussi vite qu'il pouvait*; 'as fast as possible'."[57] These examples show that the prosodeme does not necessarily signalize the number of independent words in a given speech flow; in languages such as French prosodemes signalize only the number of separate word groups within the given speech flow.

While in some languages prosodemes can correspond to units larger than separate words, namely to word groups, in other languages they correspond to units which are smaller than words, as

[57] L. V. Ščerba, *Fonetika francuzskogo jazyka* (Moscow, 1948), p. 82.

well. Let us take, for instance, the German word *Wachsfiguren-kabinett* 'cabinet for wax figures'. In this word there occur three stresses, a primary one on the first syllable, and two secondary ones on the syllables *-nett* and *-gur-*. This example shows that in German, stress signalizes not only the number of separate words in a given speech flow but also the number of parts in a composite word. Comparing the function of stress in German with the function of stress in Russian, A. Martinet writes: "In languages such as German the situation is clear: every element of the composite word preserves the stress which characterizes it as an individual word; the second syllable of the word *Figur* 'figure' always preserves its stress, independently of whether the word *Figur* constitutes an autonomous member of a sentence or a component of a composite word. Quite different is the situation in such languages as Russian where all components of the composite word, with the exception of one, lose their proper stress: the word *nos* 'nose' loses its stress and the timbre of its vowel when it becomes a component of the composite word *nosorog* 'rhinoceros'; in the German equivalent of this word, *Nashorn*, on the contrary, every one of the components preserves its proper stress; there occurs only the subordination of the stress of the component *-horn* to the stress of the component *Nas-*. Thus the *accentual unit* in Russian is the word, and in German the lexeme."[58]

Thus, prosodemes correspond not only to words but also to units which are larger or smaller than words — on the one hand to

[58] A. Martinet, *op. cit.*, p. 89. — As far as Russian language data are concerned, A. Martinet inaccurately points out that in Russian all components of a composite word, with the exception of one, lose their proper stress because in Russian there also exist composite words every element of which preserves its proper stress, either as a primary or as a secondary stress, as for instance *kònefȇrma* 'horse farm', *pàrnokopýtnye* 'artiodactyla', *slàborázvityj* 'underdeveloped', and others (cf. *Russkoe literaturnoe proiznošenie i udarenie*, reference dictionary under the edition of R. I. Avanesov and S. I. Ožegov, Moscow, 1960). However, in spite of the inaccuracy A. Martinet grasped the phonological essence of the phenomenon: since in Russian the components of composite words preserve their proper stress only in a few cases, the number of stresses in the sentence does not enable us to judge the number of lexemes within that sentence and, therefore, from the phonological standpoint, in Russian the accentual unit is not the lexeme but the word.

groups of words, and on the other hand, to lexemes. In the preceding section it was pointed out that every prosodeme is a construct; this means that the prosodeme does not possess any physical substratum which embodies it but that it possesses only a culminative function, i.e. that it signalizes the number of units in the speech flow. If there indeed exists no physical substratum of the prosodeme, then, naturally, there arises the question whether the concept of prosodeme could not be broadened so as to include also vocality as a feature of vowel phonemes. By the same token, if the culminative function consists of the signalization of the number of units in the speech flow then, naturally, vocality of the vowel phoneme should be regarded as a prosodeme since the number of vowel phonemes in the speech flow indicates the number of syllables — phonological units — in that speech flow. If we take, for instance, Russian, we see that the number of words in a sentence equals the number of stresses, and the number of phonological syllables equals the number of vowel phonemes. The fact that vocality and stress are two different acoustic entities is of no significance since the prosodeme, as a construct, can in principle be embodied in any form of physical substance.

Hence our reply to the above posed question is affirmative: if prosodemes are regarded as constructs, then the concept of prosodeme can include vocality as a phonological element which signalizes the number of phonological syllables in the speech flow.

The interpretation of vocality as prosodeme touches, however, upon the following two difficulties.

In the first place it appears incorrect to place side by side the phonological syllable which is a unilateral unit, and the lexeme, the word, and groups of words which are bilateral units; the latter group differentiates two aspects, the signifiant and the signifié, while phonological syllable belongs to only one aspect of a linguistic sign, the signifiant.

In order to eliminate these difficulties we shall execute the following mental experiment. Taking the word *smola* 'resin' we will replace its initial consonantal phoneme with the consonantal phonemes *p*, *b*, *n*, *ž*, *x*, *v*, thus obtaining *pmola*, *bmola*, *nmola*, *žmola, xmola, vmola.* Although in Russian these chains do not constitute meaningful words, there exists a fundamental difference between *pmola, bmola,* and *nmola* on the one hand, and *žmola, xmola* and *vmola* on the other hand. The latter three phonemic chains do not possess any meaning but, in principle, they could constitute Russian words; the former three phonemic chains are, however not only meaningless, but incapable, in principle, of constituting Russian words. This difference is conditioned by the fact that the Russian language does permit the consonant clusters *žm, xm, vm* before vowels in initial position, while this does not apply to the consonant clusters *pm, bm, nm.* Concrete words of any given language are the initial basis for the separation of permissible and non-permissible consonantal clusters within that language: the object of phonology seems to be, however, not the empirically given fact but the potentiality of the language to utilize phonemic chains as actual words. This potentiality of language necessitates the introduction of the concept of phonological word which should be distinguished from the concept of grammatical word. Grammatical words are bilateral units which comprise both the signifiants and the signifié. Phonological words are unilateral units which consist of phonemic chains permissible in a given language that can be converted into grammatical words. Hence, from the phonological point of view, the essential factor in respect to the word *smola* is not the possession of a definite meaning but the possession of a definite structure which permits its utilization as a grammatical word. As far as phonology is concerned, *smola* as well as *žmola, xmola,* and *vmola* are phonological words to an equal degree, while this is not the case with *pmola, bmola* and *nmola.*[59] If we accept the concept of phonological word then we are justified in placing the phonological syllable side by side with the phonological word since both are unilateral units which possess a definite linear structure. In this respect the difference between the

[59] Cf. G. L. Trager and L. Smith, *An Outline of English Structure* (Oklahoma, Norman, 1951). — In this book we find an analogous demarcation of two types of words which differs, however, considerably from ours since its authors do not connect this demarcation with the differentiation of potentiality and actuality in language.

phonological syllable and the phonological word relates only to their size: although the phonological word can coincide with the phonological syllable, it can be composed of several phonological syllables as well.

The second difficulty which touches upon the interpretation of vocality as a prosodeme is contained in the fact that, as has been shown in the preceding section, the prosodeme can possess only a single, culminative function, and the interpretation of vocality as a prosodeme contradicts the already established concept of vocality as a distinctive feature whose function is the contraposition of vowel phonemes to consonantal phonemes.

In order to eliminate this difficulty we must prove that vocality and consonantness should not be regarded as distinctive features of phonemes. In order to do this we have to pose the question: can vowel and consonantal phonemes occur in the same environment?

This question has been answered negatively by some linguists, as J. Kuryłowicz or J. Prieto, and positively by others, as R. Jakobson, G. Fant, M. Halle.[60] Neither of them question the demarcation of the abstraction levels since there exists the impression that these contraposed points of view are mutually exclusive. Actually both points of view can be reconciled if we split the concept of phonological environment into the concept of subphonological environment and concept of proper phonological environment. Subphonological environment relates to the level of observation while phonological environment relates to the level of constructs. Let us consider a concrete example. R. Jakobson, G. Fant and M. Halle, in proving that vowels and consonants can occur in identical phonological environment, cite such English contrapositions as: *wet* [u'et], *yet* [i'et] and *vet*, *set*, *net*, or *he* [h'ii] and *his* [h'iz], *hit* [h'it].[61] We believe that in this case we obtain, through direct observation, not phonological but subphonological environment. Phonemoids of

[60] Cf. J. Kuryłowicz, *Esquisses linguistiques* (Wrocław-Kraków, 1960), p. 11; Luis J. Prieto, "Traits oppositionnals et traits contrastifs", *Word*, X, 1 (1954); R. Jakobson, C. G. Fant, M. Halle, *Preliminaries to Speech Analysis: the Distinctive Features and Their Correlates* (= *Massachusetts Institute of Technology Technical Report*, No. 13), 3rd ed. (Boston, 1955).

[61] R. Jakobson, C. G. Fant, M. Halle, *op. cit*, p. 20.

both vocalic and consonantal phonemes occur in this case in the same subphonological environment; vocalic and consonantal phonemes, however, occur in different phonological environments while neither phonemes nor phonological environment are directly observable, and represent only hypothetical elements.

What constitutes the objective basis, we may ask, of the need to split the concept of phonological environment into the concepts of subphonological environment and proper phonological environment? Would it not be easier, starting from the just mentioned English data, and analogous data in other languages, to assert that vowel and consonantal phonemes can occur in the same phonological environment?

In order to substantiate the necessity of the splitting of this concept we must rely on the differentiation of two types of statements in modern logic of science. We have in mind the differentiation of abstract hypotheses and the so-called registration laws. The Polish logician K. Ajdukiewicz defines registration laws as follows: "The first stage on which empirical sciences rely by means of deductions are the so-called registration laws. Registration laws are universal or nearly universal statements which are derived from premises that serve as concrete cases of these laws and are based directly on experiment. For example, the nearly universal statement that man has, as a rule, 32 teeth represents a registration law since it is derived from premises which state that this or that man has 32 teeth, from premises which represent concrete cases of this statement and are based directly on experiment. The general statement that a specific weight of any gas is lighter than the specific weight of water also represents a registration law, etc."[62] Registration laws originate as a result of induction, while abstract hypotheses are postulated by us as statements about constructs for the clarification of the registration laws.

In connection with the problem under investigation we shall establish the following registration laws in phonology.

(1) Every independent chain of phonemoids must contain at

[62] K. Ajdukiewicz, *Język i poznanie*, I (Warsaw, 1960), p. 297.

least one phonemoid which serves as a substratum of a vowel phoneme.

(2) In the case of two independent chains of phonemoids any two phonemoids which serve as substrata of phonemes, appearing in identical phonological positions, can be mutually substituted.

We will observe the contraposition of the words *um* 'mind' and *da* 'yes' from the point of view of these phonological registration laws, assuming that the initial and terminal phonemoids of the second word occur in the same phonological positions as the initial and terminal phonemoids of the first word:

P_1	P_2
u	*m*
d	*a*

According to the second phonological registration law we are justified in substituting phonemoid *d* of the word *da* for phonemoid *u* of the word *um*; we are also justified in substituting phonemoid *m* of the word *um* for phonemoid *a* of the word *da*. In either case we obtain the chain of phonemoids *dm* which, however, according to the first phonological registration law is not permissible.

Let us examine likewise the contraposition of the words *dno* 'bottom' and *isk* '(legal) suit'. We will assume that the first, second and third phonemoid of the word *isk* occur in the same phonological positions as the first, second and third phonemoids of the word *dno*:

P_1	P_2	P_3
d	*n*	*o*
i	*s*	*k*

According to the second phonological registration law we are justified in substituting the phonemoids *k* and *s* of the word *isk* for the corresponding phonemoids *o* and *n* of the word *dno*; we are also justified in substituting the phonemoids *d* and *n* of the word *dno* for the corresponding phonemoids *i* and *s* of the word *isk*. As a result of these substitutions we obtain the phonemoidal chains *dnk* and *dsk* which are, however, not permissible in respect to the first phonological registration law.

It would be possible to introduce a number of other analogous examples which bear out the contradiction between the above postulated phonological registration laws. In order to eliminate this contradiction it becomes necessary to split the concept of phonological positions into the concept of proper phonological positions and the concept of subphonological positions.

If we perform such a split of the concept, then the above given examples can be re-interpreted thus: phonemoids which occur in identical subphonological positions embody in some cases phonemes occurring in identical phonological positions, and in other cases phonemes occurring in different phonological positions; at the same time vowel and consonantal phonemes cannot occur in identical phonological positions. On the basis of such re-interpretation we can represent the given two examples in the following diagrams:

Subphonological positions

P_1	P_2
u	*m*
d	*a*

Phonological positions

"P_1"	"P_2"	"P_3"
Ø	"*u*"	"*m*"
"*d*"	"*a*"	Ø

Subphonological positions

P_1	P_2	P_2
d	*n*	*o*
i	*s*	*k*

Phonological positions

"P_1"	"P_2"	"P_3"	"P_4"	"P_5"
"*d*"	"*n*"	"*o*"	Ø	Ø
Ø	Ø	"*i*"	"*s*"	"*k*"

In order to differentiate phonemes and phonological positions, on the one hand, and phonemoids and subphonological positions, on the other hand, the symbols which designate phonemes and phonological positions have been placed in quotation marks.

These schemes show clearly the principal difference between phonological and subphonological positions. Phonological positions are constructs which are not directly observable but are postulated for the clarification of observed facts.

In order to clarify observed facts it was necessary to postulate an abstract hypothesis which states that vowel and consonantal phonemes cannot occur in identical positions. This abstract hypothesis explains the aforementioned registration laws which represent the generalization of directly observed facts.

Hence, vowel and consonantal phonemes cannot occur in identical positions. If this abstract hypothesis is taken to be correct we should abandon the established idea of vocality as a distinctive feature which effects the contraposition of vowel and consonantal phonemes. On the basis of the above discussion we arrive inevitably at the conclusion that vocality possesses merely a culminative function; vocality signalizes the number of phonological syllables in the speech flow, and hence should be regarded as a prosodeme. However, since the use of the term "prosodeme", as applied to vocality, could lead to terminological disagreements, we introduce as a general designation the term "culminator". The concept of culminator embraces all phonological elements which possess a culminative function, among them vocality. We shall regard prosodemes and vocality as different types of culminators: prosodemes are culminators which signalize the number of lexemes, words, or word groups in the speech flow; vocality is a culminator which signalizes the number of phonological syllables in the speech flow.

Since every culminator represents a construct which possesses some form of physical substratum, then in order to identify this physical substratum of the culminator we introduce the term "culminatoid".

It is necessary to differentiate concrete culminators and culminatoids and abstract culminators and culminatoids. This can be shown on an example which applies to vocality. The Russian words *stol* 'table', *rak* 'crayfish', *mul* 'mule', *vid* 'appearance', *beg* 'race', and other monosyllabic words have individual vocalities V_1, V_2, V_3, V_4, V_5, ..., V_n. These individual vocalities represent concrete culminatoids which serve as substrata of the concrete vocalities, the culminators "V_1", "V_2", "V_3", "V_4", "V_5", ..., "V_n" (by means of the quotation marks we differentiate culminators from culminatoids). Since the concrete vocalities-culminators "V_1", "V_2", "V_3", "V_4", "V_5", ..., "V_n" are identical in regard to their monosyllabicity, they unite into a class which is designated as the abstract vocality-culminator "V".

In the preceding section we have seen an example of the differentiation of concrete prosodemoids and prosodemes on the one hand, and abstract prosodemoids and prosodemes on the other. Since prosodemoids are a variety of culminatoids and prosodemes are a variety of culminators, we can refer here to that very same example in illustrating the differentiation of concrete culminatoids and culminators from abstract culminatoids and culminators.

The two level system of culminators and culminatoids can be illustrated in the following table:

Level of constructs	*Concrete culminators*	*Abstract culminators*
Level of observation	*Concrete culminatoids*	*Abstract culminatoids*

15. BOUNDARY SIGNALS

Phonological elements whose function is to demarcate linguistic units within the speech flow are usually called boundary signals; we refer to them as possessing a demarcative or delimitative function.

A detailed classification of boundary signals can be found in N. S. Trubeckoj, who classifies them from four points of view: (1) in respect to their relation to the demarcative function; (2) in respect to their simplicity or complexity; (3) in respect to whether they indicate the presence or absence of a boundary; (4) in respect to the nature of the linguistic units whose boundaries they designate. Correspondingly, this quadruple classification differentiates the following types of boundary signals: (1) phonematic and aphonematic, (2) single and composite, (3) positive and negative, (4) word-demarcative and morpheme-demarcative. These types of boundary signals can overlap each other.

Those phonemes which possess a demarcative function are phonematic boundary signals. For instance, the phoneme *h* in English signalizes also the beginning of a morpheme; similar cases occurred in ancient-Greek. Those specific phonemic variants which occur only at the juncture of linguistic units are aphonematic boundary signals: for instance, in Tamil the phonemes *p*, *t*, *k* have aspirated variants only in initial positions, and since these variants occur only in the initial position of the word they do possess a demarcative function. Bound stress, for instance the bound stress of Czech which falls on the first syllable of the word, and the bound stress of Turkish which falls on the last syllable, can also fulfill the role of an aphonematic boundary signal.

Single boundary signals can be either separate phonemes or variants of separate phonemes. Examples of single boundary signals are, for instance, the above mentioned phoneme *h* in English and ancient-Greek, and the aspirated phonemic variants *p*, *t*, *k* in Tamil. Composite boundary signals can be also phonematic or aphonematic. Phonematic composite boundary signal is a group of phonemes possible only at the juncture of two linguistic units; for example, in German we find the groups "consonant + *h*" (*ein Haus*, *an-halten*, *Wesen-heit*, *der Hals*, *ver-hindern*, *Wahr-heit*, etc.), "nasal + liquid" (*an-liegen*, *ein-reden*, *irrtüm-lich*, *um-ringen*, etc.), and a number of other phonematic composite signals. In connection with aphonematic composite boundary signals one should introduce the following statement. "In English", writes N. S. Trubeckoj, "one can point out the demarcation of two types of *l*: the rule says that *l* which preceeds vowels is called "clear", while *l* which preceeds consonants and terminal *l* are called "dark". It would be, however, more exact to say "before a vowel fo the same word" instead of 'before vowels', since this rule does not apply beyond the limits of the word: thus, the *l* in *we learn* is clear (phonetically *wilə:n*), but the *l* in *will earn* is dark (phonetically *wil̥ə:n*). Consequently, the "clear" *l* and the "dark" *l* in English are nothing but two combinatory variants of a single phoneme, but in the phoneme sequence "vowel+*l*+vowel" the opposition of the "clear" and "dark" variants fulfills a delimitative function: the "dark realization" of the phoneme *l* signifies that between *l* and the following vowel there lies a word boundary. In Russian (as in German or English) the opposition of the palatal and velar *k* is aphonematic: before *e*, *i* the sound *k* is pronounced as a palatal; elsewhere it is pronounced as a velar. This rule does not, however, extend beyond the limits of the word. If one word terminates in *k* and the following word begins with *e* or *i*, then *k* remains velar while the vowels *i*, *e* become correspondingly retracted (*e* > *E*, *i* > *ɯ*): for instance, *k ètomu* 'to this' is pronounced *kEtəmŭ* (while *keta* 'salmon' is pronounced *k'etă*); *mog èto* 'could he [do] this' is pronounced *məkEtə*, *k izbam* 'to the huts' is pronounced *kɯzbəm* (while *kis by* 'would sour' is pronounced *k'izby*), *drug i prijatel'* 'comrade and friend' is pronounced *drùkɯ pr'ĭjæ̀t'ĭl'* (while *ruki prijatelja* 'friend's hands' is pronounced *ruk'ĭ pr'ĭjæ̀t'ĭl'ə*). Thus in Russian the combinations *kE*, *kɯ* are composite signals which indicate the existence of a word boundary between the phoneme *k* and the immediately following vowels *e*, *i*."[63]

So far all of the discussed boundary signals have been positive. They indicated that in a definite place within the speech flow there occurs a boundary of a word or a morpheme. Alongside positive boundary signals there exist also negative boundary signals which indicate the absence of a boundary in a definite place. Paralleling boundary signals with traffic signals, N. S. Trubeckoj compares positive boundary signals to red traffic light (stop) and negative boundary signals to green traffic light (go). Negative boundary signals are subdivided into general negative boundary signals and restricted unilateral negative boundary signals. The latter only point out the fact that words can neither commence nor terminate in

[63] N. S. Trubeckoj, *op. cit.*, p. 300.

a given place within the speech flow. Negative boundary signals can be phonematic or aphonematic, composite or single. The following are some examples. In the Kazakh language *γ* and *g* are permissible only in medial positions; this is an example of a phonematic general negative single signal. In German, English, Dutch, Norwegian and Swedish *ŋ* is permissible only in medial and final positions; this is an example of phonematic restricted unilateral negative single signal. In Russian strident consonants in final position are always voiceless, and therefore the combination "voiced strident + vowel" indicates in all cases that between the components of this combination there cannot occur a word boundary (phonematic general negative group signal). Every phonematic positive boundary signal, is, as a rule, opposed to an aphonematic negative boundary signal. Thus, while in Tamil the aspirated variants of the phonemes *p*, *t*, *k* which appear in initial positions are aphonematic positive signals, the fricative variants of the same phonemes which are permissible only in medial positions should be regarded as aphonematic negative signals. While in English the combination "dark *l* + vowel" is an aphonematic positive composite signal, the combination "clear *l* + vowel" which indicates the absence of a word boundary between its components should be regarded as an aphonematic negative composite signal.

In respect to the types of linguistic units whose demarcation is effected by boundary signals one finds great differences between individual languages. In some languages the function of boundary signals constitutes the demarcation of the boundaries between morphemes, while in other languages their function effects the demarcation of the boundaries between words. German, for instance, belongs to the first type, since here signals which demarcate words apply to the demarcation of morphemes as well and since some signals are limited specifically to the demarcation of morphemes. In Finnish, on the contrary, morpheme boundaries are never marked, and only word boundaries are indicated. Many languages belong to a mixed type: they possess special signals for the demarcation of the morphemic boundaries and special signals for the demarcation of word boundaries.

Speaking of boundary signals on the whole, it should be emphasized that compared to other phonological phenomena boundary signals are not absolutely essential to the language. In principle it is possible to imagine a language in which boundary signals are entirely absent. Boundary signals represent a facultative superstructure over basic phonological phenomena which derive from the essence of language as tools of communication. Pointing to the facultative character of boundary signals, N. S. Trubeckoj writes: "They could well be compared with street traffic signals. Until lately such signals were nonexistent even in large cities and even today they have not been introduced everywhere. In general, it is possible to get along without them: it is necessary only to be more careful and alert. Therefore they have not been established at every intersection but only at some. Similarly, linguistic means of delimitation do not usually occur in all positions where they would be, in principle, possible, but instead only here and there. The difference between the two kinds of signals consists only in the fact that traffic signals are always installed at "especially dangerous" intersections, while the placement of boundary signals in the majority of languages appears to be highly accidental; this, obviously, is the result of an artificial and rational regulation of traffic on the one hand, and an organic formation and development of language on the other. However, in respect to their psychological nature, linguistic means of delimitation resemble traffic signals: both of them are calculated to interrupt the span of our attention at corresponding intervals."[64]

This, in short, is the description of boundary signals put forth by N. S. Trubeckoj. Our task consists in determining the necessary corrections which should be introduced into this description from the standpoint of the two-level theory of phonology which was discussed in the preceding sections.

Because of their semiotic nature, boundary signals should be regarded as superimposed phonological constructs whose substrata are the basic phonological constructs, phonemes and culminators. Both phonemes and culminators are in relation of

[64] N. S. Trubeckoj, *op. cit.*, p. 291.

inclusion to boundary signals. In this situation the substratum of a construct is no longer merely a physical substance but another construct.

If boundary signals are to be, in fact, regarded as superimposed phonological constructs, it becomes necessary to re-examine the principle of the division of boundary signals into phonematic and aphonematic. According to N. S. Trubeckoj, who regards variants as physical realizations of the phoneme, variants are beyond the limits of the phoneme, and therefore those phonemic variants which possess a demarcative function are related to aphonematic boundary signals. Actually, if the phoneme is to be interpreted as a construct, phonemic variants do not represent sounds, but phonemes as well, and namely concrete phonemes which are varieties of the abstract phoneme. In the preceding sections, we have indicated that both abstract and concrete phonemes relate equally to the level of constructs. Therefore one should not speak about phonematic and aphonematic boundary signals, but about interphonemic and intraphonemic boundary signals. Interphonemic signals are those boundary signals whose substrata are various abstract phonemes. Intraphonemic signals are those signals whose substrata are various concrete phonemes which represent varieties of one specific abstract phoneme. From our point of view truly aphonematic boundary signals can be only those signals whose substrata are culminators, since culminators represent phonological elements which differ from phonemes basically in respect to their function.

Let us consider now the character of linguistic units which are demarcated by boundary signals. According to N. S. Trubeckoj, both morphemes and words are bilateral units which consist of a signifier and a signified. However, we believe in the necessity of a strict differentiation between the concepts of phonological word and phonological morpheme and the concepts of grammatical word and grammatical morpheme. In the preceding section we have pointed out that from the phonological standpoint the chains *žmola* and *xmola* do not, in principle, differ from the chain *smola*. In respect to their phonemic structure all three chains are phonological to an equal degree. The same applies to the chains of phonemes which serve as morphemes: from the phonological standpoint the chains *žmol-*, *xmol-* are morphemes in an equal degree as the chain *smol-*. The chains *pmol-*, *bmol-*, however, are not morphemes from the phonological standpoint, since their phonemic structure is not permissible by the Russian phonological system. Thus, the function of boundary signals, as phonological constructs, is not the demarcation of bilateral units, i.e. grammatical words and grammatical morphemes, but the demarcation of unilateral units, i.e. phonological words and phonological morphemes. It is obvious that this approach does not solve the problem of the connection of boundary signals with grammatical words and grammatical morphemes at the morphonological plane of language, and that this problem lies beyond the limits of phonology, being related to morphonology. The basic difference between phonology and morphonology lies in the fact that phonology explores the potential of language through the utilization of phonological means in the formation of grammatical morphemes and grammatical words, while morphology explores the actual utilization of this potential by the language. Any phonological morpheme or phonological word is a potential grammatical morpheme or grammatical word.

The preceding section has shown that the phonological syllable can be placed side by side with the phonological word, since both the phonological syllable and the phonological word represent unilateral units which differ mutually only as to size and phonemic structure. Consequently it was necessary to include the phonological syllable among units which possess a culminative function. Hence, it is now necessary to include the phonological syllable among units which are demarcated by boundary signals. If the phonological syllable, as a unilateral unit which possesses a definite phonemic structure, can be, in principle, placed side by side with the phonological morpheme and the phonological word, then it naturally follows that phonemes which meet at the juncture of two phonological words, can be interpreted as composite boundary signals of a special kind.

16. MORPHOPHONEMES AND MORPHODIFFERENTORS

Although morphonological problems are beyond the scope of this text, there exists an important factor belonging to the area of morphonology which we must necessarily consider. We have in mind the problem of morphonological identity. If we should disregard this question, some aspects of the problem of phonological identity might remain unclear, since the essence of phonological identity can be understood fully only through a comparison of phonological and morphonological identities.

The identity of phonemes should be viewed at two planes: the plane of phonological words and morphemes, and the plane of grammatical words and morphemes.

At each of these two planes we must differentiate two kinds of identity which we will call summarizing identity and generalizing identity.[65]

In explaining the difference between summarizing identity and generalizing identity we will commence with the famous saying of Heraclitus: "you cannot bathe in the same river twice". How should this saying be understood? Let us imagine that before us lies the river Volga. Can we enter the river Volga twice? In order to answer this question it is necessary to remove the ambiguity which is connected with the expression "the river Volga". The expression "the river Volga" can be interpreted in two ways. In the first place, we can define the river Volga as the stage of this river at any given moment, and since these stages replace one another we must differentiate a successive number of stages: $r.\ Volga_1$, $r.\ Volga_2$, $r.\ Volga_3 \ldots r.\ Volga_n$. In the second place, we can define the river Volga as the sum of these stages, i.e. as one unit. In this case $the\ river\ Volga = r.\ Volga_1 + r.\ Volga_2 + r.\ Volga_3 + \ldots + r.\ Volga_n$. Now it becomes easy to perceive that in the saying of Heraclitus the expression "the same river" should be interpreted not as one and the same river, i.e. a sum of its separate stages, but rather as one and the same separate stage of the river. In this sense it is actually im-

[65] For the origin of these two kinds of identity cf.: W. V. O. Quine, *From a Logical Point of View* (Cambridge (Mass.)), 1953, pp. 65-79; W. V. O. Quine, *Methods of Logic* (London, 1952), pp. 208-215.

possible to enter the same river twice. There exists also another variant of Heraclitus' saying which states: "We enter the same river yet we do not enter it, we bathe in the same river and yet we do not bathe in it". The contradiction which is contained in this version of the saying can be easily removed if we keep in mind the double meaning of the expression "the same river". If we say that we enter the same river and bathe in it then we speak about the sum of the separate stages of the river: if these facts are denied, then we speak about a separate stage of the river.

This semantic analysis of Heraclitus' saying allows us to clarify summarizing identity. Under summarizing identity we understand the identity of separate stages of an entity. Every entity represents the sum of its own separate stages. For instance, the entity designated by the term "this river" is the sum of the stages of the given river; the entity, designated by the term "this factory" is the sum of the stages of that factory; the entity designated by the term "I" is the sum of my own stages. The concept of stage should be understood not merely in the sense of duration but also in the sense of space. Thus, the term "this river" represents not only the sum of the durational stages of a given river but the sum of its spacial stages as well: at any place, upstream, downstream — everywhere there exist special stages of that river. Similarly, the given factory can be likewise transported from one place to another and, consequently, the term "this factory" should comprise the sum of the spacial stages of the factory as well. The individual designated by the pronoun "I" can change his location and, therefore, the pronoun "I" should also comprise the sum of the spacial stages of the individual who is identified by this pronoun. Hence, summarizing identity is a spacial-durational identity of the separate stages of the given entity. Unlike summarizing identity which unites separate stages of the entity into one whole, generalizing identity is not concerned with the separate stages of one and the same entity but with different entities belonging to the same class. At the level of generalizing identity entities are regarded as elements which cannot be further divided and which possess definite common traits that unite them into a class. If, for instance, we take separate entities designated by the term "this river", let us say Volga, Seine, Mississippi and others, then, discarding the individual traits of these entities, we unite them, on the basis of their common traits, into one class of entities designated by the term "river". Here we deal no longer with the separate stages of the Volga, the Seine, etc., but with the Volga, the Seine and other entities as indivisible elements which cannot be further subdivided and between which there exists a generalizing identity that unites them into a single class of entities.

Having clarified the difference between summarizing and generalizing identity we shall now survey the question of the identity of phonemes from this standpoint.

First of all, we will focus our attention on the identity of phonemes on a purely phonological level. This necessitates a clarification of the meaning of the expression "one and the same phoneme", using the following phrase as an example: *Segodnja dnëm on kupil sebe novyj kostjum i novyj galstuk*, 'during the day today he bought himself a new suit and a new tie'. In this phrase the word *novyj*, 'new', is used twice; so is every one of its separate phonemes. Let us take the phoneme *o*. This phoneme can be found also in the word *on* and in the word *dnëm*; in all these cases we speak about one and the same phoneme *o*. Here it is, however, necessary to differentiate two kinds of identity. When we say that the first word *novyj* and the second word *novyj* contain one and the same phoneme *o*, we refer to a summarizing identity, that is to two different stages of one and the same phoneme, we speak only of o_1, which will be henceforth designated by the corresponding indexes in parentheses: $o_{1(1)}$, $o_{1(2)}$. When we speak about one and the same phoneme in the words *novyj, on, dnëm*, we refer to a generalizing identity in this case the concrete phonemes o_1, o_2, o_3 unite into one and the same class which is designated by the abstract phoneme *o*.

At this point we will introduce the definitions of summarizing and generalizing identities.

Summarizing phonemic identity is the identity of the separate stages of a concrete phoneme, conditioned by their affiliation with one and the same phonological word or morpheme.

Generalizing phonemic identity is the identity of concrete phonemes which unite into one and the same class on the basis of an identical function of differentiation of phonological words and morphemes.

At a purely phonological level, the problem of generalizing phonemic identity is of basic importance for linguistic analysis. The problem of summarizing phonemic identity on the other hand, does not pose any difficulties and, therefore, does not warrant special consideration. This situation changes, however, when we enter the level of bilateral linguistic units, i.e. the level of grammatical words and morphemes. At this level the principal role is, indeed, played by summarizing phonemic identity which relates in this case to the phenomenon of phonological neutralization. We shall turn to a concrete example.

In specific positions in the speech flow members of certain phonological oppositions cease to differ. Let us take, for instance, the Russian words *kust* 'bush' and *gust* 'thick'; here we encounter the opposition "*k*"–"*g*". The differentors which ascertain this opposition are voicedness and voicelessness. But in Russian contraposed voiced and voiceless consonantal phonemes cease to differ whenever they occur in final position or, in other words, the oppositions of voiceless and voiced consonantal phonemes become neutralized. Thus, in the words *luk* 'bow' and *lug*, 'meadow', the opposition "*k*"–"*g*" is replaced by a single archiphoneme *K* which comprises both members of the opposition. The archiphoneme *K* differs fundamentally both from the phoneme "*k*" and from the phoneme "*g*" since, compared to them, it has a smaller number of differentors. The differentors of the archiphoneme *K* do not comprise either voicedness or voicelessness, while voicelessness does belong among the number of differentors of the phoneme "*k*", and voicedness does belong among the differentors of the phoneme "*g*".

From the phonological point of view, the phonemic chains *luK* in the words *luk* and *lug*, *luk-* in the words *luka*, *luku*, *lukom*, etc., and *lug-* in the words *luga*, *lugu*, *lugom*, etc., are fundamentally different. But from the point of view of grammar we have to identify the chain *luK* with the chain *luk-* on the one hand, and with the chain *lug-* on the other. As a consequence of this identity the archiphoneme *K* can be, in turn, identified with the phoneme "*k*" on the one hand, and with the phoneme "*g*" on the other. However, if the archiphoneme *K* differs fundamentally from the phoneme "*k*" as well as from the phoneme "*g*" how, we can ask, can we identify it with these phonemes? The need to justify this identity gives rise to the necessity to postulate a specific construct for whose designation we will utilize the already existing term "morpho-phoneme". From our point of view, the above given examples contain two morpho-phonemes [*k*] and [*g*] (in order to differentiate morpho-phonemes from phonemes we place the symbols for morpho-phonemes in square brackets). The morpho-phoneme [*k*] represents the sum of its two basic stages — [k_1] (in oblique cases of the word *luk*) and [k_2] (in the nominative case of the word *luk*). Similarly, the morpho-phoneme [*g*] represents the sum of [g_1] (in oblique cases of the word *lug*) and [g_2] (in the nominative case of the word *lug*). The substratum of [k_1] is the phoneme "*k*" while the substratum of [k_2] is the archiphoneme *K*. The substratum of [g_1] is the phoneme "*g*" while the substratum of "g_2" is the archiphoneme *K*. If we designate the relation of embodiment by the already utilized symbol *I*, then the above shown correspondences can be expressed in the language of symbolic logic by the following formulae:

$$I(\text{“}k\text{”}, [k_1]) \qquad I(\text{“}g\text{”}, [g_1])$$
$$I(K, [k_2]) \qquad I(K, [g_2])$$

We see that at the morphonological level there exists a summarizing identity of phonemes which are substrata of one and the same morpho-phoneme.

The concept of morpho-phoneme gives rise to a parallel concept which we call the morpho-differentor. Indeed, if in the quoted examples the phonemes "*k*" and "*g*", mutually contraposed because of their differentors of voicedness and voicelessness, are substrata of the morpho-phonemes [k_1] and [g_1], it is obvious that the differentors of voicelessness and voicedness should constitute the substrata of corresponding abstract elements which we term the morpho-differentors of voicedness and voicelessness.

Within the framework of the previously formulated two-level system of phonological concepts we regard morpho-phonemes and morpho-differentors as constructs of a higher plane of abstraction than phonemes and differentors. Morpho-phonemes and morpho-differentors are constructs of a second plane which relates phonology to grammar. The laws which deal with this relationship belong, within the scope of morphonology.

The differentiation of phonemoids, phonemes and morpho-phonemes confronts structural linguistics with the basic and important problem of the formulation of three types of scientific linguistic transcription, which can be called phonemoidal, phonemic and morpho-phonemic transcriptions. Detailed formulation of these types of scientific linguistic transcription will be of primary importance in the progress of research in the area of structural linguistics.[66]

17. THE TWO-LEVEL THEORY OF PHONOLOGY AND THE CONCEPT OF STRUCTURE

The above discussed two-level theory of phonology has indicated that phonological reality is not obtained through direct observation but that it belongs to the level of constructs.

Since phonology is a part of structural linguistics, it is necessary to consider the nature of the contribution of the above conception of phonological reality to a deeper understanding of the structure of language. We will concentrate first of all on the definition of the concept of structure in contemporary mathematics.

The following definition of the mathematical concept of structure is taken from the work of N. Bourbaki: "A common feature of

[66] Of special importance for the formulation of the shown types of scientific linguistic transcription, especially in connection with this topic, is: R. I. Avanesov, "O trex tipax naučno-lingvističeskix transkripcij", *Slavia*, XXV, 3 (1956); of great interest are also the works of A. I. Smirnickij which stress the necessity of a strict differentiation between the phonological and morphonological levels. Cf.: A. I. Smirnickij, "Fonetičeskaja transkripcija i zvukovye tipy", *Vestnik Moskovskogo universiteta*, 7 (1949); A. I. Smirnickij, *Morfologija anglijskogo jazyka* (Moscow, 1959), pp. 27-42.

various concepts designated by this generic name is their relation to sets of elements of indefinite nature; in order to define a structure one sets up one or more relations between these elements, then postulates the known conditions which these relations ought to satisfy (enumerating them) and which serve as axioms of the examined structure. The formulation of an axiomatic theory of a given structure consists of the deduction of logical consequences from the axioms of the structure, and rejection of all hypotheses dealing with the origin of the examined elements (especially all hypotheses dealing with the origin of their proper nature)."[67]

This statement prompts us to concentrate in particular on the fact that structure is related to sets of elements of indefinite nature. Actually, the structural point of view requires us to regard any element solely as a point of intersection of known relations, all other characteristics of the element being unessential.

The concept of structure, thus defined, is of fundamental significance to all abstract theoretical sciences which deal with constructs. Thus, if constructs are concepts which deal with objects that cannot be directly observed, it is obvious that one can discuss such objects rationally only at the structural plane. Indeed, abstract hypotheses which deal with constructs receive their explanatory power from their relationship to the directly observed data because the symbols which represent constructs are ascribed definite structural parameters that point out the place and role of constructs in the abstract theoretical system, permitting us to deduce from the abstract hypotheses the necessary consequences that lead to the clarification of directly observable facts and phenomena. Let us see how the English logician R. B. Braithwaite characterizes the structural description of constructs, using the example of Schrödinger's wave-function: "It is instructive to notice that one of the most important theoretical terms used in contemporary physics — Schrödinger's wave-function — is frequently called the "ψ-function", being referred to merely by means of the symbol ψ

[67] N. Bourbaki, "L'architecture des mathématiques", *Les grands courants de la pensée mathématique*, presentés par F. Le Lionnais, Cahiers du Sud, 1948, pp. 40-41.

which it is customary to use in the calculus of wave mechanics. I suspect that no physicist would wish directly to answer questions like: What is the concept denoted by the symbol ψ? Does Schrödinger's ψ-function really exist? The physicist will almost certainly prefer to give the indirect answer of explaining how the symbol ψ is used in his calculus... For a physicist, to think about ψ-functions is to use the symbol ψ in an appropriate way in his calculus. When he has explained this appropriate way, there is nothing further to say upon what the propositions expressed by the formulae containing ψ are about. Once the status within a calculus of a theoretical term has been expounded, there is no further question as to the ontological status of the theoretical concept."[68]

Having clarified the concept of structure, as it is interpreted in modern mathematics and the logic of science, we now see that the two-level theory of phonology does satisfy the requirements of structural description. As has been shown in preceding sections, phonemes, differentors, culminators and boundary signals — all these phonological elements represent purely abstract objects which are defined only as points of intersection of known relations. From our point of view, a correct description of phonological reality should comprise only a systematic description of abstract operations which utilize symbols. At this plane the terms "phoneme", "differentor", "culminator" can be interpreted as abbreviated designations of operations which utilize purely abstract symbols. "The concept", writes P. W. Bridgeman, "is synonymous with the corresponding set of operations".[69] If operations are to be understood, in the abstract theoretical system, as denoting operations which utilize symbols, then the definition of every theoretical concept should be reduced to a symbolic indication of the set of operations. Here lies the core of structural description, particularly of the kind of description of phonological reality which we encounter in the two-level theory of phonology.

[68] R. B. Braithwaite, *op. cit.*, pp. 81-82.

[69] P. W. Bridgman, *The Logic of Modern Physics* (New York, 1928) (reprinted in H. Feigl and M. Brodbeck, eds., *Readings in the Philosophy of Science* (New York, 1953), p. 36).

We have stated above that structural description should possess explanatory power. This means that structural description should clarify facts and phenomena which are obtained through direct observation. Otherwise structural description would constitute a useless abstraction which would lack any cognitive value. This aspect of the case is taken into account by any abstract theoretical science; it is taken into account by the two-level theory of phonology as well. The concepts of phonemoid, differentoid, and culminatoid represent connecting links between the sphere of abstract phonological universals and the sphere of the sensory perception of the sound aspect of language.

Unlike the two-level theory of phonology, some variants of the relational-physical theory of phonemes and distinctive features do not satisfy the requirements of structural description because the concepts used by the relational-physical theory have not been liberated from physical substance.

It is our belief that only that description which is liberated from physical substance, the strictly structural description, is able to disclose to us the immanent essence of the sound aspect of language.

Since phonology is a part of structural linguistics, it is clearly necessary that those principles which are the basis of the two-level theory of phonology should be applied to all of structural linguistics. In his time F. de Saussure had characterized the essence of linguistic reality in the statement: "Language is form, not substance".[70] We believe that a consistent deduction of all essential consequences from this revolutionary statement would lead to the formulation of a two-level theory of structural linguistics.

18. RESULTS OF INVESTIGATION

In conclusion, we shall sum up the general characteristics of the two-level theory of phonology.

[70] F. de Saussure, *op. cit.*, p. 169.

The core of the two-level theory of phonology comprizes two main theories: the theory of phonological units which possess a demarcative function, and the theory of phonological units which possess a culminative function. The system of concepts belonging to the theory of phonological units which possess a demarcative function can be summed up in the following table:

LEVEL OF CONSTUCTS	Constructs	*Concrete differentor*	*Abstract differentor*	*Concrete phoneme*	*Abstract phoneme*
LEVEL OF OBSERVATION	Relational physical concepts	*Concrete differentoid*	*Abstract differentoid*	*Concrete phonemoid*	*Abstract phonemoid*
	Purely physical concepts	*Concrete acoustic property*	*Abstract acoustic property*	*Concrete sound*	*Abstract sound (sound type)*

Let us consider this system of concepts from the standpoint of the general processes of concept development in sciences.

One of the more important processes in concept development is the splitting of concepts. For instance, in physics there was a time when the concepts of heat and temperature did not differ from each other: at first, there existed only the concept of heat which, due to the progress of physics, was later split into the concept of heat and the concept of temperature. In physics, the original concept of mass was later split into the concepts of gravitational mass, inertial mass, mass of the moving body and mass at rest.

If we compare the above system of phonological concepts with the original concepts utilized by linguistics in the study of the sound aspect of language, it is possible to propose the following general schemes which represent the splitting of the basic concepts that relate to the study of the sound aspect of language:

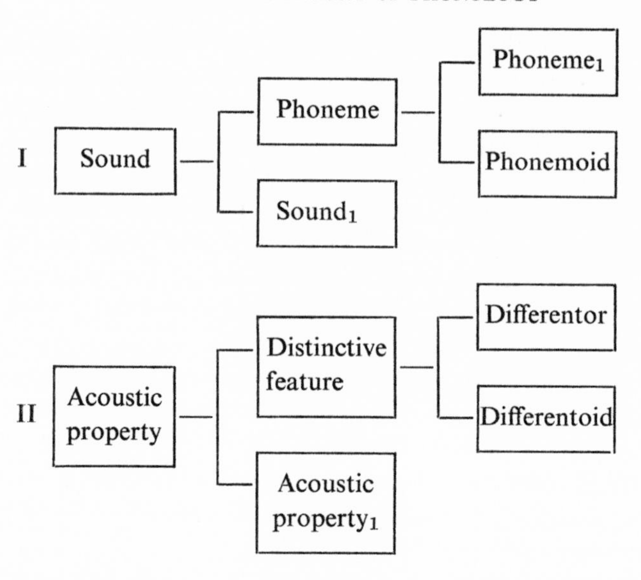

The first diagram shows that the original, undifferentiated concept of sound in linguistics was split, as a result of the progress of the science, into the concept of phoneme and the concept of sound as a purely physical phenomenon (the number index in the term "sound_1" is used to differentiate sound as a purely physical concept from the original undifferentiated concept of sound in phonetics). However, as we have attempted to point out in the present chapter, the concept on phoneme required a further splitting into the concept of phoneme as a construct and the concept of phonemoid (the number index in the term "phoneme_1" is used to differentiate phoneme as a construct from the traditional relational-physical concept of phoneme).

The second diagram shows the splitting of the original, undifferentiated concept of acoustic property into the concept of distinctive feature and the concept of acoustic property as a purely physical phenomenon (acoustic property_1), and a further splitting of the concept of distinctive feature into the concept of differentor and the concept of differentoid, the essentiality of which we have attempted to point out in this text.

The given schemes indicate that the process of the split-up of phonological concepts has been accompanied by an elevation of these concepts to a higher level of abstraction.Thus, phoneme is a more abstract concept than sound, and $phoneme_1$ is a more abstract concept than phoneme; distinctive feature is a more abstract concept than acoustical property, while differentor is a more abstract concept than distinctive feature. At this point is is possible to establish three logical stages in the history of phonological concepts: (1) the primitive stage (primitive, undifferentiated concept of sound and primitive, undifferentiated concept of acoustic property), (2) the relational stage (the concept of phoneme and the concept of distinctive feature), and (3) the stage of constructs (the concept of $phoneme_1$ and the concept of differentor). We will transfer now our attention to the theory of phonological units which possess a culminative function. The system of concepts encompassed by this theory is summed up in the following table:

LEVEL OF CONSTRUCTS	Constructs	*Concrete culminator*	*Abstract culminator*
LEVEL OF OBSERVATION	Relational physical concepts	*Concrete culminatoid*	*Abstract culminatoid*
	Purely physical concepts	*Concrete acoustic property*	*Abstract acoustic property*

The concept of culminator represents the result of a generalization, at the level of constructs, of the relational-physical concept of prosodic feature. As a result of this generalization the concept of prosodic feature has been, on the one hand, freed of physical substance while, on the other hand, it has enlarged its scope to cover a phonological element which has been assigned, up to now, a covered function, namely vocality. By the same token, the number of differentors has been narrowed down as a result of the exclusion of vocality and non-vocality.

Differentors and culminators correspond to each other as paradigmatic and syntagmatic phonological constructs. Differentors are mutually contraposed on the paradigmatic axis, while culminators are mutually contraposed on the syntagmatic axis.

Above the system of phonemes and differentors and the system of culminators there exists a superimposed facultative system of boundary signals. The function of boundary signals, which are regarded as phonological constructs, is to demarcate not only words and morphemes but phonological syllables as well.

At the morphological plane phonemes and differentors are the substrata of morpho-phonemes and morpho-differentors.

In comparison to phonemes and differentors, morpho-phonemes and morpho-differentors should be regarded as linguistic constructs of a second degree.

II

RULES OF CORRESPONDENCE FOR THE PARADIGMATIC AND SYNTAGMATIC IDENTIFICATION OF PHONEMES

1. THE PROBLEM

In Chapter I we have presented a general outline of the two-level theory of phonology. The following discussion will endeavor to apply the general principles of the two-level theory of phonology to an analysis of the basic problems of synchronic phonology.

This chapter will deal with the paradigmatic and syntagmatic identification of phonemes. The term paradigmatic identification of phonemes denotes an investigation of conditions operative in the case where two sounds that occur in different positions, i.e. that belong to different paradigmatic axes, should be regarded either as substrata of different phonemes, or as substrata of identical phonemes. This is a problem of phonological identity. The term syntagmatic identification of phonemes denotes an investigation of conditions operative in the case where two sounds that follow one another in the speech flow, i.e. that lie on the same syntagmatic axis, are either substrata of two phonemes or substrata of a single phoneme; here belongs also the investigation of the conditions under which one sound is a substratum of one phoneme, and of the conditions under which the same sound is a substratum of two phonemes.

Operations which enable us to determine the substrata of identical or different phonemes on the paradigmatic axes, and the substrata of one or two phonemes on the syntagmatic axis, are, in principle, nothing else but correspondence rules which facilitate identification of phonemes in sounds which embody them. Our problem is contingent upon finding these correspondence rules, and comparing them with the existing methods used in the definition of phonological identity and differentiation of phonemes in the speech flow.

2. OPERATOR METHOD OF THE PARADIGMATIC IDENTIFICATION OF PHONEMES

For the definition of the substrata of identical and different phonemes on the paradigmatic axes we propose the following operations:

1. Selection of a standard.
2. Establishment of homogeneous sets of sounds.
3. Measurement of the action of positional operators.
4. Establishment of paired sounds.

In order to clarify the essence and the application of these operations, let us return to the example cited in Chapter One which deals with the definition of identical substrata of vowel phonemes in Russian.

As a standard we had selected a set of sounds with a minimal palatal shading: M_1 — a_1, o_1, u_1, i_1, e_1. The position in which these sounds were mutually contraposed was designated by the symbol P_1.

Further, we had established homogenous sets of sounds: M_2 — a_2, o_2, u_2, i_2, e_2 (in position P_2), M_3 — a_3, o_3, u_3, i_3, e_3, (in position P_3), M_4 — a_4, o_4, u_4, i_4, e_4 (in position P_4). What is the criterion of homogeneity? The criterion of homogeneity should be the dependence of sound changes on the influence of positional conditions. Thus, for instance, the above sets of sounds are homogeneous because the changes in the sound sets M_2, M_3, M_4 in comparison with the standard, the set M_1, are positionally determined; the sound set M_2 has a palatal shading in the terminal phase of its duration under the influence of successive sharp consonants, the set M_3 has a palatal shading in the initial phase of its duration under the influence of preceding sharp consonants, and the set M_4 has a palatal shading over the entire segment of its duration under the influence of preceding and successive sharp consonants. If, by means of a mental experiment, we remove the influence of positional conditions, then the sets M_2, M_3, M_4 should coincide with their standard, the set M_1. According to the principle of homogeneity, all sounds of any language are divided into vowels and consonants. Comparing various sets of vowels and consonants in various positions, we can always reduce the sets of vowels to a single set of vowels (standard set of vowels), and the sets of consonants to a single set of consonants (standard set of consonants). Sets of vowels and sets of consonants cannot be mutually reduced since the differences between vowels and consonants are not dependent on positional conditions. According to the principle of homogeneity, vocalic and consonantal sounds belong to different systems of contrasted sounds, the system of vocalic sounds and the system of consonantal sounds. Finally, even within these systems there may occur cases when the difference between sounds is not positionally determined. For instance, in German, the consonantal sound *h* is found only preceding vowels with the exception of the unstressed *e* and *i*, while, conversely, the consonantal sound *ŋ* is encountered only preceding the unstressed vowels *e* and *i*, preceding consonants and in terminal position. Thus, the consonantal sounds *h* and *ŋ* occur in mutually exclusive positions. Nevertheless, these consonantal sounds cannot be mutually reduced since the difference between them cannot be regarded as being positionally determined. A similar case of a lack of positional motivation in the system of consonantal or vocalic sounds is seldom seen: the difference between sets of sounds within the system of vocalic or consonantal sounds is, as a rule, positionally determined.

Before we examine the measurement of the action of the operators, i.e. in our case, the measurement of the action of the positions P_2, P_3, P_4 on the vowels a_1, o_1, u_1, i_1, e_1, we will consider the logical characteristic of measurement in general.

Measurement can be reduced, in facto, to the establishment of a definite ordering relation between known elements.[1] Let us take,

[1] Cf. J. G. Kemeny, *A Philosopher Looks at Science* (New York, 1959), Ch. 8: "Measurement", pp. 141-155.

for instance, measurement of temperature. By comparing daily thermometer readings throughout the year it is possible to divide the days of the year according to a diagram of comparative temperature level. Such diagram should satisfy three basic requirements. First of all, if we have stated that, let us say, May 20th was warmer than May 21st, we have to exclude the possibility of a simultaneous statement that May 21st was warmer than May 20th. If *A* is warmer than *B*, then *B* cannot be warmer than *A*. In mathematical logic such property is called asymmetry. Further, asserting that May 20th was warmer than May 21st, and that May 21st had been warmer than May 10th, we can also state that May 20th had been warmer than May 10th. In other words, if *A* is warmer than *B*, and *B* is warmer than *C*, the *A* is warmer than *C*. In mathematical logic this property is called transitivity. Finally, comparing the days of the year to each other from the standpoint of temperature level, we should be able to select for the comparison any two days. In mathematical logic this property is termed connectivity. We see that the relation "to be warmer" is assymmetrical, transitive, and connected. Such asymmetrical, transitive, and connected relations are called, in mathematical logic, simple orders. Any simple order can be expressed through a linear scheme. If a relation is asymmetrical and transitive but not connected it is referred to, in mathematical logic, as a partial order. Let us take, for instance, the relation "to be older" in respect to the employees of any chosen establishment; the relation is defined on the basis of two factors, age and duration of employment. From this point of view an employee who is 38 years old and has been employed for 10 years should be regarded as being older than an employee who is 36 years old and has been employed for 8 years. But we cannot compare any two employees in accordance with such a principle; for instance, an employee who is 50 years old and has been working in the establishment for 10 years cannot be compared with an employee who is 45 years old and has worked in the establishment for 20 years.

We will now concentrate on the measurement of the action of the operators in the example under consideration. Here the action of the operators can be expressed as the degree of palatalization.

Hence, one end of the scale will be occupied by operator P_1 (minimal palatalization), and the other end of the scale by operator P_4 (maximal palatalization). Although this scale enables us to compare operators P_1 and P_2, P_1 and P_3, P_2 and P_4, P_3 and P_4, P_1 and P_4, we cannot compare operators P_2 and P_3. In the first place, in any chosen pair the operators differ as to the degree of palatalization. In the second place, P_2 and P_3 differ not as to the degree, but as to the placement of their palatalization; the set of vowels M_2 in position P_2 and the set of vowels M_3 in position P_3 differ not in respect to the degree of palatalization but in respect to the fact that the set of vowels M_2 has a palatal shading in the terminal phase of its duration while the set of vowels M_3 has a palatal shading in the initial phase of its duration. Hence, the relation of the degree of palatalization on our scale is not connected, since it does not allow us to compare every possible pair of given operators. But this relation is asymmetrical and transitive. It is asymmetrical because if one of its operators, let us say P_4, possesses a greater degree of palatalization than another, let us say P_2, we cannot assert the converse, i.e. that P_2 possess a greater degree of palatalization than P_4. It is transitive since, if we state that, let us say, P_3 possesses a greater degree of palatalization than P_1, and P_4 possesses a greater degree of palatalization than P_3 we can assert, on the basis of these two statements, that P_4 possesses a greater degree of palatalization than P_1. Since the relation of the degree of palatalization is both asymmetrical and transitive, but not relevant, it represents a partial order. As has been said above, any simple order can be represented through a linear scheme; partial order, on the other hand, can be represented by means of a branching diagram, i.e. through a so-called tree diagram. The correspondence of the above operators can be illustrated in the following branching diagram:

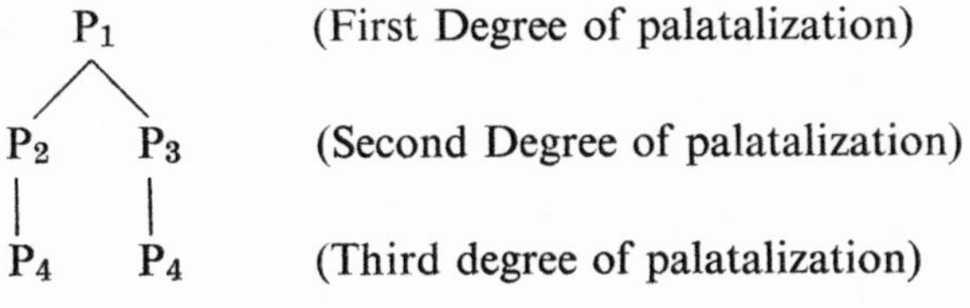

If we examine other cases of the action of positional operators we see that simple order of operators can occur side by side with partial order. For example, it is possible to imagine a language where sets of vowels in different positions would differ only in the degree of their duration. In this case it would be possible to establish a scale of the degree of duration, in respect to which one would mutually compare any two vowels occuring in different positions. Such a scale would represent a simple order of operators.

We shall now transfer our attention to the operation of establishment of paired sounds. The operation of establishment of paired sounds is based on a law which we call the law of reduction. The law of reduction can be formulated as follows: *if a given set of sounds* M_1 *is taken as a standard, then for every sound* a_1 *of this set one can find a corresponding sound* a_j *of the set* M_j, *whose difference from the sound* a_1 *can be attributed solely to the action of the positional operator* P_j.

We will concentrate on the application of the law of reduction to our example. As has been said above, we have taken as a standard a set of vowel sounds M_1 containing the vowels a_1, o_1, u_1, i_1, e_1. The set of vowels M_1 was then compared with sets of vowels M_2 M_3, M_4. As a result of this comparison, it was established that in the case of the set M_2 the differences between vowels a_2 and a_1, o_2 and o_1, u_2 and u_1, i_2 and i_1, and e_2 and e_1 can be reduced to the action of the positional operator P_2, i.e. to the forward and upward movement of articulation in the terminal phase of pronunciation. In the case of the set M_3 the differences between the vowels a_3 and a_1, o_3 and o_1, u_3 and u_1, i_3 and i_1, e_3 and e_1 can be reduced to the action of operator P_3, i.e. to the forward and upward movement of articulation in the initial phase of pronunciation. In the case of the set M_4 the differences between the vowels a_4 and a_1, o_4 and o_1, u_4 and u_1, i_4 and i_1, e_4 and e_1 can be reduced to the action of the operator P_4, i.e. to the upward and forward movement of articulation (in the case of back vowels) or simple upward movement of articulation (in the case of front vowels) over the entire segment of duration. By means of a mental experiment we had removed the action of the operators P_2, P_3, P_4 obtaining, as a result, the following pairs of sounds which constitute substrata of identical individual phonemes:

$$\begin{array}{lll} a_1 = a_2 & a_1 = a_3 & a_1 = a_4 \\ o_1 = o_2 & o_1 = o_3 & o_1 = o_4 \\ u_1 = u_2 & u_1 = u_3 & u_1 = u_4 \\ i_1 = i_2 & i_1 = i_3 & i_1 = i_4 \\ e_1 = e_2 & e_1 = e_3 & e_1 = e_4 \end{array}$$

Since the relation of identity is transitive, the above pairs of sounds yield additionally the following pairs of sounds:

$$\begin{array}{lll} a_2 = a_3 & a_2 = a_4 & a_3 = a_4 \\ o_2 = o_3 & o_2 = o_4 & o_3 = o_4 \\ u_2 = u_3 & u_2 = u_4 & u_3 = u_4 \\ i_2 = i_3 & i_2 = i_4 & i_3 = i_4 \\ e_2 = e_3 & e_2 = e_4 & e_3 = e_4 \end{array}$$

As a result we obtain classes of individual phonemoids which embody identical individual phonemes. The classes of individual phonemoids and the identical individual phonemes embodied by the phonemoids can be represented in the following table:

$$\begin{array}{l} a_1 \rightarrow \text{“}a_1\text{”} = a_2 \rightarrow \text{“}a_2\text{”} = a_3 \rightarrow \text{“}a_3\text{”} = a_4 \rightarrow \text{“}a_4\text{”} \\ o_1 \rightarrow \text{“}o_1\text{”} = o_2 \rightarrow \text{“}o_2\text{”} = o_3 \rightarrow \text{“}o_3\text{”} = o_4 \rightarrow \text{“}o_4\text{”} \\ u_1 \rightarrow \text{“}u_1\text{”} = u_2 \rightarrow \text{“}u_2\text{”} = u_3 \rightarrow \text{“}u_3\text{”} = u_4 \rightarrow \text{“}u_4\text{”} \\ i_1 \rightarrow \text{“}i_1\text{”} = i_2 \rightarrow \text{“}i_2\text{”} = i_3 \rightarrow \text{“}i_3\text{”} = i_4 \rightarrow \text{“}i_4\text{”} \\ e_1 \rightarrow \text{“}e_1\text{”} = e_2 \rightarrow \text{“}e_2\text{”} = e_3 \rightarrow \text{“}e_3\text{”} = e_4 \rightarrow \text{“}e_4\text{”} \end{array}$$

In the above table the phonemes are placed in quotation marks for the purpose of distinguishing them from the phonemoids. The arrow designates the relation of embodiment; for instance, $a_1 \rightarrow$ “a_1” should be read as: phonemoid a_1 embodies phoneme “a_1”.

These, in short, are the operations which are used in defining phonemoids that embody identical phonemes; they touch upon the problem of the identity of sounds occuring in different positions. In traditional phonology this problem has been defined as the problem of the definition of combinatory variants of the phoneme. In the two-level theory of phonology there is, however, no place for the concept of combinatory variant of the phoneme since, according to this theory, individual phonemes are constructs, and as constructs cannot be subject to positional changes. Positional changes can affect only the substrata of individual phonemes. Individual phonemes themselves represent ideal diacritical elements which differ from each other only in respect to their placement in phonemic chains.

In traditional phonology, side by side with the problem of the definition of combinatory variants of the phoneme, there exists also the problem of the definition of the so-called facultative variants of the phoneme. Within the framework of the two-level theory of phonology this problem can be reformulated as follows: in one and the same position in the speech flow, one should differentiate two types of difference among sounds: unmotivated difference, and difference which is determined by definite social or individual conditions. Those sounds whose mutual differences lack motivation are called physical substrata of different individual phonemes. Those sounds whose mutual differences are determined by definite conditions are called physical substrata of identical individual phonemes. Our problem lies in the establishment of an operation which is instrumental in defining the substrata of identical individual phonemes.

Similarly as in the case of the definition of the substrata of identical individual phonemes in different positions, we have to turn, first of all, to the operation of standard selection. As a standard we accept normal pronunciation. For instance, in French the uvular pronunciation of the sound *r* is considered to be normal.

The second operation concerns the measurement of the action of contextual operators. The term contextual operators is used in connection with social, dialectic, stylistic, and individual conditions which influence the pronunciation of sounds. Thus, in French the uvular pronunciation of the sound *r* is the norm; however, there exists likewise an apico-dental pronunciation of *r* which represents a dialectal deviation from the literary norm. Hence, in French the difference between the uvular and the apico-dental *r* is determined by the location of the speakers in relation to the literary norm of the language. It should be added that the apico-dental pronunciation of *r* is encountered as an archaism on the French scene; here the contextual operator is the declining tradition in France of the archaic scenic pronunciation. In Russian, side by side with the normal explosive pronunciation of the sound *g* there exists a fricative pronunciation of this sound. The contextual operator of the fricative pronunciation is the affiliation of the speakers with definite dialectal areas of the Russian language.

The third operation consists of the establishment of paired sounds which belong to different contexts. As in the case of the establishment of paired sounds belonging to different positions, this operation is based on the above formulated law of reduction. After removing the action of contextual operators, by means of a mental experiment, we establish the pairs of sounds which constitute substrata of identical individual phonemes. Thus, if in the above example we designate the normal context of the pronunciation of the sound *r* in French by the symbol C_1 (uvular pronunciation), the dialectal context by the symbol C_2, and the scenic context by the symbol C_3, then, having removed by means of a mental experiment the action of the latter two contexts, we establish pairs of sounds r_1 and r_2, and r_1 and r_3 which constitute substrata of identical individual phonemes "r_1", "r_2", "r_3".

By analogy, the problem of identity in the remaining cases of the action of contextual operators is resolved accordingly.

This method of the paradigmatic identification of phonemes is called the operator method of the paradigmatic identification of phonemes since it is based on a systematic analysis of the action of positional operators.

3. THE PRINCIPLE OF COMPLEMENTARY DISTRIBUTION

We will now compare the operator method with the methods of the paradigmatic identification of phonemes prevalent in modern phonology, namely the method based on the principle of complementary distribution, and the method based on an analysis of distinctive features. Since the operator method has been presented within the framework of the two-level theory of phonology and since modern phonology does not adhere to the demarcation of the two abstraction levels adopted by us in the above discussion, we ought to, in comparing the operator method with the methods of the identification of phonemes current in modern phonology, express the essence of the latter two methods in the terminology of the two-level theory of phonology as well. In this section we will concentrate on the method of the paradigmatic identification of phonemes based on the principle of complementary distribution.[2]

The principle of complementary distribution can be formulated as follows: *the two sounds A and B are in relation of complementary distribution to each other if in the speech flow of a language L these sounds cannot occur in identical positions.*

On the basis of the principle of complementary distribution, phonological identity of sounds is defined as follows: *the two sounds A and B are combinatory variants of one and the same phoneme X if they are in relation of complementary distribution to each other.*

In the terminology of the two-level theory of phonology this definition can be reformulated as follows: *the two sounds A and B are combinatory substrata of identical phonemes "A" and "B" if these sounds are in relation of complementary distribution to each other.*

The definition of phonological identity of sounds on the basis of the principle of complementary distribution is subject to two kinds of criticism. In the first place, the sounds *A* and *B* can be in mutual relation of complementary distribution yet can, nonetheless, constitute physical substrata of different phonemes. In the second place, it is possible for the sounds *A* and *B* not to be in mutual

[2] About the principle of complementary distribution cf.: B. Bloch, "A Set of Postulates for Phonemic Analysis", *Language*, 24 (1948); Charles Hockett, *A Manual of Phonology* (Baltimore, 1955); Z. Harris, *Methods in Structural Linguistics* (Chicago, 1951); K. L. Pike, *Phonemics: a Technique for Reducing Languages to Writing* (Ann Arbor, 1947).

relation of complementary distribution and, nonetheless, to constitute physical substrata of identical phonemes.

In respect to the first possibility we will consider two varieties of the Russian vowel sounds: (1) between plain consonants and (2) between sharp consonants. These two positions are illustrated in the following table:

Between plain consonants		Between sharp consonants
y	↔	*i*
ε	↔	*e*
a	↔	*ä*
o	↔	*ö*
u	↔	*ü*

The arrows connect substrata of identical phonemes.

A quick glance at this table convinces us that the relation of complementary distribution can apply not only to the substrata of identical phonemes but to the substrata of different phonemes as well. Thus, in the position between plain consonants not only the pair *i* and *y*, but the pairs *i* and *ε*, *i* and *a*, *i* and *o*, and *i* and *u*, are mutually exclusive as well. In the position between sharp consonants not only the pair *ε* and *e*, but the pairs *ε* and *i*, *ε* and *ä*, *ε* and *ö*, and *ε* and *ü* are mutually exclusive as well.

Let us now turn our attention to the second possibility. We can imagine a language in which in position P_i there exist the sounds *A* and *B*, while in position P_j there exist the sounds *B* and *C*. We will allow, at the same time, that the difference between the sound *A* in position P_i and the sound *B* in position P_j, and between the sound *B* in position P_i and the sound *C* in position P_j is motivated solely by the action of these positions. In this case, it is natural to regard the sound *A* in position P_i and the sound *B* in position P_j as substrata of identical phonemes. By the same token, one should regard the sound *B* in position P_i and the sound *C* in position P_j as substrata of identical phonemes. This reasoning can be illustrated by the following table:

P_i		P_j
A	↔	*B*
B	↔	*C*

The arrows connect substrata of identical phonemes.

This table shows at a glance that although the sounds *A* and *B* are not in a relation of complementary distribution, nonetheless they constitute not only substrata of different phonemes, but substrata of identical phonemes as well.

Our abstract example can be supported by a concrete one, borrowed from the work of R. Jakobson, G. Fant and M. Halle.[3] In Danish, the pronunciation of consonantal sounds varies sharply, depending on their occurence in so called strong or weak positions. In monosyllabic words the strong position occurs at the beginning of the word, and the weak position at its end. Consequently, the Danish sounds *d* and *t* in strong positions, will be corresponded in weak positions by the sounds *d* and *ð*, as illustrated in the following table:

Strong position		Weak position
t	↔	*d*
d	↔	*ð*

Although the sounds *t* and *d* are not in a relation of complementary distribution, nonetheless they serve not only as the substrata of different phonemes, but as substrata of identical phonemes as well.

The above discussion leads to the conclusion that the method of the paradigmatic identification of phonemes based on the principle of complementary distribution, is fundamentally unsound.

4. PARADIGMATIC IDENTIFICATION OF PHONEMES BASED ON THE ANALYSIS OF DISTINCTIVE FEATURES

Side by side with the principle of distribution in modern phonology there exists also another point of view in regard to the method of the definition of phonological identity. According to this point of

[3] R. Jakobson, C. G. Fant, M. Halle, *op. cit.*

view, which is supported by W. Twaddell, A. Martinet, R. Jakobson, and many other linguists, definition of phonological identity of given sounds is contingent on the fact that they possess identical distinctive features. In terms of the two-level theory of phonology this requirement can be reformulated as follows: the given sounds constitute substrata of identical phonemes if they are substrata of identical bundles of differentors.

Adherents of this point of view insist that without recourse to the analysis of distinctive features the problem of phonological identity is unsolvable. Thus, R. Jakobson and M. Halle write: "Each venture, however, to reduce language to its ultimate invariants, by means of a mere analysis of their distribution in the text and with no reference to their empiric correlates, is condemned to failure. The comparison of two English sequences — /ku/ and /uk/ — will yield no information on the identity of the first segment in one of these samples with the second segment in the other sample, unless we bring into play sound properties common to initial and final /k/ and those common to /u/ in both positions. The confrontation of the syllables /ku/ and /ki/ does not authorize us to assign both initial segments to one phoneme /k/ as two variants appearing to their mutual exclusion before two different vowels, unless we have identified the common features, unifying the retracted and advanced variety of the phoneme /k/ and differentiating it from all other phonemes of the same language. Only through such a test are we able to decide whether the retracted [k—] in /ku/ implements the same phoneme as the advanced [k+] in /ki/ and not the advanced [g+] in /gi/."[4] A. Martinet writes: "The identification of the phoneme results from the enumeration of its distinctive features which cause it to differ from all remaining phonemes of the given language."[5]

Until the appearance of our work which introduced for the first time the operator method of the paradigmatic identification of phonemes[6] we had also regarded the definition of phonological

[4] R. Jakobson and M. Halle, *Fundamentals of Language* (The Hague, 1956), pp. 15-16.

[5] A. Martinet, "Où en est la phonologie", *Lingua*, I, 1, p. 44.

[6] S. K. Šaumjan, "Dvuxstupenčataja teorija fonemy i differencial'nyx èlementov", *Voprosy jazykoznanija*, No. 5 (1960).

identity as being contingent only on the basis of an analysis of distinctive features. At the present time, however, we question whether a reference to distinctive features, in the definition of phonological identity, does not fail to solve the problem of phonological identity by simply shifting it to another plane. Indeed, in assuming that phonological identity is established by means of a reference to the identity of distinctive features, we assume that the given sounds are phonologically identical if they possess identical distinctive features. However, we may ask: how can we prove the identity of distinctive features? Clarification of the phonological identity of sounds by means of a reference to the identity of distinctive features is analogous to the clarification of the origin of life on Earth with reference to the fact that simple organisms have been transferred to Earth from other planets. Of course, it is possible to allow that simple organisms were actually carried over to Earth from other planets; however, this assumption leads directly to the question: what was the origin of life on other planets? The problem is not solved, it is only postponed.

Although in natural languages phonemes, as a rule, break up into definite distinctive features (in our terminology — differentors), we can theoretically imagine a language whose phonemes do not break up into distinctive features, in other words, a language whose phonemes coincide with distinctive features. An example of such a hypothetical language can be found in one of the works of A. Martinet. "Let us imagine", writes A. Martinet, "a language without phonological vowels, where for example, every consonant is always followed by a vowel of a neutral timbre. Such a language can contain 16 phonemes, each characterized by a specific relevant and unique feature. These are 1) labial, 2) labio-dental, 3) apical, 4) sibilant, 5) hushing, 6) lateral, 7) trilled, 8) palatal, 9) retroflex, 10) dorso-velar, 11) uvular, 12) nasal, 13) pharyngeal, 14) laryngeal, 15) inspiratory and 16) clicked."[7] In natural languages such phonemes as *r* and *l* often represent

[7] A. Martinet, *Economie des changements phonétiques* (Berne, 1955), p. 105.

insoluble units which coincide with the trill or the lateral distinctive feature. A. Martinet invented his hypothetical language for another purpose, but we employ it in connection with the problem under discussion. If one allows the theoretical possibility of the existence of a language whose phonemes would coincide with distinctive features then, obviously, the problem of the identity of phonemes would not differ in any way from the problem of the identity of distinctive features. Hence, any reference to the identity of distinctive features in connection with the resolution of the problem of phonological identity of sounds is basically faulty since the identity of distinctive features is not self-evident but is, itself, in need of proof.

The paradigmatic identification of phonemes should be carried out independently of the analysis of distinctive features. In respect to the distinctive features, we will employ (as we have shown in section 11 of chapter I) the same operator method which we have proposed for the paradigmatic identification of phonemes.

5. OPERATOR METHOD OF THE SYNTAGMATIC IDENTIFICATION OF PHONEMES

Up to now we have spoken only about positional operators. In considering the problem of the paradigmatic identification of phonemes we have regarded sounds as operands which, as a result of the action of positional operators, undergo a change within the speech flow. But in the speech flow the function of the operator can be fulfilled not only by positions, but by certain sounds in relation to other sounds on the syntagmatic plane as well. Let us take, for example, the sound *t*. If the sound *t* is exposed to the action of the sound *k* from the right we obtain the sound chain *tk*. However, if the sound *t* is exposed to the action of the sound *k* from the left, we obtain the chain *kt*. We can consider the sound *t* to be an operand which is subject to the action of an operator, the sound *k*. The action of this operator produces the chains *kt* and *tk*. These chains, in turn, can be regarded as new operands which are subject to the action of new operators. Thus, if the chain *kt* is exposed to the action of the operator *a*, we obtain new chains *kta* and *akt*, which, in turn, can be considered as new operands, etc.

The just observed action of the operators upon the operands is termed "application". The term "application" is taken over from mathematical logic. In mathematical logic application is defined in the following way: "If *a* and *b* are entities then "|*ab*" shall denote the application of *a* to *b*. We may conceive of the entities as operators or functions, and |*ab* as the result of operating on *b* with *a*."[8] As we see from this definition, application represents nothing else but the operation of joining one element to another.

There arises the question: if in a given speech flow one considers the sound chain *AB*, how can one define which of these sounds acts as the operand and which as the operator?

In order to establish criteria for the differentiation of operands and operators, we propose an operational test which examines each of these elements as to the possibility of its elimination from the speech flow. This operational test can lead to one of the following results:

(1) Neither *A* nor *B* are eliminable, i.e. *B* is inadmissible without *A*, while *A* is inadmissible without *B*.

(2) *A* is eliminable, but *B* is ineliminable, i.e. *B* is admissible without *A*, while *A* is inadmissible without *B*.

(3) *A* is ineliminable but *B* is eliminable, i.e. *A* is admissible without *B*, while *B* is inadmissible without *A*.

(4) Both *A* and *B* are eliminable, i.e. *A* is admissible without *B*, and *B* is admissible without *A*.

On the basis of this operational test we establish the following criteria for the differentiation of operands and operators:

(1) If neither *A* nor *B* are eliminable, the chain *AB* is indivisible and, consequently, the question of the differentiation of the operand and the operator is in this case meaningless.

(2) If *A* is eliminable and *B* is ineliminable, then *B* is the operand and *A* is the operator.

[8] P. Rosenbloom, *Elements of Mathematical Logic* (New York, 1950), p. 111.

(3) If *A* is eliminable and *B* is ineliminable, then *A* is the operand and *B* is the operator.

(4) If both *A* and *B* are eliminable, then *A* and *B* represent mutual operators.

In the case of mutual operators we introduce the operational test. If the mutual operators do not concede permutation and the chain *AB* constitutes the only possibility, they are called unilateral mutual operators (*A* acts on *B* only from the left while *B* acts on *A* only from the right). If the mutual operators concede a permutation and the chain *BA* can occur side by side with the chain *AB*, they are called bilateral mutual operators (*A* and *B* act on each other both from the right and from the left).

Having established the criteria for the differentiation of operands and operators we will introduce the following correspondence rules between sounds and phonemes on the syntagmatic axis.

(1) If the chain *AB* is indivisable, or if only one of its elements, *A* or *B*, is the operator, the chain is a physical substratum of one phoneme "*X*".

(2) If the elements *A* and *B* of the chain *AB* are bilateral mutual operators, *A* is a physical substratum of the phoneme "*A*", while *B* is the physical substratum of the phoneme "*B*".

(3) If the elements *A* and *B* of the chain *AB* are unilateral mutual operators then, depending on the structure of the phonological system of the given language, *AB* can be interpreted either as a physical substratum of one phoneme "*X*", or as a physical substratum of two phonemes, "*A*" and "*B*".

Let us clarify the above rules using a concrete example, the sound chain *tš*. According to the above rules, this chain can have the following interpretations depending on the various languages it occurs in:

(1) If the chain *tš* is indivisable, i.e. if in the given language *š* is inadmissible without *t* and *t* is inadmissible without *š*, then the chain *tš* represents a physical substratum of the phoneme "č". Such case is purely hypothetical since, to our knowledge, there exists no natural language in which both elements of the chain *tš* could not be eliminated. However, there are cases where *t* serves as the operand

and *š* as the operator, as for instance in the Spanish word *chino* [*tšino*] 'Chinese'. Eliminating the element *š* we obtain *tino* [*tino*], 'tact'. The element *t*, however, cannot be eliminated, since in Spanish words of the type [šino] are not admissible. This means that in the Spanish chain *tš*, *t* represents the operand and *š* the operator and, consequently, that the chain is a physical substratum of the phoneme "č".

(2) In German both elements of the chain *tš* can be eliminated, i.e. *t* is admissible without *š*, while *š* is admissible without *t*. Let us take, for instance, the German word *Kutschen* [*kutšen*] 'carriages'. Eliminating the element *š* we obtain *Kutten* [*kuten*], 'cowls'; eliminating the element *t* we obtain *kuschen* [*kušen*] 'to lie down (about a dog)'. Thus in German, *t* and *š* are mutual operators, and namely bilateral mutual operators, since here the chain *št*, can coexist with the chain *tš*, as for example, in the word *Stand* [*štant*] 'position, stand'. Since in German the elements *t* and *š* of the chain *tš* are bilateral mutual operators, the chain *tš* represents here a physical substratum of two phonemes, the phoneme "*t*" and the phoneme "*š*".

(3) In English both elements of the chain *tš* can be eliminated. Let us take, for instance, the word *chop* [*tšop*]; eliminating *š* we obtain *top* [*top*], and eliminating *t* we obtain *shop* [*šop*]. Hence, in English *t* and *š* represent mutual operators. Since in this language the chain *št* is fundamentally inadmissible, the elements *t* and *š* represent unilateral mutual operators. According to the third correspondence rule, if the elements *A* and *B* are unilateral mutual operators then, depending on the structure of the phonological system of the given language, *AB* can be interpreted either as a physical substratum of one phoneme "*X*", or as a physical substratum of two phonemes, the phoneme "*A*" and the phoneme "*B*". Therefore, in the case of the chain *tš* in English we have the choice of interpreting this chain either as a physical substratum of one phoneme "*č*" or as a physical substratum of two phonemes, "*t*" and "*š*". The structure of the phonological system of English dictates a choice of the first of the two possibilities: since English possesses the phoneme "*ǯ*", the methodological principle of simplicity

prompts us to interpret the chain *tš* as a physical substratum of the phoneme "*č*" which constitutes a voiceless paired phoneme in respect to the voiced phoneme "*ǯ*".

This, in short, constitutes the correspondence rules between sounds and phonemes on the syntagmatic axis. Let us now turn our attention to some of the special questions related to the application of these rules.

In various languages one encounters cases where the operational test for the possibility of eliminating the elements *A* and *B* from the chain *AB* yields, at first glance, positive results, while the chain itself appears to be, in fact, indivisable. Let us take, for instance, the Polish word *czy* [*tši*] 'if'. At first glance, in this word both *t* and *š* submit to elimination. A comparison between the words *czy* and the word *trzy* 'three' shows, however, that in reality the chain *tš* in the word *czy* is indivisable since it is contraposed to the chain *t-š* (the hyphen points out a weaker linear cohesion between *t* and *š*) whose elements, because of their weaker linear cohesion, can be regarded as physical substrata of the phonemes "*t*" and "*š*". Since the chain *tš* in the word *czy* is indivisable, it should be regarded as physical substratum of a single phoneme, the phoneme "*č*". Similar indivisable chains are encountered in the first words of the following Polish word pairs: *czech*, 'Czech' — *trzech*, 'three', *czysta*, 'clean' — *trzysta*, 'three hundred', *paczy*, 'warp' — *patrzy*, 'it looks', *oczyma*, 'through the eyes' — *otrzyma*, 'to obtain'. Thus, when we apply the operational test for the possibility of eliminating the elements *A* and *B* of the chain *AB* we should also consider the possibility of contrasting the strong and weak linear cohesions between the elements *A* and *B*. Different cohesive strength between the elements *A* and *B* in the chain *AB* can be dependent not only on purely physical properties, utilized functionally by the language, but also on whether between the elements *A* and *B* there occurs a morpheme juncture. If in one case such a morphemic juncture between the elements *A* and *B* fails to occur while in another case such a juncture is present, and this phenomenon is utilized functionally by the language, then in the first case there exists a strong cohesion between the elements *A* and *B*, while in the second case this cohesion is weak.

Such contrasting of strong and weak cohesion between the elements *A* and *B*, based on the absence or presence of morpheme juncture, occurs, for example, in the following word pairs: *podrzeć* [*podžeńś*], 'to tear up' — *podżegacz* [*pod-žegatš*] 'instigator', *ocaleć* [*otsal'eńś*], 'to remain whole' — *odsadzać* [*ot-sadzańś*], 'to drive back', *dzwon*, [*dzwon*], 'bell' — *podzwrotnikowy* [*pod-zwrotnikowi*], 'subtropical'. The sound chains *dž*, *ts*, *dz* in the words *podrzeć*, *ocaleć*, *dzwon*, owing to the strong cohesion between the elements *d* and *ž*, *t* and *s*, *d* and *z*, constitute physical substrata of the phonemes "ǯ", "c", and "ʒ". The sound chains *d* — *ž*, *t* — *s*, *d* — *z* in the words *podżegacz*, *odsadzać*, *podzwrotnikowy*, owing to the weak cohesion between the elements *d* and *ž*, *t* and *s*, *d* and *z*, constitute physical substrata of phonemic chains "*dž*", "*ts*", "*dz*".

At this point let us concentrate on cases where some positions justify a single solution while other positions allow a double solution; as an English example we will take, on the one hand, words of the type *job* [*džob*], *jug* [*džʌg*] and, on the other hand, words of the type *ledger* [*ledžə*]. These words contain the sound chain *dž* in initial and medial positions. The operational test enables us to ascertain that in initial position the element *d* cannot be eliminated, since in English words of the type [*žob*], [*žʌg*] are inadmissible. Hence it follows that in the case of the chain *dž* in initial position, the element *d* must be regarded as the operand and the element *ž* as the operator and, consequently, that the chain *dž* in initial position must be regarded as a physical substratum of the phoneme "ǯ". Application of the operational test to the chain *dž* in medial position yields, however, another result. In medial position we eliminate not only the element *ž* but the element *d* as well: here words of the type *header* [*hedə*] occur concurrently with words of the type *leisure* [*ležə*]. Since, at the same time, the chain *dž* in medial position does not concede interchange of its elements, the elements *d* and *ž* in medial position should be regarded as unilateral mutual operators. Consequently, in English the chain *dž* permits a single solution in initial position and a double solution in medial position. In the first case the chain *dž* should be interpreted as a physical substratum of the phoneme "ǯ", while in the second case it can be interpreted in two ways: either as a physical substratum of the phoneme "*ǯ*" or as a physical substratum of two phonemes, the phoneme "*d*" and the phoneme "*ž*". Wherein lies the solution to the problem of the syntagmatic identification of phonemes in respect to the chain *dž* in English? It is obvious that this solution cannot be founded on a rule established specially for the English language. Since the case when one and the same chain of elements *AB* permits in some positions a single solution and in other positions a double solution are encountered in various languages of the world, it is possible to formulate a general principle for the resolution of this problem in similar cases; this principle is termed the PRINCIPLE OF UNIFICATION. The principle of unification can be formulated as follows: *if some positions in the speech flow permit a single solution to the problem of the syntagmatic identification of phonemes while other positions permit a double solution, then the double solution should be reduced to a single one.* On the basis of this general principle the chain *dž* in English should be interpreted in all positions as a physical substratum of the phoneme "*ǯ*".

6. SYNTAGMATIC IDENTIFICATION OF PHONEMES ON THE BASIS OF COMMUTATION OR SUBSTITUTION

In an article devoted to the special problem of the syntagmatic identification of phonemes A. Martinet writes: "It is possible to state with certainty that two consecutive sounds represent two different phonemes only in the case when both of them are subject to commutation, that is, if it is possible to obtain a new word through substitution of another sound."[9]

The principle of commutation on which A. Martinet bases his solution to the problem of syntagmatic identification of phonemes gives rise to a number of objections.

Commutation is defined thus: "COMMUTATION occurs between two elements of the signifiant whose mutual interchange effects an interchange of the corresponding elements of the signifié

[9] A. Martinet, "Un ou deux phonèmes?", *Acta Linguistica*, I, 1 (1939), p. 96.

or between two elements of the signifié whose mutual interchange may bring on the mutual interchange of the corresponding elements of the signifiant."[10] The definition of commutation dictates that if we depend on commutation for the resolution of phonological problems we should turn to the semantic aspect of language. However, as we have attempted to point out in Chapter One of the present text, phonology should be formulated without any recourse to the semantic aspect of language. Depositions of the linguistic informant should constitute the protocol basis of phonological analysis. In place of commutation it is, therefore, expedient to speak about substitution (as this term is used in descriptive linguistics) since in descriptive linguistics substitution does not imply any reference to meaning.

Therefore, we will allow that in resolving the problem of the syntagmatic identification of phonemes we will refer not to commutation, but rather to the concept of substitution which is much stricter in respect to its application to phonology. We may ask if this is satisfactory. In the preceding section we have introduced an operational test for the resolution of this problem whose function is to determine the possibility of eliminating the elements *A* or *B* in the chain *AB*. In testing for substitution the test would not be concerned with elimination but rather with simple substitution of the element *A* or *B* with other elements, let us say *C*, *D*, *E*, etc. The criterion of simple substitution seems to be, however, too weak for the resolution of the problem under consideration. An instructive example of the weakness of this criterion is inherent in the history of Slavic languages. In the phonological system of Proto-Slavic, within a definite era, there arose the situation where soft and hard consonants could occur only before vowels and, therefore, where the softness or hardness of consonants was conjoint with the quality of the successive vowel. We will observe, for instance, the chains *ra* and *r'ȧ*, during the era in question. If in the chain *ra* the vowel *a* is replaced by the vowels *u*, *o*, *ъ*, *y*, we obtain the chains *ru*, *ro*, *rъ*, *ry*; if in the same chain we substitute the consonant *r* with the con-

[10] L. Hjelmslev, "Langue et parole", *Cahiers Ferdinand de Saussure*, II (1942) p. 32.

sonants *t, d, s, z*, we obtain the chains *ta, da, sa, za*. If in the chain *r'ȧ* the vowel *ȧ* is replaced by the vowels *u̇, ȯ, ь, i*, we obtain the chains *r'u̇, r'ȯ, r'ь, r'i*; if in the same chain the consonant *r'* is replaced by the consonants *t', d', s' z'*, we obtain the chains *t'ȧ, d'ȧ, s'ȧ, z'ȧ* (the dot above the vowel transcription symbols represents palatal quality of the corresponding vowels). Thus both the element *r* and the element *a* are subject to substitution by other elements in the chain *ra*, and both the element *r'* and the element *ȧ* are subject to substitution in the chain *r'ȧ*. On the basis of the criterion of substitution we can regard *r* and *a* as substrata of different phonemes in the chain *ra*, while *r'* and *ȧ* are regarded as substrata of different phonemes in the chain *r'ȧ*. In reality this is, however, not admissible since the hardness and softness of the consonants *r* and *r'* is contingent on the velar and palatal quality of the vowels *a* and *ȧ* while, vice versa, the valar and palatal quality of the vowels *a* and *ȧ* is contingent on the hardness and softness of the consonants *r* and *r'*. The chains *ra* and *r'ȧ* must be considered indivisable in the phonological sense since their elements react negatively to the operational test which probes the possibility of their elimination. In our opinion R. I. Avanesov characterizes correctly the situation which applies to the chains *ra* and *r'a* and to analogous chains within the era of the Proto-Slavic language in question, in his statement: "The question of what we face — different consonantal phonemes plus the identity of succeeding vowels, or different vowel phonemes plus the identity of preceding consonants — remains open. And this question remains open not because the imperfection of our knowledge or of our method, but as a result of the fact that it has not been differentiated within the system itself. It is believed that the most effective state of affairs would be the positing of an *interdependence*, and not the establishment of a unilateral dependence of vowels on preceding consonants, or the reverse. In view of the impossibility of isolation one could consider the function of the differentors of meaning to be carried, as a unit, by the combination of the consonant with the succeeding vowel, i.e. the entire syllable."[11]

[11] R. I. Avanesov, "Iz istorii russkogo vokalizma", *Vestnik Moskovskogo universiteta*' No. 1 (1947), p. 48.

Thus, an example from the history of Slavic languages has convinced us of the inherent weakness of the criterion of commutation or substitution. Still, the criterion can be defended on the basis of new propositions. Defenders of this criterion can posit that in some cases, similar to the above examined one, the criterion becomes inapplicable; but they will say that such cases are quite infrequent. Although the criterion of commutation or substitution is not always applicable, they will say, it can still be applied in the majority of cases.

Actually cases which are similar to the above examined example from the history of Slavic languages are quite rare. However, the criterion of commutation or substitution is subject to one additional objection which, we believe, strips it ultimately of any possible theoretical value. The objection, which to us seems decisive, is that the criterion of commutation or substitution cannot differentiate between two kinds of linearity, phonological linearity and subphonological linearity (i.e. between linearity at the level of constructs and linearity at the level of observation in phonology).

Let us consider a concrete example, selecting the chain *kl* in Russian. Through substitution we can exchange *k* for *p*, and *l* for *r*. In the first case we obtain the chain *pl*, in the second case the chain *kr*. And now let us take the sound *g*. Through substitution it is possible to exchange voicedness for voicelessness, and velarity for apicality or labiality. In the first case we obtain *k*, in the second *d* or *b*. Here arises the question why the features which comprise the sound *g* should not be regarded as substrata of different phonemes but the features which comprise the sound chain *kl*, on the contrary, should be regarded as substrata of different phonemes since both the features comprising the sound *g* and the features comprising the sound chain *kl* undergo the exchange for other elements to an equal degree. The answer to this question seems to be self-evident: the features which comprise the sound *g* are simultaneous while the features which comprise the sound chain *kl* are linear. This answer is, however, unsatisfactory. Indeed, if simultaneous physical features cannot constitute substrata of different phonemes, why is it possible to interpret the sound *b*', depending on the phonological structure of the language in question, in two ways, either as a substratum of the phoneme "*b*" or as a substratum of two phonemes "*bj*"? The features which comprise the sound *b*' are, as we know, simultaneous. It is essential to strictly differentiate, and to avoid the confusion of the two kinds of simultaneity and linearity: simultaneity and linearity at the level of observation, and simultaneity and linearity at the level of constructs. At the level of observation the features comprising the sound *b*' are simultaneous, while the features which comprise the sound chain *kl* are linear; but after transition to the level of constructs we can treat a complex of simultaneous acoustic properties — the sound *b*' as the substratum of linear features, of the phonemic chain "*bj*" and, conversely, a complex of linear acoustic properties, the sound chain *kl*, as the substratum of a complex of simultaneous features, of a single phoneme which we designate by the symbol "*kl*". The sound *g* is, in practice, never regarded as the substratum of two phonemes but since its features are subject to substitution by the other features no less than are those features which comprise the sound *b*', it could, in principle, be interpreted as the substratum of two phonemes. The basic shortcoming of the criterion of commutation or substitution in the syntagmatic identification of phonemes is inherent in its conception of phonological simultaneity and linearity as directly observable entities, while phonological simultaneity and linearity should be postulated at the level of constructs.

What are the objective reasons which form the basis for the postulation of phonological simultaneity and linearity? In our opinion these basic reasons are found in the operator method of the syntagmatic identification of phonemes which was introduced in the preceding section. As was shown above, the operational test for the permutation of elements in the sound chain *AB* is a constitutive part of the operator method. According to this operational test we should regard the sound chain *AB* as the physical substratum of two phonemes, "*A*" and "*B*", only in the case when these elements permit permutation, i.e. if the given language admits, side by side with the sound chain *AB*, also the chain *BA*. Returning to the aforementioned concrete example we should regard the sound chain *kl* as the physical substratum of two phonemes "*kl*" only in the case when the sounds *k* and *l* permit permutation. In the case of Russian the sound chain *lk* is admissible side by side with the sound chain *kl* (cf. *klad* 'treasure' and *palka* 'stick'). Therefore, here the sound chain *kl* should be regarded as the physical substratum of two phonemes, "*kl*". In those languages where the elements of the sound chain *kl* do not permit permutation we can, but are not obliged to, interpret *kl* as the physical substratum of two phonemes "*kl*". Therefore, depending on the phonological structure of the given language the sound chain *kl* can be regarded as either the physical substratum of two phonemes or as the physical substratum of one phoneme. This reasoning is applicable also to a complex of simultaneous physical properties, let us say, to the sound *b*'. Since the question of element permutation becomes meaningless in respect to a complex of simultaneous physical properties, these complexes resemble sound chains which do not permit permutation of elements. If this is the case, complexes of simultaneous physical properties, similarly as sound chains which do not permit permutation, can be interpreted, depending on the phonological structure of the given language, in some cases as substrata of two phonemes and in other cases as substrata of a single phoneme. Consequently, the aforementioned sound *b*' can be regarded in one language as the physical substratum of two phonemes "*bj*" and in another language as the physical substratum of a single phoneme "*b*'".

Thus we see that the operator method of the syntagmatic identification of phonemes gives a sufficiently reliable basis for the demarcation of two kinds of simultaneity and linearity, phonological and subphonological.

7. RESULTS OF INVESTIGATION

Investigation of the problem of the paradigmatic and syntagmatic identification of phonemes within the framework of the two-level theory of phonology had led us to the creation of the operator method.

The backbone of the operator method is a strict differentiation of the two abstraction levels, the level of observation and the level of constructs.

In the case of the paradigmatic identification of phonemes the operator method has been contrasted with methods based on the principle of complementary distribution and on the analysis of distinctive features.

The method of the paradigmatic identification of phonemes based on the principle of complementary distribution differs sharply from the method of the paradigmatic identification of phonemes based on the analysis of distinctive features; they not only have nothing in common but are actually directly opposite to one another. At the same time both methods possess one common feature: the failure to differentiate the two abstraction levels, the level of observation and the level of constructs. And precisely this failure to differentiate the two levels is the source of the shortcomings common to both methods.

The method of the paradigmatic identification of phonemes based on the principle of complementary distribution interprets phonological identity as an empirical phenomenon which derives from the fact that certain sounds are mutually exclusive in the same position. This chapter has pointed out, however, that such an interpretation of phonological identity tends to contradict the true facts of language. We have seen that sounds can be mutually exclusive in the same position and, nevertheless, constitute physical substrata of different phonemes and, vice versa, that sounds can fail to be mutually exclusive in the same position and, nevertheless, constitute physical substrata of identical phonemes. In order to resolve correctly the problem of the paradigmatic identification of phonemes it is necessary to reject the interpretation of phonological identity as an empirical phenomenon and to ascend to the level of constructs by means of a mental experiment. This mental experiment constitutes, in effect, the indispensable feature of the operator method used in the resolution of the problem of the paradigmatic identification of phonemes. The mental experiment facilitates correlation of differences between specific sounds with the action of positional operators and thus enables us to regard these sounds as physical substrata of identical individual phonemes. Since identical phonemes have been postulated as constructs, phonological identity should be interpreted as a construct as well.

In the case of the paradigmatic identification of phonemes based on the analysis of distinctive features the failure to differentiate the two abstraction levels leads to absoluteness of the disparity between distinctive features and phonemes as primary and secondary units. Indeed, if we regard phonemes as empirical, directly observed elements, it is mandatory to define distinctive features as primary units and phonemes, bundles of distinctive features, as secondary units. From this standpoint the difference between the distinctive feature as the primary and simple unit and the phoneme as the secondary and composite unit appears absolute. Consequently, this implies the feasibility of concluding that phonological identity should be postulated on the basis of the reduction of composite, secondary units — phonemes — to simple, primary units, distinctive features. In reality, however, the matter stands differently. If distinctive features and phonemes are, in fact, constructs, then as constructs in any science, distinctive features and phonemes are not absolute entities which possess permanent, absolute characteristics; they are abstract entities whose function is to explain the directly observed phenomena and which can vary in their characteristics in accordance with the different methods of approach to each particular problem. The split of constructs into composite and simple, secondary and primary, is always relative. Constructs which are composite from one point of view can appear simple from another standpoint and, vice versa, simple constructs can appear composite. As has been pointed out above, it is not mandatory to interpret phonemes as bundles of distinctive features. A phonological postulation of phonemes themselves, rather than distinctive features, as primary elements which do not permit further subdivision is fully justified. And if there exists the contingency of such phonological postulation we must, obviously, search for a different solution to the problem of phonological identity which would supercede the reduction of phonemes to equivalent bundles of distinctive features. Moreover, even if one accepts the phonological postulation of distinctive features as primary units and of phonemes as secondary units, i.e. bundles of distinctive features, the definition of the identity of phonemes by means of a reference to the identity of distinctive features is unproductive since it raises a new question: how should one define the identity of distinctive features themselves? If distinctive features are constructs, their identity is not ascertained by means of direct observation but must be deduced on the basis of an analysis of the investigated empirical data. Thus reference to distinctive features fails to resolve the problem of phonological identity and succeeds only in transposing it onto another plane. This chapter attempts to show that the operator method of the paradigmatic identification of phonemes furnishes us with an escape from all these difficulties.

The operator method of the paradigmatic identification of phonemes is closely paralleled by the operator method of the syntagmatic identification of phonemes which is included in the discussion; this latter method is contraposed to the method of the syntagmatic identification of phonemes based on commutation or substitution.

As in the case of the non-operator methods of the paradigmatic identification of phonemes, the shortcomings of the method of the syntagmatic identification of phonemes based on commutation or substitution originate in the failure to differentiate the level of observation and the level of constructs. The inherent feature of the operator method of the syntagmatic identification of phonemes is a strict differentiation of two kinds of simultaneity and linearity: subphonological, i.e. belonging to the level of observation, and phonological, i.e. belonging to the level of constructs. Neither commutation not substitution permit differentiation of subphonological and phonological simultaneity and linearity; this fact underlies the theoretical inconsistency on the part of the method of the syntagmatic identification of phoneme based on commutation and substitution.

III

THE TWO-LEVEL THEORY OF PHONOLOGY AND THE METHOD OF BINARY PATTERNING OF PHONOLOGICAL OPPOSITIONS

1. THE PROBLEM

Every science is compelled to differentiate two distinct aspects: (1) an explicit aggregate of the technical modes of investigation, of specific technical regulations or, in other words, all that is, as a rule, termed the method, and (2) an explicit system of concepts, a conceptual apparatus which forms the theoretical basis of science. Both these aspects, the method and the conceptual apparatus of science are closely interrelated: advances in the technical modes of investigation lead to changes in our conceptual apparatus and, vice versa, intensified logical analysis of the conceptual apparatus exerts an essential influence on the development of the technical modes of investigation.

The two-level theory of phonology formulated in Chapter One of this text is the result of an intensified investigation into the semiotic nature of the sound aspect of language. This investigation necessitated the creation of a corresponding conceptual apparatus which, at the present time, appears to reflect adequately the phonological reality.

Chapter Two attempted to explore the application of the two-level theory of phonology to the method of the paradigmatic and syntagmatic identification of phonemes. Conclusions drawn in this chapter can serve as examples of the influence of the conceptual apparatus of science on the method. As we have tried to point out, the acknowledgment of the conceptual apparatus of the two-level theory of phonology leads inevitably to the supercession of the current methods of the paradigmatic and syntagmatic identification of phonemes by new methods which have been termed the operator methods of the paradigmatic and syntagmatic identification of phonemes.

Chapter Three scrutinizes the method of binary patterning of phonemic oppositions from the standpoint of the two-level theory of phonology. At this point it is necessary to stress the following points: as has been shown in Chapter One, the splitting of the concept of phoneme into the concept of phoneme as a construct, and the concept of phonemoid, and the splitting of the concept of distinctive feature into the concepts of differentor and differentoid are irresolubly bound with an analogical splitting of the concept of phonemic opposition into the concept of phonemic opposition as a construct, and the concept of phonemic contrast, as a sound contraposition at the level of observation. The necessity of a strict distinction between phonemic opposition and phonemic contrast which constitutes one of the cornerstones of the two-level theory of phonology does not in itself predetermine the resolution of the problem of the essence of a phonemic opposition in regard to the number of its constituent members. On the basis of an investigation into the semiotic nature of the sound aspect of language, the two-level theory of phonology has deduced the necessity of a strict distinction between phonemic oppositions and phonemic contrasts, regarding the latter as physical substrata of the former; the two-level theory of phonology does not affect, however, the question whether all phonemic oppositions should be regarded as binary or whether there exist, side by side with binary oppositions, oppositions which are polynomial. Moreover, if phonemic oppositions are, in effect, constructs, it becomes apparent that phonological reality can, in principle, be described by means of various patterns of phonemic oppositions. This conclusion is in harmony with the prevalent methodological statement of the modern logic of science which postulates that at the level of constructs one and the same sphere of investigation can yield several acceptable descriptions depending on the model being used, and that the choice of the model should be governed by the actual goals of that particular investigation. We cannot, therefore, agree with R. Jakobson and M. Halle who, in discussing the question "whether the dichotomous scale is the pivotal principle which the analyzer can profitably impose upon the linguistic code or whether this scale is inherent in the structure of language", come to the conclusion that "there are several weighty arguments in favor of the latter solution".[1] There exists, of course, the possibility of accepting or rejecting the binary model of phonemic oppositions; however, whether we accept or reject this model, we will still lack a basis for proving its applicability or inapplicability to the nature of language. Models cannot be, as a rule, classified as being regular or irregular; they only can exhibit, to a smaller or greater degree, correspondence to the particular goals of scientific investigation.

While we are not regarding the binary model of phonemic oppositions as the only possibility, we prefer it to other models owing to the following reasons which, in our opinion, are of fundamental significance:

(1) Contemporary logic of science asserts that scientific progress is dependent on the successful reduction of external complexity of the studied entity to simpler entities and on their interrelations which function as the foundation of science. This is the so-called principle of simplicity. From the standpoint of this principle which constitutes an important statement of general methodology, the binary model of phonemic oppositions, being a simpler model in comparison to other models of phonemic oppositions, ought to meet our requirement to the fullest degree.

(2) One of the most important qualities of the binary model of phonemic oppositions is its inherent link with acoustic phonetics. The binary model of phonemic oppositions owes its acceptance to the successes of acoustic phonetics. While other models are based on physiological phonetic data, the binary model of phonemic oppositions which is based on the spectrographic analysis of speech sounds bridges the gap between phonology and acoustic phonetics and transforms the latter into an experimental basis of phonology.

(3) As a result of its close bond with the spectrographic analysis

[1] R. Jakobson and M. Halle, *op. cit.*, p. 47.

of speech sounds the binary model of phonemic oppositions has admitted phonology into the sphere of important applied problems of cybernetics which are concerned with the acoustic analysis and synthesis of speech sounds. This sphere embraces such progressive areas of great social significance as the construction of automatic computing and stenographic installations, automatic installations for machine communication control, etc. The binary model of phonemic oppositions can furnish a sound basis for the cooperation of the representatives of the various scientific fields within the aforementioned applied areas of cybernetics — linguists, physicists, communication and electronics engineers, mathematicians, specialists in mathematical logic and in semiotics.

The present chapter will examine critically the methodology of binary patterning of phonemic oppositions, will point out the theoretical difficulties inherent in this methodology in its present stage and, referring to the conceptual apparatus of the two-level theory of phonology, will attempt to propose a way to surmount these difficulties.

2. CURRENT STATE OF THE METHOD OF BINARY PATTERNING OF PHONOLOGICAL OPPOSITIONS

The classification of phonemes according to the manner and point of articulation distinguishes binary and polynomial oppositions of phonemes. Classification of consonantal phonemes according to the manner of articulation yields in most cases binary oppositions, as for example the oppositions stops – constrictives, sharp – plain, nasal – non-nasal, voiced – voiceless; classification according to the point of articulation, on the other hand, yields usually polynomial oppositions as, for instance, the ternary opposition of labial, dental and velar stops. The opposition of vowels according to the point of articulation can be binary as, for example, in the opposition of front and back vowels, or polynomial as in the ternary opposition of back, central and front vowels; the opposition of vowels according to the manner of articulation is, as a rule, also binary, as can be illustrated by the opposition of low and high vowels (in regard to the degree of jaw opening), or polynomial as in the case of the ternary opposition of low, middle and high vowels.

It has already long been established that in various languages the velar consonants undergo a change to labial consonants and, conversely, the labial consonants change to velar. Changes of the former type can be found, for example, in Rumanian (e.g. Rumanian *lapte* "milk" and Latin *lactem*), changes of the latter type, for example, in the Celtic languages (e.g. Celtic *-cht-* corresponds to the Indoeuropean *-pt-*). These changes, however, can not be explained in terms of the above mentioned classification scheme of phonemic oppositions since the diachronic phonetic theory adheres to the principle that all sound changes must be gradual. According to this principle phonemes cannot undergo changes by means of an arbitrary shift of any one distinctive feature to any other distinctive feature; their changes must be relative to the change of this or that distinctive feature into its contiguous distinctive feature. Thus, the changes of voiceless consonantal phonemes into voiced ones and, conversely, of voiced consonants into voiceless are common phenomena since voicedness and voicelessness are regarded as contiguous distinctive features. On the other hand, labial and velar distinctive features are not contiguous since, according to the above given classification scheme, they are separated by the velar and the palatal distinctive features. One can explain fully the change of *p* into *t* within the framework of the formulated classification scheme; however, there exists no possible explanation for the change of *p* into *k* and, conversely, of *k* into *p*. Such cases which defy classification within the framework of the above classification scheme pose the question of the feasibility of altering this scheme in such a way so as to permit the labial and velar distinctive features to be regarded as contiguous. The answer to this question lies obviously in the reduction of the polynominal oppositions to binary ones.

Additionally, we shall direct our attention to another fundamental difficulty linked with the phonemic classification according to the manner and point of articulation, namely to the fact that polynomial oppositions established by the above classification yield a number of disjunctive distinctive features which are not related to each other. Thus the analysis of consonant according to the point of articulation furnishes us with polynomial oppositions which contain a total of eight disjunctive distinctive features: labial, labio-dental, linguo-dental, alveolar, palatal, velo-palatal, velar and glottal. Furthermore, for instance, the liquids /r/ and /l/ are considered to be disjunctive phonemes as well. The presence of a large number of disjunctive features contradicts, however, the postulate of the systematic character of language: if language is, in effect, a system and if the relationship among the units of language (including phonemic units) comprises oppositions, then it is natural to expect that linguistic oppositions (i.e. also phonemic oppositions) must be characterized by a certain amount of regularity, a certain degree of order: the presence of a large number of disjunctive features represents a factor which tends to disrupt the regularity of the system, injecting into it an element of chaos. Hence the contradiction between the postulate of the systematic character of language and the antisystematic character of the disjunctive features gives rise to the fundamental dilemma which confronts the scheme of phonemic classification according to the manner and point of articulation. It is clear that the resolution of the problem lies in the reduction of the polynomial oppositions to binary ones.

In this context there arises the basic question whether the reduction of polynomial phonemic oppositions to binary ones lies within the realm of feasibility.

This question was posed for the first time by R. Jakobson in his report to the Third International Congress of Phonetic Sciences in Ghent in July 1938.[2] His answer was affirmative. He pointed out that for every language may be adopted a new classification scheme of phonemic oppositions based on the principle of binarity.

[2] R. Jakobson, "Observations sur le classement phonologique des consonnes", *Proceedings of the Third International Congress of Phonetic Sciences held at the University of Ghent 18-22 July 1938* (Ghent, 1939), pp. 34-41.

Let us examine the conclusions arrived at by Jakobson.[3]

The main difficulty connected with the reduction of polynomial oppositions to binary ones lies in the analysis of phonemic oppositions according to the point of articulation. If we consider, for instance, the Serbocroatian opposition *p* : *t* : *ћ* : *k*, a reduction of this quadratic opposition to a binary one is difficult to conceive.

The method which leads to the surmounting of this difficulty is suggested by the aforementioned phenomenon of wide-spread changes of velar consonants into labials and, conversely, of labials into velar consonants which have been encountered in various languages of the world. These changes demonstrate that certain features are common to both velar and labial consonants.

Indeed, a single indivisible oral resonator is a feature which is common to both velar and labial consonants. On the other hand, during the articulation of the palatal and linguo-dental consonants the apex of the tongue divides the oral cavity into two short resonators.

These two parts of the oral cavity possess specific acoustic characteristics. From the acoustic point of view velar and labial consonants are characterized by a lower tonality as compared to the palatals and linguo-dentals.

Hence, the differences among the four types of consonants — the velar, palatal, linguo-dental and labial — dissolve themselves, in effect, into two types of binary oppositions: on the one hand, the palatal and linguo-dental and, on the other hand, the velar

[3] The current approach to the methodology of binary patterning of phonological oppositions is put forth in the following works: R. Jakobson, C. G. Fant, M. Halle, *op. cit.*; R. Jakobson and M. Halle, *op. cit.*; R. Jakobson and M. Halle, "Phonology in Relation to Phonetics", *Manual of Phonetics* (Amsterdam, 1957), Ch. 14; in Russian there have appeared three works which apply the methodology of binary paterning to concrete languages: S. K. Šaumjan, *Istorija sistemy differencial'nyx èlementov v pol'skom jazyke* (Moscow, 1958); V. V. Ivanov and V. N. Toporov, *Sanskrit* (Moscow, 1960); T. Ja. Elizarenkova, "Differencial'nye èlementy soglasnyx fonem xindi", *Voprosy jazykoznanija*, No. 5 (1961); the problems of the methodology of binary patterning of phonemic oppositions are discussed also in the following works: V. V. Ivanov, "O priemlemosti fonologičeskix modelej", *Trudy Instituta točnoj mexaniki i vyčislitel'noj texniki AN SSSR*, 2 (Moscow, 1961); R. G. Piotrovskij, "Ešče raz o differencial'nyx priznakax fonemy", *Voprosy jazykoznanija*, No. 6 (1960).

and labial consonants. The latter are called grave, the former acute consonants.

The differences among the aforementioned four types of consonants can be reduced to two types of binary oppositions on the basis of yet another criterion. The velar and palatal consonants (including the sibilants) can be contraposed to the linguodentals and labials in respect to the differentiation of the back and front parts of the oral cavity; the former are formed in the back part, the latter in the front part of the oral cavity. The back consonants are characterized by a higher degree of audio-perceptibility or, in other words, by a greater "phonetic power" in comparison with the front consonants. Thus, for instance, *k* and *ħ* have a higher degree of audio-perceptibility than *t* and *p*; similarly, *g* and *ђ* have a higher degree of audio-perceptibility that *d* and *b*. The differences between the low and high degree of audio-perceptibility are coupled with corresponding specific differences in the acoustic spectrum: the back consonants have compact acoustic spectra while the spectra of the front consonants are diffused. Consequently, the back consonants are termed compact and the front ones diffuse. "Compact phonemes are characterized by the relative predominance of one centrally located formant region (or formant). They are opposed to diffuse phonemes in which one or more non-central formants or formant regions predominate."[4]

Thus polynomial oppositions of consonants according to the point of articulation dissolve themselves into binary oppositions on the basis of distinctive features: grave – acute and compact – diffuse. These binary oppositions of consonants are complemented by the binary oppositions of back – front vowels and low – high vowels (in regard to the degree of jaw opening); the back vowels are characterized by a lower tonality in comparison with the front vowels while the acoustic spectra of the low vowels are compact in comparison with the spectra of the high vowels which are diffuse. In respect to their acoustic characteristics the back vowels are termed grave, the front vowels acute; the low vowels are termed compact and the high vowels diffuse.

[4] R. Jakobson, C. G. Fant, M. Halle, *op. cit.*, p. 27.

In this way the tonality feature grave – acute and the acoustic spectrum feature compact — diffuse represent binary distinctive features which are common to both consonantal and vowel phonemes. Discovery of these binary distinctive features has facilitated the establishment of triangular and rectangular isomorphic patterns of consonantal and vowel phonemes in various languages.[5]

Triangular isomorphic patterns of consonantal and vowel phonemes can be applied, for example, to the consonants *k*, *t*, *p* in English and the vowels *a*, *i*, *u* in Arabic. Let us examine a schematic illustration of the isomorphism between the English consonants and the Arabic vowels.

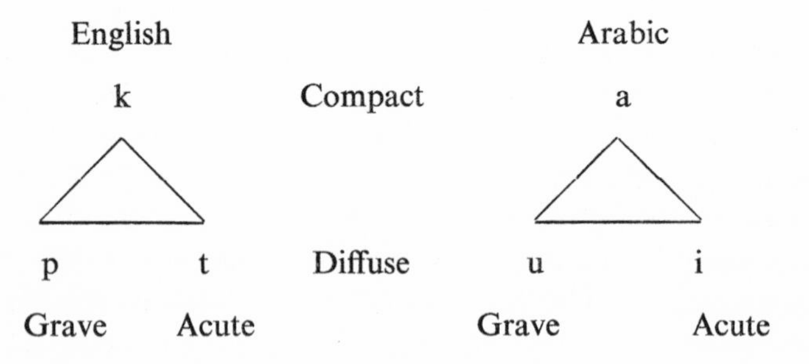

It is evident that as far as the acoustic spectrum opposition compact – diffuse is concerned the relationship of the English consonantal phoneme *k* to the consonantal phonemes *p* and *t* parallels the relationship of the Arabic vowel phoneme *a* to the vowel phonemes *u* and *i*. In respect to the tonality opposition grave – acute the relationship of the English consonantal phoneme *p* to the consonantal phoneme *t* is analogous to the relationship of the Arabic vowel phoneme *u* to the vowel phoneme *i*.

Exemplary of the rectangular isomorphic patterns of consonantal and vowel phonemes are the Serbocroatian consonants *k*, *ћ*, *t*, *p*, and the vowels *a*, *æ*, *i*, *u* of the Amerindian language Wichita.

[5] R. Jakobson, C. G. Fant, M. Halle, *op. cit.*, pp. 33-34.

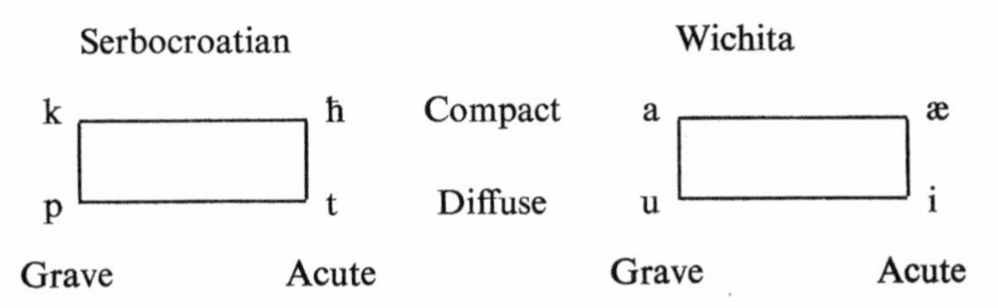

It is apparent that in regard to the acoustic spectrum opposition compact – diffuse in Serbocroatian the consonantal phonemes *k* and *ħ* are to the phonemes *p* and *t* what in Wichita the vowel phonemes *a* and *æ* are to the phonemes *u* and *i*.

In regard to the tonality opposition grave – acute the Serbocroatian consonantal phonemes *k* and *p* are to the phonemes *ħ* and *t* what the Wichita vowel phonemes *a* and *u* are to the phonemes *æ* and *i*.

In certain languages we encounter ternary oppositions of vowels. How can these ternary vowel oppositions be converted to binary oppositions? Let us take, for example, the ternary opposition of the Russian vowel phonemes *a* : *o* : *u*. The members of this opposition exhibit three distinct degrees of compactness: the vowel phoneme *a* has a maximal degree of compactness and the phoneme *u* a minimal degree of compactness, i.e. diffuseness. Since the phoneme *o* occupies a central position between the phonemes *a* and *u* we can regard it as diffuse in comparison to the phoneme *a* and as compact in comparison to the phoneme *u*. Consequently, this ternary opposition can be split into two binary oppositions in respect to the binary distinctive feature compact – diffuse: *a* : *o* and *o* : *u*. Since the phoneme *o* is present in both oppositions it possesses both compactness and diffuseness as a complex distinctive feature.

A systematic conversion of polynomial oppositions of consonantal and vowel phonemes to binary oppositions has resulted in the substantiation of the following twelve pairs of distinctive features which apply to all the languages of the world:

(1) Vocalic – Non-vocalic
(2) Consonantal – Non-consonantal

(3) Interrupted – Continuant
(4) Checked – Unchecked
(5) Strident – Mellow
(6) Voiced – Voiceless
(7) Compact – Diffuse
(8) Grave – Acute
(9) Flat – Plain
(10) Sharp – Plain
(11) Tense – Lax
(12) Nasal – Oral.[6]

Let us examine these distinctive features in greater detail: *Vocalic – Non-vocalic and Consonantal – Non-consonantal.* These distinctive features underlie the differentiation of the following four classes of phonemes: vowels, consonants, liquids and the so-called glides. While vowels possess the vocalic feature and lack the consonantal feature, consonants, vice versa, possess the consonantal and lack the vocalic feature. Both the vocalic and consonantal features are present in the liquids, i.e. *r* or *l*, and both are lacking in the glides (which include the phonemes *h*, *w* and *j*).

Interrupted – Continuant. Continuant phonemes include all fricatives and, additionally, the liquid phoneme *l*. Interrupted phonemes comprise, beside the stops, also the liquid phoneme *r*. During the articulation of continuant phonemes the air stream flows uninterruptedly while during the articulation of interrupted phonemes the air stream is cut off one or more times (several interruptions occur during the articulation of the phoneme *r*).

Checked – Unchecked. Checked phonemes are marked by a specific abruptness of articulation which is caused by the accompanying glottalized stop. The checked phonemes are usually stops and very rarely fricatives. The opposition between checked and unchecked phonemes is encountered in Caucasian, Indian, African and Far East languages.

Strident – Mellow. These distinctive features are encountered in fricatives, in stops, and in liquid phonemes. The articulation of

[6] R. Jakobson, C. G. Fant, M. Halle, *op. cit.*, p. 40.

strident consonants is characterized by a supplementary obstruction of the air stream which creates a specific harsh noise. This noise effect is absent in the articulation of mellow consonants. The following subdivision of consonants is well known: the labials are split into bilabials and labio-dentals, the linguo-dentals into linguo-dentals proper and linguo-dental sibilants, the palatals into palatals proper and palatal sibilants, and the velars into velars proper and uvulars. The first member of each one of these consonantal pairs is mellow, the second is strident. The essential feature of this differentiation lies in the fact that the articulation of bilabial consonants employs only the lips while the articulation of labio-dentals utilizes teeth as well; the articulation of linguo-dentals proper utilizes the tongue and the upper teeth while the articulation of the linguo-dental sibilants makes use of the lower teeth as well; the articulation of palatal sibilants employs, besides the central part of the tongue, also the lower teeth; the articulation of uvulars uses the glottis in addition to the back part of the tongue and the soft palate. Affricates belong likewise to strident consonants; their corresponding pair-mates, the stops, are mellow. Examples of the opposition of strident and mellow consonants are: in English *sing – thing*, in German *Zeilen* 'lines' – *teilen* 'to divide'; *Pfanne* 'pan' – *Panne* 'breakdown'.

Flat – Plain. The articulation of flat consonants and vowels, in contrast to plain consonants and vowels, is supplemented by labialization. Since labialization causes a sharp downward shift in the tonality of vowels and consonants, it is conventional to employ a musical term for the labelling of this feature. Hence one uses the subscript musical flat ♭ as the diacritical sign for the designation of labialized consonants.[7]

Sharp – Plain. The basic articulation of sharp consonants, in contrast to plain consonants, employs a supplementary palatalization. Since palatalization introduces a sharp upward shift in the tonality of the consonants, again we utilize a conventional musical term for the labelling of this feature.

There is no need to reexamine any additional terms employed in

[7] R. Jakobson, C. G. Fant, M. Halle, *op. cit.*, p. 31.

the labelling of binary distinctive features, since compact – diffuse as well as grave – acute have been discussed in the preceding section, and the remaining terms, voiced – voiceless, tense – lax and nasal – oral correspond to the generally accepted classification.

As to the origin of the terms denoting distinctive features it is necessary to keep in mind the following considerations expressed by the authors of the *Preliminaries to Speech Analysis*: "The names of the distinctive features are meant to denote linguistic discriminations: in other words, the significant discriminations utilized in the code common to the members of the speech community. The stage of the speech event to which a given term is etymologically connected is much less important. Thus a term which alludes to the articulation may at times be used if the articulatory fact in question is common to all the manifestations of the given feature, e.g. the nasalization feature. Similarly, it is not important whether the term refers primarily to the physical or perceptual level, as long as the feature is definable on both levels. In cases where no generally acceptable term was available, we have used names for certain distinctive features which may later be supplanted by more suitable ones. Nevertheless, a discussion of the features themselves seems to us more pertinent than an argument over their labels."[8]

The aforementioned twelve pairs of distinctive features are regarded by R. Jakobson, G. Fant and M. Halle as inherent distinctive features. Besides inherent distinctive features the authors distinguish also prosodic distinctive features. The difference between prosodic and inherent distinctive features is defined as follows: "A prosodic feature is displayed only by those phonemes which form the crest of the syllable and it may be defined only with reference to the relief of the syllable or of the syllable chain, whereas the inherent feature is displayed by phonemes irrespective of their role in the relief of the syllable, and the definition of such a feature does not refer to the relief of the syllable or of the syllable chain."[9] Prosodic distinctive features are subdivided into three types: tone, quantity and force. Each of these types comprises two varieties:

[8] R. Jakobson, C. G. Fant, M. Halle, *op. cit.*, p. v.
[9] R. Jakobson, M. Halle, *op. cit.*, p. 22.

intersyllabic and intrasyllabic distinctive features; in the first case the crest of one syllable is compared to the crest of other syllables; in the second case one portion of the crest of the syllable is compared to other portions of the same crest.

The authors emphasize that the three types of prosodic features, tone, force and quantity, correspond to the three attributes of sensation voice pitch, voice loudness and subjective duration. These three attributes of sensation possess the following physical correlates: the dimensions of frequency, amplitude and intensity, respectively.[10]

The aforementioned twelve pairs of distinctive features which form a panchronic system for the languages of the world fail to comprise a number of binary features, as for instance aspiration – non–aspiration,which had been listed in N.S.Trubeckoj's *Grundzüge der Phonologie*. Those distinctive features which had been regarded by N. S. Trubeckoj as distinctive are defined by R. Jakobson, G. Fant and M. Halle as redundant and, consequently, do not enter into the given classification system. As to the demarcation between distinctive and redundant features, the authors advance the following principle: "If two or more allegedly different features never co-occur in a language and if they, furthermore, yield a common property distinguishing them from all other features, then they are to be interpreted as different implementations of one and the same feature, each occuring to the exclusion of the others and, consequently, presenting a particular case of complementary distribution."[11] On the basis of this principle the above mentioned twelve pairs of distinctive features are considered to be the universal invariants of the binary oppositions found in the languages of the world. Let us examine actual examples of the reduction of binary oppositions to invariants.

Since no language contains, within the same environment, a co-occurence of the oppositions pharyngeal – non-pharyngeal and labial – non-labial, these two oppositions are contracted into a single invariant, the opposition flat – plain.

[10] R. Jakobson, M. Halle, *op. cit.*, p. 22.
[11] R. Jakobson, M. Halle, *op. cit.*, pp. 27-28.

The oppositions tense – lax, intensive – non-intensive, aspirated – non-aspirated, and pre-aspirated – non-pre-aspirated, identified by N. S. Trubeckoj as four separate oppositions,[12] are never encountered under the same phonological conditions and are, therefore, reduced to a single invariant, the opposition tense – lax. Analogical reduction of other binary oppositions to invariants leads to the establishment of the aforementioned twelve pairs of universal binary distinctive features.

Thus, those phonological oppositions which had been traditionally regarded as polynomial have been reformulated in terms of binary oppositions. Consequently, the principle of binarity can be viewed as the basic principle of phonological analysis.

The principle of binarity allows us to identify phonemes on the basis of their logical description.[13]

What is the basis of the logical description of phonemes?

It is generally known that logic employs the principle of dichotomy which, when applied to class theory, is posited as follows: an object is either a member of the class *A* or a member of the class non-*A*. This principle can be represented by the interrogative formula "yes or no?" which permits only two alternatives ("yes" or "no"). Utilizing this interrogative formula it is possible to identify every separate component of the system of any given set. E. Cherry, M. Halle and R. Jakobson illustrate the application of this method[14] to a set of eight objects which are subject to identification by means of logical description : *A*, *B*, *C*, ..., *H*. These objects have to be identified by the use of the interrogative formula "yes or no?". The answer "yes" is symbolized by the sign +, negative answer by the sign —. The group under investigation is, first of all, split into two parts; subsequently, we ask whether the given object is to be found on the right side (+) or not (—). Successive subdivisions will eventually identify every object. Complete

[12] Cf. N. S. Trubeckoj, *op. cit.*, pp. 165-166.

[13] Cf. E. C. Cherry, M. Halle, R. Jakobson, "Toward the Logical Description of Languages in Their Phonemic Aspect", *Language*, No. 1 (1953) (reprinted in Roman Jakobson, *Selected Writings*, I (The Hague, 1962), pp. 449-463).

[14] E. C. Cherry, M. Halle, R. Jakobson, *op. cit.*, p. 37; R. Jakobson, *op. cit.*, pp. 452-453.

identification of each object comprises a string composed of plus and minus signs, e.g. the object *F* in the above given scheme is identified by the string (+—+).

The identification scheme of objects in a set of eight has the following appearance:

A	B	C	D	E	F	G	H
—	—	—	—	+	+	+	+
—	—	+	+	—	—	+	+
—	+	—	+	—	+	—	+

How do we identify phonemes by means of their logical description?

Every phoneme, if regarded as a bundle of distinctive features, differs from any other phoneme in regard to the composition of its distinctive features. Therefore, identification of the phonemes of a given language signifies, in effect, the definition of the distinctive features of each phoneme. The definition of the distinctive features of phonemes hinges on the question whether the specific phoneme does, or does not, possess the given distinctive feature. For instance, is the given phoneme voiced — yes or no?, etc. The answers, affirmative or negative, are entered in the identification matrix as plus (+) or minus (—) signs.

There are cases where the question whether the phoneme possesses the given distinctive feature fails to yield a definite answer. Thus one may ask, for instance: Is the given phoneme voiceless? If the identification concerns phonemes of the Russian language, this question is answered affirmatively in respect to the phonemes *k*, *p*, *t*, *f*, *s*, *š* and negatively in respect to the phonemes *g*, *b*, *d*, *v*, *z*, *ž*. However, in respect to the Russian phoneme *x* the answer to the given question will be equivocal, i.e. "both yes and no." Since Russian does not possess the opposition $x : \gamma$ the phoneme *x* can be regarded equivocally as either voiceless or voiced; the choice will in no way affect the identification of this phoneme in Russian.

Whenever the question whether the phoneme possesses the given distinctive feature yields an equivocal answer we are dealing with a redundant feature of that phoneme. An equivocal answer is symbolized in the matrix of phoneme identification by the zero sign (○).

M. Halle and N. Chomsky introduced a method of transforming the matrix of phoneme identification into a branching diagram.[15] The function of the branching diagram is to define the hierarchy among distinctive features. The construction of the diagrams presupposes the existence of at least one distinctive feature in the matrix which lacks the zero sign. This distinctive feature is assigned to the first node of the diagram. After the phonemes of the given language have been split into two classes according to the presence or absence of this distinctive feature we seek out, for successive class subdivisions, those distinctive features which lack the zero sign and assign them to the corresponding nodes. Having obtained subclasses of phonemes we repeat the process in respect to these subclasses and obtain subclasses of each subclass, and so forth, until we arrive at the individual phonemes which terminate the branching. Those distinctive features which lack the zero sign and which are chosen at every stage of the branching can be either identical or different for the given subclasses of phonemes. The resulting hierarchy of distinctive features is not necessarily complete. For example, if there exist two distinctive features without a zero sign, there is no basic requirement for placing one of the features before the other. Thus, in terms of mathematical logic, one speaks not of a simple order but only of a partial order among distinctive features. The hierarchy of distinctive features can be regarded as explanation of the intuitively given gact that all distinctive features do not occupy an equal place in the phonological system. Thus, the distinction between vowels and consonants is considered to be more fundamental than, for instance, the distinction between nasal and non-nasal vowels or the distinction between voiced and unvoiced consonants.

The foregoing discussion of the method of transforming the

[15] Cf. M. Halle, *The Sound Pattern of Russian: A Linguistic and Acoustical Investigation* (The Hague, 1959).

matrixes of phoneme identification into branching diagrams can be illustrated in the following tables which appear in the aforementioned book of M. Halle:[16]

Table 1 represents a branching diagram whose subclasses are subject to further branching on the basis of identical distinctive features.

Table 1

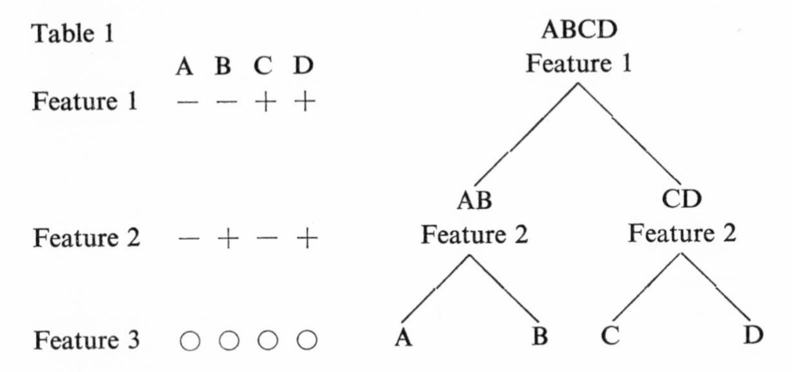

	A	B	C	D
Feature 1	−	−	+	+
Feature 2	−	+	−	+
Feature 3	○	○	○	○

Table 2 represents a branching diagram whose subclasses are subject to further branching on the basis of different distinctive features.

Table 2

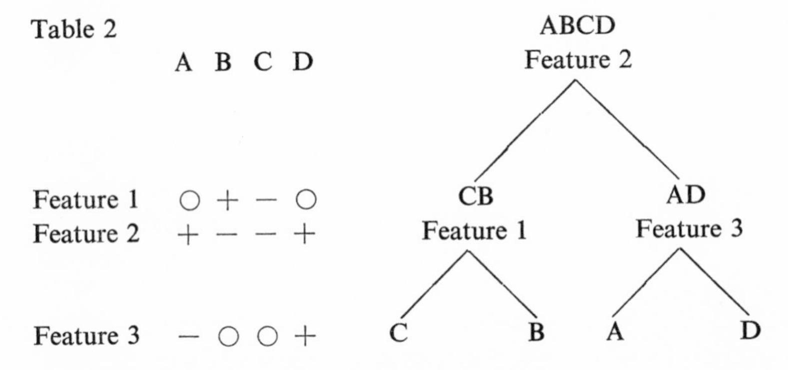

	A	B	C	D
Feature 1	○	+	−	○
Feature 2	+	−	−	+
Feature 3	−	○	○	+

Table 3 represents the case when the matrix of phoneme identification cannot be transformed into a branching diagram because it fails to contain an element lacking the zero sign.

[16] M. Halle, *op. cit.*, pp. 35-36.

Table 3

	A	B	C
Feature 1	O	+	−
Feature 2	+	O	−
Feature 3	+	−	O

Table 4 points out that the transformation of a matrix of phoneme identification into a branching diagram does not require us to establish in all portions of the branching diagram identical ordering of the questions as to the presence or absence of distinctive features.

Table 4

	A	B	C	D	E	F
Feature 1	−	−	−	+	+	+
Feature 2	O	−	+	−	+	+
Feature 3	−	+	+	O	−	+

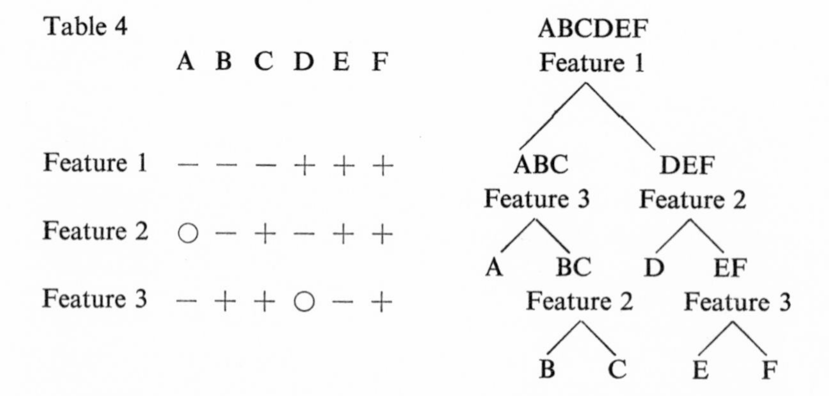

Every path, starting at the first node of the branching diagram and terminating in one of the end nodes of the diagram, defines in its entirety one specific phoneme of the phonological system.

In one of his recent articles M. Halle points out that the binary model of phonological oppositions can be utilized in measuring the simplicity of linguistic description.[17] We should regard as simpler that one of two linguistic descriptions which, under otherwise equal conditions, utilizes a smaller number of distinctive features.

[17] M. Halle, "On the Role of Simplicity in Linguistic Descriptions", *Proceedings of Symposia in Applied Mathematics*, Vol. XII: *Structure of Language and Its Mathematical Aspects* (1961), pp. 89-94.

As an example one can cite the following two descriptions of the plural formation of English substantives:

I. When forming the plural of substantives it is essential:

(1) to add *iz* to the stem when the stem terminates in a phoneme characterized by non-vocalic, consonantal, acute and strident features;

(2) to add *s* to the stem when the stem terminates in a phoneme characterized by a) non-vocalic, consonantal, voiceless and mellow features or b) non-vocalic, consonantal, voiceless, strident and grave features;

(3) to add *z* to the stem when the stem terminates in a phoneme characterized by a) a vocalic feature, b) non-vocalic, consonantal, voiced and mellow features, or c) non-vocalic, consonantal, voiced, strident and grave features.

II. When forming the plural of substantives it is essential:

(1) to add *iz* to the stem when the stem terminates in a phoneme characterized by non-vocalic, consonantal, acute and strident features;

(2) to add *s* to the stem when the stem terminates in a phoneme characterized by non-vocalic, consonantal and voiceless features;

(3) to add *z* to the stem in all other cases.

Comparison of these two descriptions of the plural formation of English substantives shows clearly that the latter requires mention of a smaller number of distinctive features and should, consequently, be regarded as the simpler of the two. It is important to note as well that the mention of a smaller number of distinctive features in the second description is due to the arrangement of its rules in accordance to the number of distinctive features that would have to be mentioned: the first rule mentions four distinctive features, the second rule three, while the third rule requires mention of none.

3. THEORETICAL DIFFICULTIES ENCOUNTERED IN THE DEMARCATION OF DISTINCTIVE AND REDUNDANT FEATURES

The preceding section has introduced a general outline of the present-day method of binary patterning of phonological oppositions. A more detailed attention was naturally given to those aspects of the method which will play a vital role in further discussion. Subsequent sections will present a critical analysis of this method, concentrating on its inherent theoretical difficulties. Referring to the conceptual apparatus of the two-level theory of phonology we will strive to overcome these theoretical difficulties in an effort to bring the method of binary patterning of phonological oppositions into conformity with the two-level theory of phonology.

Investigation of the theoretical difficulties will commence with an analysis of the difficulty arising in connection with the demarcation of distinctive and redundant features during the formulation of a universal system of distinctive features for the languages of the world. First of all, however, a few words need to be said about theoretical difficulties of a more general kind.

The method of binary patterning of phonological oppositions in its present stage is linked with the relational-physical concept of distinctive feature. Yet, as has been pointed out in Chapter One, the relational-physical concept of distinctive feature leads inevitably to the antinomies of transposition and identity. The overcoming of these antinomies requires a split-up of the concept of distinctive feature into the concept of differentor and the concept of differentoid. These antinomies represent theoretical difficulties of a general type which are independent of the manner of phonological system patterning by means of either the binary scheme of phonological oppositions or the traditional classification scheme of phonological oppositions. Hence, even without recourse to an analysis of the essence of the method of binary patterning of phonological oppositions we can posit, on the basis of considerations enumerated in Chapter One, the necessity of connecting this method with the concepts of differentor and differentoid. However, even if we sidestep these general considerations, the method of binary patterning of phonological oppositions retains an inherent theoretical difficulty the overcoming of which leads likewise inevitably to a split-up of the concept of distinctive feature into the concepts of differentor and differentoid. This theoretical difficulty relates to the method of the demarcation of distinctive and redundant features which was adopted by the authors of the binary model of phonological oppositions in connection with the formulation of a universal system of distinctive features for the languages of the world.

The preceding section introduced an accurate formulation of the principle utilized by the authors of the binary model of phonological oppositions in the demarcation of distinctive and redundant features for the languages of the world. Illustrating the application of this principle we have shown the reduction of four phonemic oppositions established by N. S. Trubeckoj, tense – lax, intensive – non-intensive, aspirated – non-aspirated, and pre-aspirated – non-pre-aspirated, to a single phonemic opposition, tense – lax. In reducing these four oppositions to a single one the authors of the binary model proceeded from the fact that the distinctive features present in these oppositions never co-occur under identical phonological conditions. For instance, while in one language the distinctive function is carried by tenseness, in a second language a corresponding role is played by aspiration, in a third language by intensiveness, and in a fourth language by pre-aspiration; or, in one and the same language, in one position one encounters tenseness while in other, corresponding positions, one encounters aspiration, intensiveness, or pre-aspiration. Having thus established a relation of complementary distribution among these four distinctive features the authors of the binary model eliminated as redundant the oppositions aspirated – non-aspirated, intensive – non-intensive and pre-aspirated – non-pre-aspirated from their universal system, and retained only the opposition tense – lax.

One may, however question the reason for the reduction of the three oppositions, aspirated – non-aspirated, pre-aspirated – non-pre-aspirated and intensive – non-intensive to the fourth opposition, tense – lax. Why should one not select any one of the four oppositions, let us say, the opposition aspirated – non-aspirated, as the basic one to which the remaining three, including the opposition tense – lax, could be reduced?

This qeustion cannot be answered since, whichever opposition may be selected as basic, the reduction of any one opposition to any other one will always remain arbitrary.

Thus, the method of the authors of the binary model encounters the following theoretical difficulty: on the one hand, the formulation of a universal system of distinctive features for the languages of the world requires elimination of some phonological oppositions as redundant while, on the other hand, any attempt at such an elimination appears to be arbitrary.

Overcoming of this difficulty is contingent on the splitting of the concept of distinctive feature into the concepts of differentor and differentoid, and the splitting of the concept of phonological opposition into the concept of phonological opposition as a construct and the concept of phonological contrast as a relational-physical concept.

If we regard the above introduced oppositions from the standpoint of the two-level theory of phonology, we can identify them as relational-physical substrata of phonological oppositions, i.e. constructs. By the same token, we are justified in equating tenseness, aspiration, intensiveness and pre-aspiration only in the case if we regard them as differentoids, i.e. features which constitute physical substrata of identical differentoids.

Designating the relation of embodiment by the sign I, tenseness by the symbol T, and the differentor which includes tenseness by the symbol D_1 we can represent the relation between tenseness and its differentor by means of the following formula:

$$I\,(T, D_1)$$

Designating aspiration by the symbol A and the differentor which embodies it by the symbol D_2, we can represent the relation between aspiration and its differentor as:

$$I\,(A, D_2)$$

Designating intensiveness by the symbol In and the differentor which includes it by the symbol D_3 we can represent the relation between intensiveness and its differentor as:

$$I\,(In, D_3)$$

Analogously, designating pre-aspiration by the symbol *Pr* and the differentor which includes it by the symbol D_4, we can represent the relation between pre-aspiration and its differentor as:

$$I\,(Pr, D_4).$$

Since D_1, D_2, D_3, and D_4 are identical it follows that *T*, *A*, *In*, and *Pr*, being substrata of D_1, D_2, D_3 and D_4, are identical as well.

Here we encounter a theoretical question as to the terms to be assigned to the differentors D_1, D_2, D_3, and D_4. Utilizing terminology adopted by the authors we can term D_1, D_2, D_3, and D_4 varieties of tenseness; in that case, however, we must distinguish strictly the term "tenseness" as a conventional designation of a specific differentor and the term "tenseness" as the designation of a relational-physical property which constitutes a substratum of that differentor. Adopting these terminological conditions we can posit that tenseness-differentor is embodied by four differentoids: tenseness, aspiration, intensiveness, and pre-aspiration.

Applying an analogous reasoning to other terms we must differentiate voicedness-differentor and voicedness-differentoid, compactness-differentor and compactness-differentoid, checkedness-differentor and checkedness-differentoid, etc. In order to avoid intermixture of differentors and differentoids, it is possible to introduce indexation: in those cases when the terminology of differentors and differentoids coincides, the differentoids will bear the index sub-1 and the differentors the index sub-2: for instance, $voiced_1$ and $voiced_2$, $compact_1$ and $compact_2$, $checked_1$ and $checked_2$, etc.

Thus, the two-level theory of phonology compels us, to split the concept of a universal system of distinctive features into two concepts — the concept of a universal system of differentors and the concept of a physical embodiment of the universal system of differentors.

4. THEORETICAL DIFFICULTIES ENCOUNTERED IN THE DEFINING OF POSITIVE AND NEGATIVE DISTINCTIVE FEATURES

The process of defining positive and negative distinctive features in the method of binary patterning of phonemic oppositions encounters a number of theoretical difficulties which have been already pointed out in the works of P. S. Kuznecov, A. A. Reformatskij, and A. Martinet.[18]

The basic difficulty is epitomized by the following question: what is the nature of the objective criteria which underlie the division of distinctive features into positive and negative?

Let us take, for example, the opposition voiced – voiceless or the opposition sharp – plain. The authors of the method of binary patterning regard voicedness and sharpness as positive distinctive features, voicelessness and plainness as negative distinctive features. However, could not this postulation be reversed; would it not be possible to regard voicelessness and plainness as positive, voicedness and sharpness as negative distinctive features? Moreover: voicedness and voicelessness, sharpness and plainness might be qualitatively equal and, therefore, could it be that the concepts of positivity and negativity are altogether inapplicable in respect to these pairs of distinctive features?

In connection with this A. A. Reformatskij rightly writes: "The most interesting are the binomials "plain – sharp" where, unfortunately, the well known theory of "marked" and "unmarked" members introduced by the Prague school phonologists (including R. O. Jakobson) obviously does not correspond to reality. The Prague formula "marked – unmarked" should correspond to the formula $a - a + 1$, while closed correlations of the type "voiced –

[18] Cf.: P. S. Kuznecov, "O differencial'nyx priznakax fonem", *Voprosy jazykoznanija*, 1958, No. 1; A. A. Reformatskij, "Dixotomičeskaja klassifikacija differencial'nyx priznakov i fonematičeskaja model' jazyka", *Voprosy teorii jazyka v sovremennoj zarubežnoj lingvistike* (Moscow, 1961); A. Martinet, *Economie des changements phonétiques*.

voiceless" should, in effect, be represented by the formula $a - a \pm 1$, since the presence of voicedness constitutes simultaneously also the absence of voicelessness, being it that "zero signs" in various systems of language structure often bear the same significance as presence. In a closed correlation of "plain – sharp" in those languages where these sound differences are not positionally determined (as, for instance, in French where these features are dependent on the following vowels or in synharmonic languages, as in Turkish, where plainness or sharpness of consonants is contingent on the palatal synharmonism of the word) but are phonemically independent and relevant, the matter is more complex: it is not possible to posit (as is often done when this question is taken at an elementary level) that in order to obtain a "soft" consonant one must necessarily add "softness". One actually must not only "add softness", i.e. palatalize by elevating the center part of the tongue to the hard palate, but "also remove hardness" as well, i.e. deprive the articulation of the given consonant of velarization by lowering of the back part of the tongue (similarly as the "conversion of a soft consonant into a hard one" requires us not only to "deprive it of its palatalization", i.e. to lower the center part of the tongue, but to invest it with velarization as well, i.e. to elevate the back part of the tongue). The above has been confirmed roentgenographically. Accordingly, the Prague school formula $a - a + 1$ lacks any ontological verification and should be replaced by the formula $a - a \pm 1$."[19]

The words of A. A. Reformatskij cannot be contested. Actually there exists no objective basis for regarding voicedness and sharpness as positive distinctive features and voicelessness and plainness as negative distinctive features. A.A. Reformatskij's reasoning can be applied to other pairs of distinctive features as well. In all cases we do not deal with positive and negative distinctive features but with distinctive features which are qualitatively equal. While agreeing with the critical considerations of A. A. Reformatskij we must, however, engage in additional discussion. These critical considerations are valid only because the authors of the binary model fail to distinguish the two levels of abstraction. Indeed, if

[19] A. A. Reformatskij, *op. cit.*, pp. 112-113.

positivity and negativity were to be regarded as directly observed entities, as objectively stated differences pertaining to the physical properties of the sounds, we would have to agree that there exist no objective criteria for the differentiation of positive and negative distinctive features. This situation becomes, however, entirely altered if we interpret distinctive features as constructs rather than as physical facts. Interpretation of distinctive features as constructs leads to a frank declaration that the definition of positive and negative distinctive features is in no way contingent upon the presence of any objective criteria but constitutes, instead, a matter of agreement, a matter of definite convention. However, this situation does not undermine the cognitive value of the differentiation of positive and negative distinctive features. From the cognitive standpoint its essence does not lie in the choice of certain distinctive features as positive and others as negative; instead, it lies in the postulation of the presence of certain distinctive features opposed to each other. For instance, the objective fact which relates both to voicedness and to voicelessness is the presence of a certain opposition which is independent of our decision to regard voicelessness as the absence of voicedness or vice versa.

An analogous situation concerns the definition of magnetic poles. The accepted designation of magnetic poles is conventional, and does not reflect the inherent nature of the magnet. It is possible to reverse the accepted terminology and to rename the positive pole negative and, vice versa; the essence of the magnet will not be affected. It is not important which one of the magnetic poles will be termed positive and which negative; the importance is vested in the recognition of the fact of magnetic polarity per se.

The above discussion shows that statements concerning positive and negative distinctive features do not represent opinions whose truth or falsity can be proved or disproved but rather definitions which, as any definitions, can be only arbitrary. We believe that many statements in structural linguistics which up to the present time have been regarded from the standpoint of truth or falsity should be, in effect, reevaluated in terms of simple definitions. This step will have as great an importance for structural linguistics as analogous steps have had for other sciences, for example for physics. In this connection it is interesting to introduce the following words of H. Reichenbach dealing with the origin of the theory of relativity in physics:

"The logical basis of the theory of relativity is the discovery that many statements, which were regarded as capable of demonstrable truth or falsity, are mere definitions.

This formulation sounds like the statement of an insignificant technical discovery and does not reveal the far-reaching implications which make up the philosophical significance of the theory. Nonetheless it is a complete formulation of the *logical* part of the theory.

Consider, for instance, the problem of geometry. That the unit of measurement is a matter of definition is a familiar fact; everybody knows that it does not make any difference whether we measure distances in feet or meters or light-years. However, that the comparison of distances is also a matter of definition is known only to the expert of relativity. This result can also be formulated as the definitional character of congruence. That a certain distance is congruent to another distance situated at a different place can never be proved to be true; it can only be maintained in the sense of a definition. More precisely speaking, it can be maintained as true only after a definition of congruence is given; it therefore depends on an original comparison of distances which is a matter of definition. A comparison of distances by means of the transport of solid bodies is but one definition of congruence. Another definition would result if we regarded a rod, once it had been transported to another location, as twice as long, thrice transported as three times as long, and so on. A further illustration refers to time: that the simultaneity of events occuring at distant places is a matter of definition was not known before Einstein based his special theory of relativity on this logical discovery...

Definitions are arbitrary; and it is a consequence of the definitional character of fundamental concepts that with the change of the definitions various descriptional systems arise. But these systems are equivalent to each other, and it is possible to go from each system to another one by a suitable transformation. Thus the definitional character of fundamental concepts leads to a plurality of equivalent descriptions. A familiar illustration is given by the various descriptions of motion resulting when the system regarded as being at rest is varied. Another illustration is presented by the various geometries resulting, for the same physical space, through changes in the definition of congruence. All these descriptions represent different languages saying the same thing; equivalent descriptions, therefore, express the same physical content."[20]

By altering the definition of positive and negative distinctive features we can obtain equivalent systems of phoneme description. These systems will have one and the same phonemic content. As an illustration we can examine description of the vowel phonemes of the contemporary Polish literary language which is contained in one of the author's earlier works.[21] The description can be plotted as the following matrix:

	u	*o*	*a*	*i*	*e*	*ę*
Vocalic	+	+	+	+	+	+
Compact	—	±	+	—	±	○
Grave	+	+	○	—	—	○
Nasal	○	—	○	○	○	+

Construction of the matrix is based on the definition of vocality, compactness, gravity and nasality as positive distinctive features, and of consonantness, diffuseness, acuteness and labiality as corresponding negative distinctive features. It is, however, possible to reverse this definition and to regard consonantness,diffuseness, acuteness and labiality as positive distinctive features and vocality,

[20] H. Reichenbach, "The Philosophical Significance of the Theory of Relativity", *Readings in the Philosophy of Science*, H. Feigl and M. Brodbeck, eds. (New York, 1953), pp. 198-200.

[21] Cf. S. K. Šaumjan, *Istorija sistemy differencial'nyx èlementov v pol'skom jazyke* (Moscow, 1958), pp. 74-75.

compactness, gravity and nasality as corresponding negative distinctive features. This new definition of positive and negative distinctive features necessitates the mapping of a new matrix:

	u	*o*	*a*	*i*	*e*	*ǫ*
Consonantal	−	−	−	−	−	−
Diffuse	+	∓	−	+	∓	○
Acute	−	−	○	+	+	○
Labial (non-nasal)	○	+	○	○	○	−

Comparison of these two matrixes points out their mutual equivalence in regard to the identity of their phonological content. The point does not lie, hence, in our choice of certain distinctive features as positive and others as negative, but in a consistent application of the adopted system of designations to the description of the phonemes. Thus, if in describing vowel phonemes we have decided to regard consonantness, diffuseness, acuteness, and labiality as positive distinctive features, we have to regard them as positive distinctive features also in respect to the description of consonantal phonemes.

Hence, if we regard distinctive features as constructs, the question of the nature of objective criteria in the demarcation of positive and negative distinctive features is, indeed, meaningless. The demarcation of positive and negative distinctive features is a matter of agreement, a matter of definite convention; only the fact of the presence of polarity among distinctive features is, indeed, objective and, consequently, designation of this polarity requires us conventionally to regard one distinctive feature as positive and another as negative.

At the level of mathematical logic the definition of polar distinctive features corresponds to the definition of the truth functions in the logical operation of negation. Let us consider the matrix which represents the logical operation of negation:

X	$\bar{X}$
T	F
F	T

This matrix may be interpreted as follows: X represents a positive distinctive feature, $\bar{X}$ a negative distinctive feature, T the presence of the distinctive feature, and F the absence of the distinctive feature.

In mathematical logic there exists a law of double negation which is expressed by the formula:

$$\bar{\bar{X}} \equiv X$$

Our interpretation of this law reads: every positive feature is equivalent to the negation of a negative distinctive feature.

Let us now consider the following problem. In some languages we encounter ternary vowel oppositions (for example, $a : o : u$ in Russian) which resist reduction to binary oppositions within the framework of the binary model; this circumstance violates the consistent application of the principle of binarity. Being aware of this difficulty, the authors of the binary model employ the concept of a composite distinctive feature. A composite distinctive feature is designated by the symbol $\pm$. It should be pointed out, however, that the composite distinctive feature constitutes a heterogenous factor in the binary model of phonological oppositions and, as a result, fails to eliminate the difficulty under consideration. In our opinion the interpretation of phonological oppositions and of distinctive features as constructs points the way toward an overcoming of this difficulty. If the phonological opposition compact – diffuse is regarded as a construct we are fully justified, at the level of constructs, to split this opposition into two oppositions: compact – non-compact and diffuse – non-diffuse. This splitting guarantees a consistent application of the principle of binarity within the binary model of phonological oppositions.[22]

[22] An attempt to replace the composite distinctive feature compact — diffuse

Thus, a consistent application of the principle of binarity is fully feasible. Any phonological opposition which has been traditionally regarded as polynomial can be reduced to binary phonemic oppositions. In this connection it is essential to turn our attention to general methodological considerations raised by A. Martinet against the principle of binarity. A. Martinet writes:

"In order to be justified in asserting that all phonemic oppositions are binary it is essential either, having examined all possible cases, to assert that the situation indeed exists or to prove that man, because of his inherent nature, can organize distinctive units only in accordance with the binary principle. Who can, however, boast of being familiar with all existing or attested to languages? And what can be said about languages which have disappeared without a trace or about languages which are yet to appear on Earth in the future?"[23]

If the binary model of phonological oppositions is to be regarded as a generalization of physical data given through direct observation, then the just mentioned critical considerations would, in fact, point to a difficulty and would constitute a serious argument against the principle of binarity. If we, however, interpret the binary model of phonological oppositions as a construct which possesses an explanatory function in relation to the directly observed data, then these considerations lose their impact. By the same token, our assignment of the binary model of phonological oppositions to the level of constructs does not imply that we regard it as the only possibility. On the contrary, side by side with our interpretation of phonological oppositions as constructs there exists a definite possibility of formulating diverse models of phonological oppositions, binary as well as non-binary. Our preference of the binary model to others is not contingent on inductive considerations but on the fact that the binary model of phonological oppositions

---

by two oppositions, compact — non-compact and diffuse — non-diffuse has been already carried out, on another plane, by M. Halle and N. Chomsky (Cf. M. Halle, "In the Defense of the Number Two", *Studies Presented to J. Whatmough* (The Hague, 1957), p. 72.).

[23] A. Martinet, *Economie des changements phonétiques*, pp. 73-74.

constitutes a convenient abstract hypothesis which satisfies, to a maximal degree, the general methodological principle of simplicity and, in addition, possesses a number of other important advantages which have already been pointed out in the preceding section of this chapter.

In conclusion we will consider the problem which concerns the interpretation of the zero sign in the matrixes of phoneme identification.

As has been mentioned above, the authors of the binary model of phonological oppositions interpret the zero sign as an expression of indeterminateness; e.g. from this standpoint the question whether the Russian phoneme "*x*" is voiceless can be answered "both yes and no", i.e. the phoneme can be regarded equally as voiceless or voiced since the choice exerts no influence on its identification.

This interpretation of the zero sign encounters a serious difficulty which stems from the failure to differentiate the two abstraction levels. We are already aware of the necessity to differentiate strictly between the distinctive feature in the proper sense (i.e. differentor) and the physical substratum of distinctive feature (i.e. differentoid). The distinctive feature in the proper sense and the physical substratum of distinctive feature are two heterogenous concepts which relate to different levels of abstraction: the former relates to the level of constructs, the latter to the level of observation. By analogy, phonemes and the physical substrata of phonemes, phonemoids, are heterogeneous concepts as well. Whenever, by reason of the absence of the phonological opposition "*x*" – "*γ*", the Russian phoneme "*x*" is described indiscriminately as both voiceless and voiced, this assertion should, in effect, concern the physical substratum of this phoneme, i.e. the phonemoid "*x*", rather than the phoneme "*x*" itself. The indeterminate characteristic can apply only to the phonemoid *x* and then only in the case when voicedness or voicelessness are taken to signify acoustic properties. If the statement concerns the phoneme "*x*" then the indeterminate characteristic loses its meaning since in Russian neither voicelessness nor voicedness can be included in the category of distinctive features pertaining to the phoneme "*x*".

Hence the interpretation of the zero sign as an expression of indeterminateness leads to a confusion of distinctive features and physical substrata of these distinctive features, i.e. differentors and differentoids. In order to overcome this difficulty it is essential to refute the interpretation of the zero sign as an expression of indeterminateness, and replace it with an interpretation of the zero sign as an expression of the fact that the question of the presence or absence of the given distinctive feature is inapplicable to the given phoneme. The logic of science points out correctly that in the process of cognition there arise situations when the answer to a specific problem seems impossible, not as a result of the insufficiency of our knowledge but owing to a basic inapplicability of the posed problem to the given situations. In respect to phonemes the question of the presence or absence of a distinctive feature can be posed only in the case when the phonemes are members of a specific phonological opposition. For instance, only after we have established that the given set of phonemes belongs to the phonological opposition voiced – voiceless can we question the presence or absence of voicedness in the phonemes which are members of this phonological opposition. If one of the phonemes does not belong to the phonological opposition voiced – voiceless, the question of the presence or absence of voicedness in this phoneme becomes meaningless. In Russian, the question whether the phoneme is voiced is answered affirmatively in respect to the phonemes "*g*", "*b*", "*d*", "*v*", "*z*", "*ž*", and negatively in respect to the phonemes "*k*", "*p*", "*t*", "*f*", "*s*", "*š*". However, this question is not applicable to the Russian phoneme "*x*"; from the phonological standpoint this phoneme cannot be regarded as either voiced or voiceless, since the Russian language lacks the corresponding paired phoneme "*γ*" and, consequently, the opposition "*x*" – "*γ*".

The above discussion leads to the following conclusion: the question about the presence or absence of a given distinctive feature in a given phoneme permits three answers: (1) "yes," (2) "no," and (3) "the question is not applicable to the given phoneme". The first answer is symbolized by a plus sign (+), the second by a minus sign (—), and the third by the zero sign (○).

5. THE NECESSITY OF A HIERARCHICAL CLASSIFICATION OF BINARY PHONOLOGICAL OPPOSITIONS

The authors of the binary model of phonological oppositions do not differentiate between such oppositions as voiced – voiceless or sharp – plain on the one hand, and such oppositions as compact – diffuse or grave – acute on the other hand. All of these, as well as other oppositions, are viewed at one and the same plane as equal to one another. Such interpretation of binary phonology oppositions encounters a serious difficulty in respect to the problem of phonological neutralization.

The concept of neutralization originated with the Prague school of phonology in connection with the differentiation of the so-called bilateral and multilateral phonological oppositions. N. S. Trubeckoj defines bilateral and multilateral phonological oppositions as follows: "In bilateral oppositions the basis for comparison (that is to say, the set of features which the two members of the opposition have in common) is limited solely to these two members of the opposition and fails to apply to any other member of the same system. Conversely, the basis for comparison of a multilateral opposition is not limited exclusively to the two members of the opposition in question but extends to the other members of the same system as well. The difference between bilateral and multilateral oppositions can be illustrated on examples taken from the Latin alphabet: the opposition of the letters *E* and *F* is bilateral since the set of features common to both these letters (a vertical support with two attached horizontal bars, one affixed at the upper extremity and the other at the center of the support) are not found in any other letter of the Latin alphabet. On the other hand, the opposition of the letters *P* and *R* is multilateral since the set of features common to both these letters (a right-handed loop attached at the upper extremity of a vertical support) applies likewise to the letter *B*."[24] Referring to the differentiation of bilateral and multilateral phonemic oppositions N. S. Trubeckoj professes that neutralization can occur only in bilateral phonological oppositions. About the concept of neutrali-

[24] N. S. Trubeckoj, *op. cit.*, p. 70.

zation he writes: "First of all it is necessary to present a clear definition of this concept. Not all types of phonological oppositions can undergo "neutralization". In those positions where a neutralizable opposition is effectively neutralized the specific features of the members of the opposition lose their phonological value and only those features which the two members have in common (that is to say, the basis for comparison of that opposition) remain relevant. In the neutralized position one of the members of the opposition comes thus to represent the "archiphoneme" of that opposition: the term "archiphoneme" signifies here that set of distinctive features which the two phonemes have in common. It follows that only bilateral oppositions can be neutralized. In effect, only those oppositions possess archiphonemes which can be opposed to all other phonological units of the given system; and such is a fundamental condition for phonological existence in general. If in German the bilateral opposition *d – t* is neutralized in the terminal position, that member of the opposition which occupies the neutralization position is neither voiced nor voiceless, but rather "occlusive dental non-nasal in general," and as such is opposed, on the one hand, to the nasal dental *n* and, on the other hand, to occlusive labials and guttural non-nasals. As opposed to this the fact that in German the phonemes *t* and *d* are not admissible in initial position before *l*, while *b* and *p* do occur in this position does not permit neutralization of the oppositions *d – b* and *p – t*: in such words as *Blatt* 'leaf' the initial *b* retains all its features, that is to say, remains labial and voiced and cannot be regarded as the representative of the archiphoneme of the opposition *d – b* since the phonological content of such an archiphoneme could be only "voiced in general", while the *b* in *Blatt* cannot be treated as such owing to the fact that the phoneme *g* in the word *glatt* 'sleek' is voiced as well. Hence, true neutralization by means of which one member of the opposition becomes the representative of the archiphoneme of that opposition is applicable only to bilateral phonological oppositions. It does not follow, however, that all bilateral oppositions are, in effect, neutralizable; in nearly every language there occur constant bilateral oppositions. However, whenever a language possesses a neutralizable opposition, this opposition is always bilateral."[25]

The authors of the binary model of phonological oppositions use both the concept of neutralization and the concept of archiphoneme. However, their interpretation of all binary phonological oppositions as being equal to one another contradicts the concept of neutralization. And, de facto, there does exist a difference between the opposition $d-t$ and the opposition $d-b$, the former being neutralizable and the latter not. The binary model in its present form dissolves these specific differences between the two types of oppositions through the abstract principle of binarity. We are confronted with two choices: either to repudiate the concept of neutralization, or to establish a definite hierarchy among binary phonological oppositions from the standpoint of their neutralizability. Since the concept of neutralization constitutes one of the corner stones of contemporary phonology and, consequently, its repudiation is foreclosed, only the second path toward the overcoming of the difficulty in question remains open.

Our proposal concerns the establishment of a hierarchy of binary phonemic oppositions based on the concepts of the relation theory in mathematical logic.

In mathematical logic the concept of relation is characterized as follows: "It is characteristic of a relation to pair elements off with elements according to one or another plan. The numerical relation *less than*, e.g., pairs 0 off with 1, also it pairs 0 off with 2, also it pairs 1 off with 2, and in general it pairs x off with y wherever $x<y$. The relation *father of*, again, pairs Abraham off with Isaac, and in general it pairs x off with y wherever x is the father of y. It is thus convenient to think of each relation as a class of pairs of elements. To say that an element x bears a relation z to an element y is to say, then, that x paired with y forms a member of z... Since relations are to be classes of pairs of elements, these pairs must themselves be elements; otherwise we could not have classes of them."[26]

[25] N. S. Trubeckoj, *op. cit.*, pp. 81-82.

[26] W. V. O. Quine, *Mathematical Logic*, rev. ed. (Cambridge (Mass.), 1955), p. 198.

Relations between two objects are termed binary relations; relations among several objects are called polynomial relations. Up to the present time the theory of relations has been concerned primarily with binary relations; and it is these that interest us as well in regard to the case at hand.

Any binary relation can be represented symbolically as xRy. This formula is interpreted as follows: "Any entity x bears a relation R to any entity y." The term x is called the referent of the relation R, the term y the relatum of the relation R. The class of all possible referents of the relation R is termed the domain of R, and the class of all its possible relata is termed the converse domain of R.

Mathematical logic recognizes various properties of relations. We will, at this time, concentrate on those which are essential to our analysis of binary phonological oppositions, beginning with the paired properties of relations, *symmetry* and *asymmetry*. A relation is symmetrical when the formula xRy always implies the formula yRx. An example of a symmetrical relation is the relation "parallel to": if line A is parallel to line B it follows that line B is parallel to line A. A relation is asymmetrical when the formula xRy always implies the formula $\sim yRx$. Examples of asymmetrical relations are the relations "father of", "husband of"; if x is the father of y it follows that y cannot be the father of x; if x is the husband of y it follows that y cannot be the husband of x.

It is not difficult to see that every binary distinctive feature constitutes an asymmetrical relation. Let us take, for example, voicedness. If, let us say, the phoneme *d* bears a relation of voicedness to the phoneme *t* it follows that the phoneme *t* cannot bear a relation of voicedness to the phoneme *d*.

Several asymmetrical relations can be paired off as follows: side by side with the relation R there can exist another relation which is called the converse R and is symbolized as $\breve{R}$. Conversion is defined as follows: A relation R exists between x and y if and only if there exists a relation $\breve{R}$ between y and x (for instance, if we take the relation "husband of", the converse of this relation will be "wife of".)

The concept of conversion is applicable to distinctive features which are based on the principle of binarity: side by side with the given distinctive feature R there must exist a distinctive feature $\breve{R}$ which constitutes its converse. Thus, the converse of voicedness is voicelessness; returning to the phonemes *d* and *t*, we can make the following statement: the phoneme *t* bears the relation of voicelessness to the phoneme *d* only because the phoneme *d* bears the relation of voicedness to the phoneme *t*. Whichever pair of distinctive features we select, one of the paired distinctive features must be regarded as the converse of the other paired distinctive feature.

It has been said above that relations should be conceived as classes of paired entities. We will apply this postulate to phonemes. Since every binary distinctive feature represents a binary relation it is corresponded by a definite class of paired phonemes which will be called the range of that distinctive feature. Let us take, for instance, nasality in Russian. If we symbolize this distinctive feature by the sign N we can represent it as:

$$xNy$$

This formula is satisfied by a corresponding class which consists of the following paired phonemes:

m – b	*n – d*
m' – b'	*n' – d'*

If we now take non-nasality which constitutes the converse of nasality and symbolize it by the sign $\breve{N}$, we can represent it as:

$$x\breve{N}y$$

This formula is satisfied by a corresponding class which consists of the following paired phonemes:

b – m	*d – n*
b' – m'	*d' – n'*

It is evident that paired phonemes which constitute the range of nasality and paired phonemes which constitute the range of non-nasality coincide as to their composition but differ in respect to their structure. In fact, those phonemes which constitute the referents of relation *N* are, at the same time, the relata of relation *N*, and vice versa. The differences in the structure of the pairs are expressed by means of a direct or reverse order of the constituent phonemes. This corresponds to the general principle of the theory of relations, according to which, in the words of Quine, "pairs must be conceived in a non-commutative fashion, as *ordered* pairs; they must be distinguished not only when they differ as to their constituent elements, but when they are formed from the same elements in reverse order. We must distinguish e.g. between Abraham paired with Isaac and Isaac paired with Abraham, for the former pair is wanted as a member of *father of* whereas the latter pair is not."[27]

The theory of relations in mathematical logic makes a strict distinction between single-valued and many-valued binary relations.

A relation *R* is single-valued if in the formula *xRy* for every *y* there is only one *x*. An example of a single-valued relation: "*x* is the father of *y*" (every person *y* can have only one father *x*).

A relation *R* is many-valued if in the formula *xRy* for every *y* there are several *x*. An example of a multiple relation: "*x* is smaller than *y*" (here several *x* can correspond to *y*).

Among single-valued relations a special place is occupied by *one-one relations*. A relation *R* is a *one-one relation* if in the formula *xRy*, *y* has a unique corresponding *x* and, vice versa, if *x* has a unique corresponding *y*. An example of a one-one relation: "*x* is the father of an only *y*" (a given only son has a given father, and vice versa.) Another example of a one-one relation is the relation between a set of positive and a set of negative numbers where every positive number corresponds to one negative number, and vice versa.

Besides one-one relations, single-valued relations encompass also *one-many* and *many-one* relations. A *one-many relation* is a single-valued relation to the left, i.e. in the formula *xRy* the given *y* has a unique corresponding *x* whereas the same *x* has several corresponding *y*. A *many-one relation* is a single-valued relation to the right, i.e. in the formula *xRy* the given *x* has a unique corresponding *y* whereas the same *y* has several corresponding *x*. As an example

[27] W. V. O. Quine, *op. cit.*, p. 198.

of a one-many relation we can take the relation of a father to his children, and as an example of a many-one relation, the relation of children to their father.

When a relation is many-valued in both directions, i.e. if in the formula xRy the given x has several corresponding y and, vice versa, the given y has several corresponding x, the relation is called a *many-many relation.* An example of this type of relation is the relation "x is a teacher of y" (every teacher x can have several pupils y and, conversely, every pupil y can have several teachers x).

The above discussed properties of relations can serve as a basis for the establishment of a hierarchy of binary phonological oppositions.

Binary phonological oppositions can be subdivided into three types:

(1) binary phonological oppositions which establish one-one correspondences between their constituent phonemes;

(2) binary phonological oppositions which establish one-many or many-one correspondences among their constituent phonemes;

(3) binary phonological oppositions which establish many-many correspondences among their constituent phonemes.

The most important of these three types of oppositions are the one-one oppositions since they are the only ones which are capable of undergoing neutralization.

Neutralizable one-one oppositions will be henceforth termed correlations.

If the same phonemes are simultaneously members of two or more correlations there arises a complex of interrelated correlations which will be termed a correlational system. Depending on the number of constituent correlations one can differentiate dyadic, triadic, tetradic, etc., correlational systems. For instance, in Russian we encounter a dyadic correlational system which contains two correlations: voiced – voiceless and sharp – plain.

The aforementioned three types of oppositions must be differentiated not only at the level of constructs but at the level of observation as well. At the level of observation we differentiate three types of phonological contrasts:

(1) one-one phonemic contrasts;

(2) one-many and many-one phonemic contrasts;
(3) many-many phonemic contrasts.

Immediate observation furnishes us solely with phonological contrasts. On the basis of an analysis of phonological contrasts we then postulate the corresponding phonological oppositions and distinctive features. For instance, in Russian we determine the phonological contrast *k*:*g*, and on its basis we postulate the phonological opposition "*k*":"*g*" and ascribe to the phoneme "*k*" the distinctive feature of "voicelessness" and to the phoneme "*g*" the distinctive feature of "voicedness." On the other hand, since Russian does not possess the phonological contrast *g*:*γ* we cannot postulate, for the Russian language, the phonological opposition "*g*":"*γ*" and, consequently, the Russian phoneme "*g*" should be regarded as neither interrupted nor continuant. Similarly, since Russian does not possess the phonological contrast *x*:*γ* we are not justified in postulating for Russian the phonological opposition "*x*" : "*γ*" and, consequently, the Russian phoneme "*x*" should be regarded as neither voiceless nor voiced.

The necessity of a strict differentiation of the two levels of abstraction in the postulation of phonological oppositions and distinctive features of phonemes can be illustrated on the above introduced examples.

Answers to the question about the presence of voicedness in the phonemes "*k*", "*g*" and "*x*" can be gathered in the following table:

	k	*g*	*x*
Voiced	−	+	○

If we regard this table only at the level of phonological oppositions we have to state, if questioned ajout the presence of continuity in the given phonemes, that the phonemes "*k*" and "*g*" bear an identical relation to the phoneme "*x*". Hence we obtain the following table:

	k	*g*	*x*
Continuant	−	−	+

This table shows that the phoneme "*g*" should be regarded as an interrupted phoneme. This deduction contradicts, however, the fact that the Russian language lacks the phonological opposition "*g*" : "*γ*", and that the absence of this opposition irrevocably dictates the absence of both interruptedness and continuity in the phoneme "*g*".

Overcoming of this difficulty, and of analogous difficulties connected with the postulation of distinctive features of other phonemes, can be effected only if we differentiate the two abstraction levels. If we differentiate the two abstraction levels we proceed as follows: in reply to the question about the presence of voicedness, the phoneme "*x*" is ascribed a zero sign not because of the absence of the phonological opposition "*x*":"*γ*", but rather because of the absence of the phonological contrast *x*:*γ*. In reply to the question about the presence of continuity, the phoneme "*g*" is ascribed a zero sign not because of the absence of the phonological opposition "*g*": "*γ*", but rather because of the absence of the phonological contrast *g*:*γ*. If we proceed from an analysis of phonological contrasts there, indeed, exists no basis for ascribing to the phoneme "*g*" the feature of interruptedness since the phonological contrast *g*:*x* is not equivalent to the phonological contrast *k*:*x*.

By the same token, we cannot agree with M. Halle who, in his matrix of the identification of phonemes of the contemporary Russian language, regards the phoneme "*g*" as interrupted and the phonemes "*t*" and "*t'*" as non-nasal.[28] Referring to the analysis of phonologically contrasts we are compelled to state that the question of the presence of interruptedness in the phoneme "*g*" and of non-nasality in the phonemes "*t*" and "*t'*" has to be answered merely by the assignment of the zero sign to all three phonemes, since in Russian the interrupted sound *g* cannot be contrasted with a corresponding continuant sound, and the non-nasal sounds *t* and *t'* cannot be contrasted with corresponding nasal sounds.

6. THE UNIVERSAL MODEL OF DIFFERENTORS AND CULMINATORS

On the basis of the discussion presented in the foregoing sections

[28] M. Halle, *op. cit.*, p. 45.

and of considerations which will immediately follow, it is our intent to submit the following modification of the universal model of distinctive features introduced by R. Jakobson, G. Fant, and M. Halle.

First of all we will split the concept of distinctive feature into the concept of differentor and the concept of differentoid, and introduce special indexation which symbolizes this split-up. The term differentoid will be designated by the index sub-1, the term differentor by the index sub-2. For instance, nasality-differentoid and nasality-differentor will be written as nasality_1 and nasality_2, respectively.

The previously given system of twelve binary oppositions as differentors necessitates the introduction of the following changes. Vocalic_2 – non-vocalic_2 and consonantal_2 – non-consonantal_2 will be conjoined into a single opposition: vocalic – consonantal. This latter opposition is removed from the system of differentors and included in the system of culminators. The opposition compact_2 – diffuse_2 should be, by the same token, split into two oppositions: compact_2 – non-compact_2 and diffuse_2 – non-diffuse_2. Additionally, it is necessary to introduce into the system of differentors the following oppositions: liquid_2 – non-liquid_2, glide_2 – non-glide_2 and long_2 – short_2.

We will now consider the validity of these changes.

Initially it is necessary to stress the indispensability of introducing two particular differentors, liquidity and glide.

Liquid phonemes are such phonemes as *r* and *l*, glides such phonemes as *j* and *h*. R. Jakobson and his co-authors reduce the liquid feature to a combination of vocalic and consonantal features, and the glide feature to a combination of non-vocalic and non-consonantal features.

We can raise the question whether phonemes which are simultaneously both vocalic and consonantal and, conversely, phonemes which are neither vocalic nor consonantal can, indeed, exist.

The answer to this question is contingent upon the interpretation of the nature of the phoneme.

If we regard the phoneme as an acoustic element then we can, indeed, allow that there exist phonemes which comprise the physical properties of vowels as well as consonants or which, vice versa, comprise neither of these.

However, it has been pointed out before that the phoneme does not comprise anything physical.

If we regard the phoneme as a construct, then the answer to the posed question must be negative. It has been shown in Chapter One that vowel and consonantal phonemes, when regarded as constructs, cannot be opposed to one another in one and the same position. Therefore vocalic and consonantal features are syntagmatic rather than paradigmatic features. Hence it follows that no phonemes can unite in themselves both vocalic and consonantal features. On the other hand, there can be no phonemes which are neither vocalic not consonantal; every phoneme, as a construct, must be either vocalic or consonantal.

Hence it follows that it is impossible to posit that liquids possess both vocalic and consonantal features and that glides contain both non-vocalic and non-consonantal features. Liquids as well as glides should be regarded as independent, indivisible differentors.

Turning our attention to another question, we want to point out that in the list of phonemic oppositions drafted by R. Jakobson and his co-authors for the languages of the world there appear two oppositions, vocalic – non-vocalic and consonantal – non-consonantal, which in our opinion should be definitely reduced to a single opposition, vocalic – consonantal. One can question whether there exists an objective basis for such a reduction of two oppositions into a single one.

R. Jakobson and his co-authors found it apparently necessary to posit two oppositions (vocalic – non-vocalic and consonantal – non-consonantal) in order to be able to distinguish, side by side with the categories of vowel and consonantal phonemes, two additional categories: a category of phonemes which contain both vocalic and consonantal features, i.e. which are a mixture of vowel and consonantal phonemes (phonemes of the type *r* and *l*), and a category of phonemes which contain both non-vocalic and non-consonantal features, i.e. which are related neither to vowel nor to consonantal phonemes (phonemes of the type *h* and *j*). However, division of phonemes into these four categories fails to be convincing from a phonological point of view. Sure, from a phonetic standpoint it is possible to admit that the sounds *h* and *j* do not exhibit any relationship to either vowels or consonants and that the sounds *r* and *l* contain qualities of both vowels and consonants; in phonetics there exists, therefore, a very likely reason to differentiate between vocalic – non-vocalic and consonantal – non-consonantal features as physical properties. Phonology, however, distinguishes only two categories of phonemes in respect to their function within the syllable: either central (vowels) or marginal (consonants). Thus, from the phonological standpoint the nonvocalic feature can be identified with consonantness, and the non-consonantal feature with vocality. This reasoning underlies our decision to reduce the oppositions vocalic – non-vocalic and consonantal – non-consonantal into a single opposition, vocalic – consonantal.

In Chapter One we had pointed out that the vocalic and consonantal features are culminators rather than differentors. Hence, if we unite the oppositions vocalic – non-vocalic and consonantal – non-consonantal into a single opposition vocalic – consonantal, we have to remove this opposition from the system of differentors and introduce it into the system of culminators.

We will now turn our attention to the opposition long – short. Viewing length from a physical point of view, R. Jakobson and his co-authors relate it to prosodic features. In effect, however, if we regard length as a construct, we cannot discern any quantitative difference between long and short phonemes. Quantitative differences can exist only between corresponding phonemoids. At the level of constructs length must be, indeed, regarded not as a quantity, but rather as a quality. This fact explains the necessity of regarding length and shortness as distinctive features, on an equal level with other distinctive features.

The opposition $compact_2$ – $diffuse_2$ should be split into two oppositions, $compact_2$ – non-$compact_2$ and $diffuse_2$ – non-$diffuse_2$, if the principle of binarity is to be applied consistently (in order to avoid complex differentors bearing the sign $\pm$). This method is fully justified at the level of constructs.

Consequently, we propose a universal system of distinctive features which consists of the following 14 binary oppositions:

(1) compact_2 – non-compact_2
(2) diffuse_2 – non-diffuse_2
(3) grave_2 – acute_2
(4) flat_2 – plain_2
(5) nasal_2 – non-nasal_2
(6) continuant_2 – interrupted_2
(7) checked_2 – unchecked_2
(8) strident_2 – mellow_2
(9) voiced_2 – voiceless_2
(10) sharp – plain_2
(11) tense_2 – lax_2
(12) liquid_2 – non-liquid_2
(13) glide_2 – non-glide_2
(14) long_2 – short_2

Side by side with the universal system of differentors we postulate also a universal system of culminators. This system contains:

(1) vocality_2 (culminator of the syllable) as opposed to consonantness_2;
(2) culminator of the word (physical substratum of this culminator can be the dynamic, quantitative or tonic stress);
(3) culminator of the word group (physical substratum of this culminator can be stress or intonation);
(4) culminator of the sentence (physical substratum of this culminator is intonation).

Together these two systems constitute the universal model of differentors and culminators. In no language does one encounter this model in its entirety. One language utilizes some differentors, another language other differentors. Similarly all culminators do not occur in every language. For instance, there exist languages which have no word culminators.

This universal model of differentors and culminators should be regarded as a working hypothesis which will be, undoubtedly, subject to further modification as a result of subsequent conceptual analysis and of deeper research into empirical material.

7. RESULTS OF INVESTIGATION

The two-level theory of phonology enables us to overcome a number of serious theoretical difficulties appertaining to the method of binary patterning of phonological oppositions.

These theoretical difficulties are contingent upon the failure of the authors of the method of binary patterning of phonological oppositions to differentiate the level of observation and the level of constructs.

Theoretical difficulties arise, first of all, in connection with the demarcation of distinctive and redundant features. While posing as their problem the reduction of phonologically identical acoustic properties to invariants, the authors of the method of binary patterning define some acoustic properties arbitrarily as distinctive, others as redundant features. The reason for this lies in the fact that if we, as the authors themselves, should interpret distinctive features as physical facts, arbitrariness would be present no matter which one of the phonologically identical acoustic properties we raised to the rank of the invariant. Overcoming of this difficulty is contingent upon the splitting of the concept of distinctive feature into the concept of differentor and the concept of differentoid, introduced by the two-level theory of phonology, and the consequent interpretation of phonologically identical acoustic properties as physical substrata (i.e. differentoids) of identical differentors.

Another theoretical difficulty concerns the definition of positive and negative distinctive features. If we regard distinctive features as physical entities we are compelled to seek positivity and negativity in the acoustic properties of sound; it is easy to see, however, that any attempt to establish physical criteria for the differentiation of positive and negative distinctive features is untenable. Overcoming this difficulty is contingent upon giving up seeking positivity and negativity at the level of observation and relating these concepts to the level of constructs. At the level of constructs the concepts of positivity and negativity are purely conventional, and if distinctive features are regarded as constructs it makes no difference which of them we consider positive and which negative, the essential point being that having termed some distinctive features positive and others negative, we adhere consistently to the convention adopted and avoid clashing with the consequences of this convention.

A serious difficulty is encountered also in the interpretation of all binary phonological oppositions as equal to another. This interpretation precludes explanation of the fact that some oppositions are capable of undergoing neutralization while others are not. Overcoming of this difficulty is contingent upon the establishment of a hierarchical explanation of binary phonological oppositions. We propose to differentiate three types of binary phonological oppositions:

(1) one-one oppositions,
(2) one-many and many-one oppositions, and
(3) many-many oppositions.

Neutralization can be effected only in respect to one-one oppositions.

Neutralizable one-one oppositions are termed correlations. Correlations can be united into complexes which are called correlational systems. In accordance to the number of their members, correlational systems can be dyadic, triadic, tetradic, etc.

A critical analysis of the universal model of distinctive and prosodic features presented in the works of R. Jakobson and his co-authors causes us to introduce a universal model of differentors and culminators. This model consists of 14 pairs of differentors and four types of culminators. Our model which modifies the model introduced by R. Jakobson and his co-authors is based on the conceptual apparatus of the two-level theory of phonology and is somewhat less economical than their model which contains only 12 pairs of distinctive features. In this connection it is, indeed, necessary to point out that the logic of science stresses that economy in itself does not constitute the decisive criterion for the attribution of a greater or lesser adequacy to a model. The decisive criterion of every model is inherent in its explanatory function, i.e. its ability to explain the directly observed data. Hence, that one of two models should be selected which is capable of explaining a greater number of directly observed data and which does not encounter theoretical difficulties in the process of the resolution of any problems. In so far as considerations of the model's economy are concerned, they are applicable to a comparative evaluation of models only under identical conditions. Thus, if both models explain the directly observed data equally well and, at the same time, one of the models is more economical that the other, we should, of course, select the more economical model. However, if the more economical model encounters theoretical difficulties and presents a less thorough explanation of the directly observed data, we are compelled to select unhesitatingly the less economical model.

IV

THE TWO-LEVEL THEORY OF PHONOLOGY AND THE METHODS OF PHONOLOGICAL SYLLABLE PATTERNING

1. THE PROBLEM

There are already a great number of publications concerning methods of investigation of the phonological syllable structure. One can mention here the works of R. I. Avanesov,[1] J. Kuryłowicz,[2] L. Hjelmslev,[3] E. Fischer-Jørgensen,[4] A. Rosetti,[5] and many other scholars. The critical survey of these works does not, however, pertain to the following investigation. We shall examine the method of the phonological syllable structure patterning only from the standpoint of the two-level theory of phonology. Referring to the conceptual apparatus of the two-level theory of phonology we will construct a generative model of the phonological syllable which possesses an explanatory function. By the term 'generative model' we mean an abstract logical device which produces a definite set of linguistic entities from primitive elements by means of rules of construction, or generation. The explanatory function of the generative model is in the model's ability to reduce the

[1] R. I. Avanesov, *Fonetika sovremennogo russkogo literaturnogo jazyka* (section: "O slogorazdele i stroenii sloga v russkom jazyke", pp. 41-58).
[2] J. Kuryłowicz, "Contribution à la théorie de la syllabe", *Biuletyn polskiego towarzystwa językoznawczego*, VIII (1948) (reprinted in J. Kuryłowicz, *Esquisses linguistiques*, Wrocław-Kraków, 1960). This is an especially important work.
[3] L. Hjelmslev, "The Syllable as a Structural Unit", *Proceedings of the 3rd International Congress of Phonetic Sciences* (Ghent, 1939).
[4] E. Fischer-Jørgensen, "On the Definition of Phoneme Categories on a Distributional Basis", *Acta Linguistica*, VII (1952).
[5] A. Rosetti, *Sur la théorie de la syllabe* (The Hague, 1959).

external connection among the elements of the object under consideration to deep, inherent connections.

Investigation of the phonological syllable must necessarily distinguish two separate problems: the demarcation of phonological syllables in the speech flow, and the investigation of the internal structure of the phonological syllable. Although these two problems are interrelated, each of them can be investigated separately, the other problem being regarded as having been resolved. This investigation will not probe into the problem of the syllabic boundary. This problem will be presupposed to have been resolved, and attention will be focused solely on the internal structure of the phonological syllable per se. This investigation of the internal structure will touch also upon the problem of the definition of phonemic classes from the standpoint of the mutual connections of phonemes within the phonological syllable.

As it was shown in the foregoing sections of our investigation phonemes, differentors, and other phonological constructs examined are related to the level of observation by means of correspondence rules. The phonological syllable is likewise a construct. However, in its case it is not deemed necessary to seek correspondence rules. In order to justify the superfluousness of such a search in this case we will turn our attention to the logic of science.

The logic of science posits that not all constructs of a given science are necessarily required to possess rules of correspondence. There exist cases when constructs lack correspondence rules; those numerous cases are meant where some constructs are defined by means of other constructs. The former do not require rules of correspondence; it is sufficient that the latter constructs which are not defined by means of other constructs, possess such rules. We must distinguish two types of cases where constructs which are defined by means of other constructs become liberated from the rules of correspondence. There exist constructs which, although liberated from the correspondence rules, are, in principle, capable of possessing such rules; on the other hand, there exist constructs for which definition by means of other constructs is mandatory and which, in principle, refute correspondence rules.

Considering, first of all, the former type we will utilize as an example of a construct the concept of velocity in classical mechanics. The rule of correspondence pertaining to the concept of velocity places it into relation with the readings of the spedometer; this correspondence rule is based on the principle that the force, which the magnet exercises on the metallic part of the spedometer is proportional to the velocity of the magnet . If we, however, define the concept of velocity by means of other constructs this rule of correspondence becomes superfluous. According to a generally accepted definition, velocity v of a given body is defined by the ratio $\frac{s}{t}$, where s is a space traversed by a body during a time t. Thus velocity is expressed by the formula $v = \frac{s}{t}$. This formula shows clearly that the construct "velocity" is defined in terms of a relation between the constructs "space" and "time". The latter two constructs can be assigned rules of correspondence but they can, in turn, be defined by means of other constructs.[6]

Transferring our attention to the remaining case where the rules of correspondence are inapplicable, we will investigate those constructs which require definition in terms of other constructs because they cannot, in principle, possess correspondence rules. An example of such a construct is "velocity of a molecule". There exists no measuring device which would enable us to determine a molecule's velocity. We can define molecule velocity only by relating this construct to other constructs which can possess correspondence rules, to the concepts of pressure and density of a gas.

The above discussion of the general principles of the logic of science which deal with constructs points to the fact that in phonology, as in any other abstract science, all constructs are not required to possess correspondence rules. We are justified, then, in stating that the phonological syllable is not necessarily subject to correspondence rules. As a matter of fact, the phonological syllable

[6] Various examples of the process of defining constructs either through correspondence rules or by means of other constructs can be found in H. Margenau, *The Nature of Physical Reality* (New York, 1950), pp. 220-244.

does not constitute an indivisible unit, as does the phoneme or the differentor, but rather a unit of the quantizing of the phonemic flow into definite phonemic groups which are governed by a strict order in respect to phoneme combinations. And if this is the case, then the phonological syllable must be interpreted as a construct which is defined in terms of other constructs, in terms of phonemes and in terms of definite rules governing phoneme combinations. Therefore it is not necessary to relate the phonological syllable directly to the level of observation. Rules of correspondence are essential in the case of phonemes since it is impossible to identify phonemes in the speech flow without relating them to the level of observation. In so far as the investigation of the phonological syllable structure is concerned we regard phonemes as something already given and not requiring definition, and concern ourselves only with the determination of the rules governing the combinations of phonemes.

2. BASIC TYPES OF GENERATIVE MODELS AND THE POSSIBILITY OF THEIR APPLICATION TO THE INVESTIGATION OF THE PHONOLOGICAL SYLLABLE

The basic types of generative models have been investigated by N. Chomsky in connection with the grammar of language.[7] Generative models used in the description of the grammatical system of language are of three types: (1) the finite state model, (2) the phrase structure model and (3) the transformational model.

These models are viewed by N. Chomsky from the standpoint of the feasibility of their application to the description of the grammatical system of language. Since they are abstract they can be applied not only to the description of grammar, but to the

[7] N. Chomsky, "Three Models for the Description of Language", *Institute of Radio Engineers Transactions on Information Theory*, IT2, No. 3 (1956), pp. 113-124; N. Chomsky, *Syntactic Structures*; general discussion of linguistic models is contained also in A. A. Zinov'ev and I. I. Revzin, "Logičeskaja model' kak sredstvo naučnogo issledovanija", *Voprosy filosofii*, No. 1 (1960).

description of various other semiotic systems and, in particular, to the description of the structure of the syllable as well.

We will dwell briefly on the characteristics of these models.

(1) THE FINITE STATE MODEL. Let us assume that we are given a logical device which can be in any of a finite numbeı of states: S_0, S_1, S_2, ..., S_q. The first state, S_0, is called the initial state, the last S_q the final state. During the transition from one state to another the device produces, in a linear left-to-right sequence, the transition symbols W_0, W_1, W_2, ..., W_p which are called words. The symbols are linked together by means of the binary operation of concatenation. The strings of symbols obtained as a result of this operation are called phrases. A set of phrases generated by this logical device is called a finite state language. If the transition from one state to another is assigned, we obtain the probability variant of the finite state model which is called the Markov process model.

As N. Chomsky has rightly pointed out, the application of the finite state model to the description of the grammars of natural languages yields little fruit since natural languages which contain sentences with a complex hierarchical structure are not finite state languages. The finite state model can be utilized only for the generation of several types of simple sentences. In so far as a full description of the grammar of language is concerned, it necessitates an application of stronger generative models, the phrase structure model and the transformational model.[8]

(2) THE PHRASE STRUCTURE MODEL. This model consists of a set of symbols called an alphabet and a set of rewriting rules pertaining to the strings of symbols. The rewriting rules are designated as $X \rightarrow Y$, where both X and Y represent strings of symbols. Some of the symbols stand for words and morphemes, others stand for syntactic phrases and sentences. The former constitute the so called terminal vocabulary, the latter the non-terminal vocabulary. This generative device functions as follows: the initial string S designates the sentence; applying the first rewriting rule

[8] A similar description of a finite state model can be found in N. Chomsky and G. A. Miller, "Finite State Languages", *Information and Control*, I (1958), pp. 91-112.

$S \rightarrow Y_1$ we obtain the string Y_1. Subsequent application of the rules $Y_1 \rightarrow Y_2$, $Y_2 \rightarrow Y_3$, etc., yield the string Y_2, Y_3, etc., until the terminal string Y_n is obtained. The last string is called terminal since its symbols cannot be further rewritten. The set of strings obtained is then called the derivation of the string Y_n.

The above process of generation of grammatically correct sentences is, as a rule, illustrated graphically as mathematical branching diagrams (trees). If we assume the given rules to be:

(1) $S \rightarrow A + B$ (4) $C \rightarrow a$
(2) $A \rightarrow C$ (5) $D \rightarrow b$
(3) $B \rightarrow D + F$ (6) $F \rightarrow c$,

we obtain the following derivation:

$$S,\ A+B,\ C+B,\ C+D+F,\ a+D+F,\ a+b+F,\ a+b+c.$$

The branching diagram of this derivation has the following form:

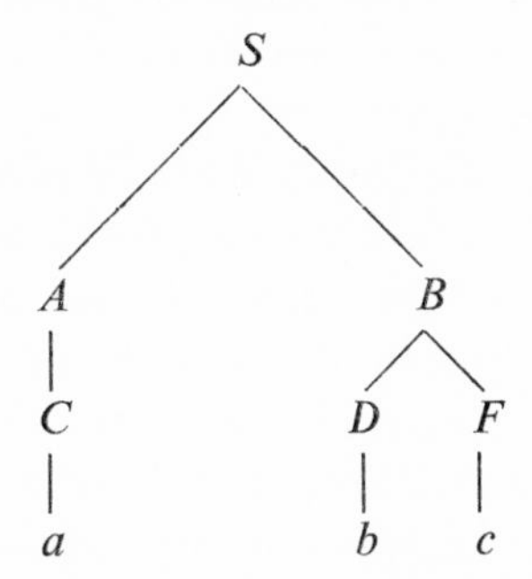

If we interpret the symbol *A* as the "noun phrase," the symbol *B* as the "verb phrase," the symbol *C* as a singular "noun", the symbol *D* as a singular "verb", the symbol *F* as an "object," the symbol *a* as the word *učenik* 'pupil', the symbol *b* as the word *čitaet* 'reads', and the symbol *c* as the word *knigu* 'book', we can regard the above derivation as the structural description of the sentence *Učenik čitaet knigu* 'The pupil reads a book'.

Application of the rules of generation is contingent upon the following conditions:

(1) Every separate rule allows the rewriting of only a single symbol; it is not possible to rewrite, simultaneously, two or more symbols;

(2) the process of rewriting does not permit permutation of symbols;

(3) the formulation of the rule of string generation takes into account only the structure of each given string; as far as the preceding strings are concerned, their structure is not taken into consideration. In other words, the history of derivation of each given string exerts no influence on the generation of successive strings.

These are the most general formal characteristics of the phrase structure generative model.[9] N. Chomsky has pointed out that although, in comparison with the finite state model, the phrase structure model has considerable power, it is still not capable of reflecting the various inherent features of natural languages. Let us take, for instance, the problem of generating passive constructions. Every passive construction is generated from an active construction; during the generative process there arises a need for symbol interchange.

E.g., formation of the phrase *Kniga napisana matematikom* 'The book has been written by a mathematician' from the phrase *Matematik napisal knigu* 'The mathematician has written a book' necessitates an interchange of the subject and the object of the latter phrase (interchange does not signify here an external change of position within the sentence but rather an internal change of position which is linked with a change in the noun cases). Such an interchange violates the above posited condition (2) which prohibits interchange of symbols during the rewriting process. Since the application of the phrase structure model encounters a number of difficulties, there arises a need for the formulation of another model which would supplement the phrase structure model. This new model is called the transformational model.

(3) THE TRANSFORMATIONAL MODEL. This model contains new

[9] A detailed formal description of the generative model of immediate constituents can be found in N. Chomsky, "On Certain Formal Properties of Grammar", *Information and Control*, II, (1959), pp. 137-167.

rules which are, in effect, an extension of the generative rules of the phrase structure model. By means of transformational rules those sentences which have been generated by the usual process of the phrase structure model are transformed into new sentences. Transformational rules are contingent upon the removal of the limitations imposed upon the phrase structure model: whereas the phrase structure model does not permit rewriting of more than one symbol at one time, the transformational model permits the rewriting of several symbols simultaneously; whereas the former model prohibits interchange of symbols, such and interchange is permitted in the latter model; whereas the former model shuns any reference to the history of derivation of the strings, the transformational model, on the contrary, requires such reference.

Transformational rules do not abolish the phrase structure model but rather introduce it into the framework of a broader grammatical system which N. Chomsky terms the transformational grammar.

Transformational grammar constitutes a system composed of three types of rules: (1) rules of the phrase structure model, (2) rules of the transformational model, and (3) morphophonemic rules.

In transformational grammar the generation of sentences adheres to the following process. Since it constitutes a logical device of a definite type, transformational grammar has at its onset the symbol *S* which represents the sentence; through a number of successive steps this symbol is rewritten in accordance with the rules of the phrase structure model into a terminal string of this model. A set of similar terminal strings forms the kernel of a language; this kernel of a language consists of simple narrative active sentences, or so-called kernel sentences. When applying the transformational rules to the kernel sentences we generate new strings which, in their stead, undergo branching in accordance with the rules of the phrase structure model. The resulting strings are rewritten at the terminal stage into a string of morphophonemes in accordance with special morphophonemic rules.

This much for the formal features of the finite state model, the phrase structure model, the transformational model, and the avenues of their application to grammar. However, the question "in what way can these models be applied to phonology?", remains open.

Although we have seen that the finite state model is limited in its application to the grammatical description of language, it can be applied to phonology with a considerable measure of success. This phenomenon can be explained by the fact that although inherent analogies between the structure of the sentence and the structure of the phonological syllable have been substantiated, the two structures exhibit, at the same time, two fundamental differences:

(1) the structure of the phonological syllable is characterized by a rigid order of its phonemes, i.e. phonemes which bear a direct relation to each other are required to stand side by side, whereas in the structure of the sentence words which are directly related may be separated by other words: for instance, an adjective can be separated from the noun it modifies by the verb (cf. *Čitaju interesnuju knigu* 'I am reading an interesting book' and *Interesnuju čitaju knigu*);

(2) the structure of a sentence can have a so-called closed-in construction (of the type *esli* ..., *to* 'if ... then') whereas the structure of the phonological syllable has no closed-in constructions. These differences between the two structures constitute the conditions which facilitate the description of any type of phonological syllable by means of the finite state model.[10]

Although the finite state model is capable of generating any type of phonological syllable, phonology cannot be satisfied with only a single model, since the finite state model regards relations between elements which it has generated as equal, so to say, on one plane (this is the result of the linear sequence of generation on the part of the finite state model). This feature of the finite state model limits its applicability in three ways:

[10] An example of a phonemic description which utilizes the finite state model is the article: S. Marcus and E. Vasiliu, "Mathématiques et phonologie: la théorie des graphes et le consonantisme de la langue roumaine", *Revue de mathématiques pures et appliqués*, V, 2 (Bucarest, Editions de l'Académie de la République Populaire Roumaine, 1957).

(1) The finite state model is not capable of distinguishing differences in the cohesive strength among the phonemes of the syllable. Thus, for instance, in the Russian syllable *sta* the cohesive strength among its phonemes is not equal: the phonemes *s* and *t* exhibit a greater mutual cohesiveness than the phonemes *t* and *a*; this fact cannot be disclosed if we use the finite state model.

(2) The finite state model is not capable of differentiating basic and derivational phonological structures. Hence all types of phonological structures are interpreted as equal to one another. However, there exists an evident hierarchy among the various types of phonological structures. For example, the structure of certain implosive groups of consonants in the pnohological syllable can be regarded as a mirror image of the structure of explosive consonants within the syllable; this means that these structures should be interpreted, in regard to their mutual relationship, as basic and derivational structures respectively.

(3) The finite state model is not capable of differentiating hierarchical relationships among the distributional classes of phonemes. Within the framework of this model all positional parameters of the distributive classes of phonemes are taken as being equal to one another; this fact leads to a failure to differentiate the basic and derivational distributive classes of phonemes.

These three deficiencies of the finite state model lead to the following conclusion: because of its linearity the finite state model is incapable of discerning the inherent, deep bonds among the elements of the phonological syllable structure and is, consequently, limited to a simple description of the external bonds among these elements.

The aforementioned discussion calls for a demarcation of two separate planes at the level of constructs, the descriptive plane and the immanent plane. At the descriptive plane we deal with the external bonds among phonemes while at the immanent plane we deal with the inherent, deep bonds among phonemes. The finite state model relates solely to the descriptive plane. In order to penetrate the immanent plane it is necessary to turn to more powerful models, the phrase-structure model and the transformational model.

On the basis of experience in application of the phrase-structure model and the transformational model to the grammatical description of language, we will construct a generative model capable of disclosing the inherent bonds among the elements of the phonological syllable. Since this model will possess an explanatory function we will call it the explanatory generative model of the phonological syllable. The generative finite state model will be termed the descriptive generative model of the phonological syllable.

The explanatory generative model of the phonological syllable does not abolish the descriptive generative model of the phonological syllable. On the contrary, both models are mutually complementary since the inherent, deep bonds among the elements of the phonological syllable can be discerned only by means of an analysis of the external bonds among the elements which, in turn, are ascertained by the descriptive generative model. Thus the descriptive and the explanatory generative models of the phonological syllable constitute a pair of related and mutually complementary models. They are related in the following manner: the descriptive model discloses facts which stand in need of an explanation; this explanation is contingent upon the exposure of the inherent, deep bonds among these facts; this exposure is effected by means of an application of the explanatory model.

Investigation of the structure of the phonological syllable requires us to keep in mind this pair of generative models. The following section will introduce the formulation of the explanatory generative model of the phonological syllable; later we will point out how this model can be substantiated by facts yielded by the descriptive model of the phonological syllable.[11]

[11] Other methods of patterning of the phonological syllable are feasible as well, as for instance the method expounded in the article: Ju. K. Lekomcev, "Ob odnom sposobe opisanija sočetaemosti fonem v sloge (na materiale klassičeskogo tibetskogo jazyka)", *Kratkie soobščenija Instituta narodov Azii*, LVII, Sbornik pamjati Ju. N. Rerixa (Moscow, 1961).

3. THE EXPLANATORY GENERATIVE MODEL OF THE PHONOLOGICAL SYLLABLE

The explanatory generative model of the phonological syllable is defined by means of a finite set of phonemes and a finite set of rules governing the generation of phonemic strings which function as phonological syllables.

The model comprizes two separate components: basic and derivational. The generative rules of the basic component are symbolized as : $X \rightarrow Y$. Each such rule constitutes an order to write Y in place of X (X and Y represent generalized symbols of phonemic strings). The basic component of the model generalizes phonemic strings through a successive branching of the symbol S which represents the phonological syllable. Phonemic strings generated by the basic component of the model are called basic phonemic strings.

In connection with the basic component of the explanatory generative model of the phonological syllable we adopt the following assumptions:

Assumption 1. The process of the generation of phonemic strings determines basic distributive classes of phonemes, since every class of phonemes occupies a specific node on the branching diagram of the generative process and this branching node constitutes the formal distributive parameter of the given class of phonemes.

Assumption 2. The length of the generated basic string cannot exceed four positions.

Assumption 3. Among the classes of phonemes there exists only a single relation which is termed domination and is defined as follows: assume that a language L possesses the phonemes A and B which form the string $A + B$; if, within this string, A can be replaced by zero while B cannot, then B dominates A ($B \gg A$); if, however, B can be replaced by zero while A cannot, then A dominates B ($A \gg B$); finally, if both A and B can be replaced by zeroes, then there is no relation of domination between A and B.

Assumption 4. The relation of domination has the following two properties:

(1) For any X_1, the relation $X_1 \gg X_1$ is not possible, i.e. no element of a language can be dominant over itself.

(2) Any pair of elements X_1 and X_2 which exhibit relation of domination cannot be simultaneously $X_1 \gg X_2$ and $X_2 \gg X_1$, i.e. only one of these elements can be dominant.

Having posited these assumptions we adopt the symbol S as the initial symbol of the branching diagram of the generative process; its branching into strings of symbols proceeds in accordance with the following rules:

1. $S \rightarrow In/O + V$
2. $In \rightarrow In_1/O + C_1$
3. $In_1 \rightarrow C_3/O + C_2$
4. $In \rightarrow C_3/O + In_2$
5. $In_2 \rightarrow C_2 + C_1$

In transcribing these rules the oblique line represents the possibility of a choice between the given symbol and zero.

Application of the above rules yields the following strings of symbols:

1. $In + V$
2. $O + V$
3. $In_1 + C_1 + V$
4. $O + C_1 + V$
5. $C_3 + C_2 + C_1 + V$
6. $O + C_2 + C_1 + V$
7. $C_3 + In_2 + V$
8. $O + In_2 + V$
9. $C_3 + C_2 + C_1 + V$
10. $O + C_2 + C_1 + V$

We see that in so far as the order of its symbols is concerned, string No. 5. is identical to string No. 9., and string No. 6. is identical to string No. 10. However, these strings differ as to their history of derivation which constitutes the basis for the postulation of a more or less compact internal cohesive strength among the symbols.

If we disregard the history of derivation of the generated strings of symbols we obtain the following four terminal strings:[12]

$$O + V$$
$$O + C_1 + V$$
$$O + C_2 + C_1 + V$$
$$C_3 + C_2 + C_1 + V$$

At this point let us introduce the interpretation of the symbols used in the above notations:

S — phonological syllable,
V — vowel phoneme,
In — string of initials (prevocalic consonants) in their universal aspect,
In_1 — left substring of initials,
In_2 — right substring of initials,
C_1 — initial preceding the vowel phoneme,
C_2 — initial preceding the initial C_1,
C_3 — initial preceding the initial C_2.

On the basis of an analysis of the terminal strings of symbols we introduce the following formula for domination:

$$C_3 \ll C_2 \ll C_1 \ll V$$

This formula points out clearly that vowel phonemes constitute the absolute dominant elements of the string. The consonantal phonemes are subdivided into three classes: C_1 constitutes a class of consonantal phonemes which are directly dominated by the vowel phonemes and which, in turn, dominate other consonants; C_2 constitutes a class of consonantal phonemes which are directly dominated by some consonants but which, in turn, dominate other consonants; C_3 constitutes a class of consonantal phonemes which are the absolute dominated elements of the string.

The aforementioned terminal phonemic strings represent basic phonemic strings from which other types of phonemic strings can

[12] Terminal strings are those strings which consist solely of terminal symbols, i.e. symbols which, in accordance with the accepted convention, cannot be replaced by new symbols. In the given case we accept the convention that symbols which designate basic distributive classes of phonemes should be considered terminal.

be derived by means of various operations; the latter strings are termed derivational phonemic strings.

The characteristics of phonemic classes from the standpoint of the relation of domination will be called the basic dominative parameters of phonemic classes.

The basic dominative parameters of phonemic classes can be assigned the following symbols:

D_0 — basic dominative parameter of the vowel phoneme,
D_1 — basic dominative parameter of the initial C_1,
D_2 — basic dominative parameter of the initial C_2
D_3 — basic dominative parameter of the initial C_3.

The definition of basic phonemic strings and basic phonemic classes necessitates the introduction of four operations which enable us to generate derivational phonemic strings and classes. These operations are: the operation of mirror reflection of strings, the operation of mapping of classes by a relation, the operation of substitution, and the operation of application.

The essence of the operation of mirror reflection of strings is the arrangement of the elements of the string in reverse order; when applied to terminal strings of phonemes it has the following appearance:

$$O + V \rightarrow V + O$$
$$O + C_1 + V \rightarrow V + C_1 + O$$
$$O + C_2 + C_1 + V \rightarrow V + C_1 + C_2 + O$$
$$C_3 + C_2 + C_1 + V \rightarrow V + C_1 + C_2 + C_3$$

Consequently, the operation of mirror reflection reverses the dominative parameters of the classes of consonantal phonemes from prevocalic to corresponding postvocalic dominative parame-meters. Postvocalic domination constitutes nothing else but the converse of prevocalic domination. We will introduce special diacritical signs to designate converse dominative parameters and finals (postvocal consonants) defined by these parameters. Mirror reflection yields the finals $\breve{C}_1$, $\breve{C}_2$, $\breve{C}_3$, and corresponding converse dominative parameters $\breve{D}_1$, $\breve{D}_2$, $\breve{D}_3$.

At this point we will transfer our attention to the operation of mapping of classes by a relation. Mapping of the class K through relation R occurs in the case[13] where there exists a class L_K any element x of which bears a relation R to one or more elements of the class K. The class L_K is called the R-image of the class K and is symbolized as "R"K. Our case will be concerned with the mapping of classes of phonemes by the relation of domination D. Proceeding from the relation of domination we can obtain D-images of the classes of phonemes C_1, C_2, C_3 and, correspondingly, $\check{D}$-images of the classes of phonemes $\check{C}_1$, $\check{C}_2$, $\check{C}_3$. Class of phonemes V yields both D-images and $\check{D}$-images.

The theoretically feasible mappings of classes of phonemes by the relations of prevocalic and postvocalic domination can be illustrated by the following two matrixes:

Matrix No. 1. *Mapping of phonemic classes by the relation of prevocalic domination:*

↓	C_3	C_2	C_1	V
D_0	C_3^0	C_2^0	C_1^0	—
D_1	C_3^1	C_2^1	—	V^1
D_2	C_3^2	—	C_1^2	V^2
D_3	—	C_2^3	C_3^1	V^3

Matrix No. 2. *Mapping of phonemic classes by the relation of postvocalic domination:*

↓	V	C_1	C_2	C_3
$\check{D}_1$	V^1	—	C_2^1	C_3^1
$\check{D}_2$	V^2	C_1^2	—	C_3^2
$\check{D}_3$	V^3	C_1^3	C_2^3	—
$\check{D}_0$	—	C_1^0	C_2^0	C_3^0

In each matrix the first left column shows the dominative parameters of the basic classes and the uppermost horizontal line shows

[13] Cf. for instance, W. V. O. Quine, *Mathematical Logic* (Cambridge, 1955), p. 209.

the basic classes of phonemes. The operation of mapping of phonemic classes by the dominative parameters generates derivational classes which are shown at the intersections of horizontal and vertical columns. Derivational classes have two numerical indexes, lower and upper. The lower numerical index indicates the basic class which was subjected to the operation of mapping by the relation of prevocalic or postvocalic domination. The upper numerical index indicates the dominative parameter which corresponds to the given actual operation of mapping. The symbol of the class of vocalic phonemes lacks the lower numerical index since, obviously, the class of vocalic phonemes is designated by a single symbol.

It is selfevident that the above derivational classes of phonemes are to be viewed only from the standpoint of the theoretical feasibility of their existence. In so far the existence of these derivational classes in natural languages is concerned, some of them either fail to occur altogether, or are encountered only in certain languages.

Let us now consider the operation of substitution. This operation facilitates the utilization of the derivational classes of phonemes obtained by means of the above discussed operation of mapping of classes by the relation of domination for the generation of new phonemic strings. The newly generated phonemic strings will be termed derivational phonemic strings.

The operation of substitution replaces the basic classes of phonemes or the converse basic classes of phonemes in phonemic strings with derivational classes of phonemes; the result is the generation of derivational phonemic strings. We will examine a concrete example of the operation of substitution, affecting the phonemic string $C_3\ C_2\ C_1$. Replacing the basic classes of phonemes with the derivational classes of phonemes C_1^0, C_1^2, C_1^3, we obtain the following phonemic strings:

$$
\begin{array}{llll}
C_3\ C_2\ C_1\ C_1^0 & \qquad & C_3\ C_1^2\ C_1\ V \\
C_3\ C_1^2\ C_1\ C_1^0 & \qquad & C_1^3\ C_2\ C_1\ V \\
C_1^3\ C_2\ C_1\ C_1^0 & \qquad & C_1^3\ C_1^2\ C_1\ V \\
C_1^3\ C_1^2\ C_1\ C_1^0 & &
\end{array}
$$

Generation of derivational strings can be effected, however, also through the operation of application.

Within the framework of the explanatory generative model of the phonological syllable, the operation of application consists of the addition, either from the left or from the right, of basic or converse basic classes of consonantal phonemes to basic phonemic strings or converse basic phonemic strings. For instance, if we take the basic string $C_3\,C_2\,C_1\,V$, and apply to it the basic class C_1 we obtain the string:

$$C^3_1\;C^2_3\;C_2\;C_1\;V.$$

Additional application of the basic class C_1 yields the string:

$$C^3_1\;C^{(3)2}_1\;C^3_3\;C_2\;C_1\;V$$

Repeated applications of this class will yield the strings:

$$C^3_1\;C^{(3)2}_1\;C^{(3)2}_1\;C^2_3\;C_2\;C_1\;V$$
$$C^3_2\;C^{(3)2}_1\;C^{(3)2}_1\;C^{(3)2}_1\;C^2_3\;C_2\;C_1\;V$$
$$C^3_1\;C^{(3)2}_1\;C^{(3)2}_1\;C^{(3)2}_1\;C^{(3)2}_1\;C^2_3\;C_2\;C_1\;V$$
$$C^1_3\;C^{(3)2}_1\;C^{(3)2}_1\;C^{(3)2}_1\;C^{(3)2}_1\;C^{(3)2}_1\;C^2_3\;C_2\;C_1\;V\text{ etc.}$$

We see that the operation of application has a recursive character: whichever basic class of consonantal phonemes we select, after applying it from the left to the string of initials, it is automatically mapped by the dominative parameter D_3, i.e. it appears in the position of the absolutely dominant class; at the same time the adjacent class of consonants is automatically mapped by the dominative parameter D_2, i.e. it appears in the position of a class of consonantal phonemes which is dominated by one class of consonantal phonemes and which, in its stead, dominates another class of consonantal phonemes. Repeated applications repeat this process: that class which is applied from the left becomes the absolutely dominant class, and the adjacent class is converted from an absolutely dominant class into a class which is dominated by one class and which, in turn, dominates another class, etc.

We see that the operation of application is closely connected with the operation of mapping of classes by the relation of domination.

In summing up: the operations of mirror reflection, of mapping of classes by relation, of substitution, and of application make it possible to generate from a finite number of basic syllabic phonemic strings and basic distributive classes of phonemes an essentially infinite number of derivational syllabic phonemic strings and derivational classes of phonemes.

4. SUBSTANTIATION OF THE EXPLANATORY GENERATIVE MODEL OF THE PHONOLOGICAL SYLLABLE

The explanatory generative model of the phonological syllable described in the preceding section is regarded as a hypothesis which is subject to verification by factual data at the descriptive plane of investigation of the phonological syllable. The problem concerns the substantiation of the explanatory model by the descriptive generative model of the phonological syllable.

The descriptive generative model of the phonological syllable is defined with the help of a finite set of phonemes and the binary operation of concatenation which unites phonemes, set up by that model, in a linear sequence from left to right. During the process of the generation of phonemic strings the model runs through a finite number of states, S_0, S_1, S_2, ..., S_q. Switching from the initial state S_0 to state S_1 the model produces the first phoneme, F_0. Passing from state S_1 into structure S_2, the model yields a second phoneme, F_1, etc. Switching to the final structure S_q, the model yields the last phoneme, F_p. Consequently, in the end we obtain the phonemic string F_0, F_1, F_2, ..., F_p.

Our problem concerns the need to investigate the specific features of the structure of phonemic strings generated by the descriptive model, and to derive them from the explanatory generative model of the phonological syllable.

We will commence with a question: which feature of the structure of phonemic strings generated by the descriptive model induces us to formulate the rule $S \rightarrow In/O + V$ in the explanatory model?

This rule can be substantiated by the generally known empirical fact that in all languages of the world the limitations in the selection of consonants and vowels are minimal specifically at the point of contact between a vowel phoneme and a prevocalic group of consonantal phonemes. It is in this position that the consonantal paradigm encounters the greatest number of oppositions.

The following four rules belonging to the basic part of the explanatory model stipulate that limitations in the selection of consonants are unequal at the point of contact of various positions within a group of consonants. The general principle holds that, being given three consonantal phonemes *X*, *Y*, *Z*, where between *X* and *Y* there exists a lesser freedom of selection in respect to the replacement of these consonants by other consonants than between *Y* and *Z*, we postulate a greater cohesive strength between *X* and *Y* than between *Y* and *Z* and, consequently, unite *X* and *Y* into one group which is contraposed to the phoneme *Z*. On the other hand, if we discover that a lesser freedom in respect to the replacement of one phoneme by another exists at the contact point of the phonemes *Y* and *Z*, then in this case, vice versa, we unite into one group the phonemes *Y* and *Z*, and contrapose this group to the phoneme *X*. As a result, we obtain two different branching diagrams of the generation of the phonological syllable:

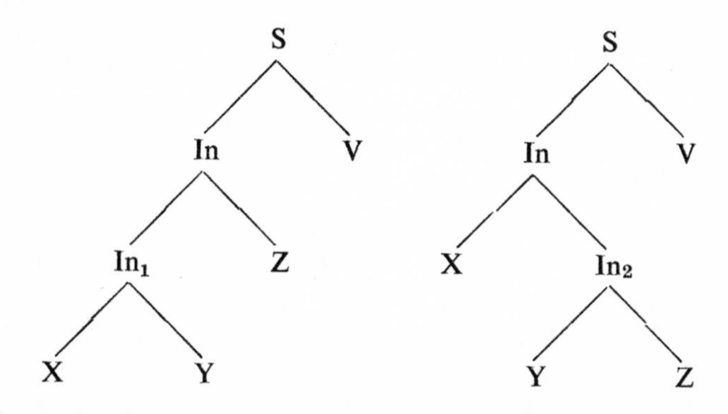

It is necessary to point out that our scheme of the generation of the phonological syllable is of an ideal type, and in its abstract form is certainly not suitable to every natural language. For instance, there exist languages in which the prevocalic group cannot contain more than two consonants; in this case the just examined problem disappears. As any ideal scheme, our scheme should be regarded simply as an abstract basis for the construction of concrete schemes of the generation of a phonological syllable which depends on the empirical features of this or that natural language.

We will now concentrate on the nature of the empirical basis for the postulation of the relation of domination.

Notwithstanding which language we select, we are bound to encounter some phonological syllables of the following types: $C_3C_2C_1V$, C_2C_1V, C_1V, V, or VC_1, VC_1C_2, $VC_1C_2C_3$. In all these phonological syllables the obligatory element is V; C_1, C_2, and C_3 are facultative elements. Furthermore, if we compare the strings $C_3C_2C_1$, C_2C_1, C_1, C_1C_2, $C_1C_2C_3$ we realize that in all these strings C_1 constitutes the obligatory element and the remaining elements are facultative. Thus, C_1 is optional in relation to V but constant in relation to the other elements of the phonological syllable. Further, comparing the strings C_3C_2, C_2, C_2C_3, we conclude that in these strings C_2 constitutes the obligatory element and C_3 the facultative element. Consequently, C_2 is simultaneously a facultative and a obligatory element; in relation to V and C_1 it is facultative, in relation to C_3 obligatory. We also see that C_3 is facultative in all cases. On the basis of these empirical facts we then postulate the relation of domination for the elements of the phonological syllable, regarding V as the absolute dominant element, C_1 and C_2 as relative dominant elements, and C_3 as the absolute dominated element.

Let us now consider the nature of the empirical basis which underlies the operation of mapping of classes by the relation of domination.

The empirical basis which underlies the operation of mapping of classes by the relation of domination is contingent on the fact that one and the same phoneme can possess simultaneously several dominative parameters. For instance, the ancient-Greek phoneme *s* had two dominative parameters, D_3 and D_1. The Czech liquid phonemes *r* and *l* have dominative parameters of both consonantal and vowel phonemes. If all dominative parameters of a given phoneme were to be regarded as equally important in regard to the determination of its membership in any one class, then the distributive classification of phonemes would become superficial and trivial; such an approach to the distributive classification of phonemes would fail to point out the inherent relationships among phonemes within the system of the phonological syllable. In order to enable the distributive classification of phonemes to expose the inherent relationships among phonemes it is essential to isolate from the number of dominative parameters of the given phoneme a single parameter which is decisive in regard to the determination of the membership of that phoneme in a specific phonemic class; the remaining dominative parameters of the phoneme should be regarded as the results of the subjection of the phonemic class to which the phoneme belongs to the operation of mapping of classes by the relation of domination. This reasoning leads us to divide dominative parameters into basic and mapping. A phonemic class is defined only by its basic dominative parameter; the mapping parameters produce *D*-images of the given phonemic class. The division of dominative parameters into basic and reflected has, additionally, a relative character: a dominative parameter which is basic in respect to one phonemic class constitutes the mapping parameter of another phonemic class, and vice versa.

There arises the question of the nature of the objective criteria to be considered in the definition of basic and mapping dominative parameters of this or that phonemic class. These criteria are to be found in the concept of quantity of information. In order to clarify the resolution of our problem by the use of the concept of quantity of information we will examine the meaning of information within the sphere of information theory.

In the information theory the concept of information has nothing in common with the general concept of information as communication which contains a definite semantic content. The information theory views information as the degree of indeterminateness among the possible choices. For example, if in answering a question we are confronted with an equal possibility of choice between the answers "yes" and "no", then both these words possess equal information. However, if we were to answer always "no", then the word "no" would possess no information at all, since in all cases only one answer would be expected, i.e. any uncertainty as to the choice of an answer would be eliminated. In old chronicles in which all sentences began with the conjunction *and*, this conjunction held no information since at the beginning of a sentence no other word but this conjunction was expected. If the possibility of a choice between "yes" and "no" would permit the calculation of a greater probability of "yes", it would follow that "yes" possesses less information than "no". These considerations enable us to formulate the following principle: the greater the probability of the appearance of the given element the smaller its information and, conversely, the smaller the probability of the appearance of the given element, the greater its information.

We will apply this principle to the resolution of our problem. Observation of the facts of language leads to the establishment of the fact that one and the same phoneme which is characterized by several dominative parameters has an unequal probability of appearance in respect to the different dominative parameters. Maximal probability of the appearance of the given phoneme is subject to minimal limitations on the part of the phonemic context and vice versa, minimal probability of the appearance of the given phoneme occurs in those cases where the phoneme is subject to maximal limitations on the part of the phonemic context. Since the individuality of each phoneme is best revealed in those cases where the phoneme is subject to minimal limitations on the part of the phonemic context, i.e. where the given phoneme possesses minimal information, these cases should, indeed, be adopted as the basic dominative parameter of the given phoneme. The cases where the phoneme possesses greater information should be, correspondingly, regarded as the mapping dominative parameters of that phoneme.

In order to further clarify the above discussion we will return to the earlier introduced examples. The ancient-Greek phoneme *s* had, as has already been pointed out, two dominative parameters, D_1 and D_3. In respect to D_3 the phoneme *s* possessed smaller information than in respect to D_1 (since in the position immediately preceding vowels the phoneme *s* could occur only after the stops *p* and *k*, it was thus subject to maximal limitations on the part of the phonemic context). Consequently, D_3 should be regarded as the basic dominative parameter of the ancient-Greek phoneme *s*, and D_1 as the reflected dominative parameter of that phoneme. Aš was said above, the Czech liquid phonemes *r* and *l* possess dominative parameters of both consonantal and vowel phonemes. However, *r* and *l* behave as vowel phonemes only between consonants, between zero and a consonant, or between a consonant and zero, while they behave as consonantal phonemes between vowels, between zero and a vowel, between a vowel and zero, between a consonant and vowel, and finally between a vowel and a consonant. Hence it is possible to conclude that the phonemes *r* and *l* possess maximal information in respect to D_0 since in that case they are subject to maximal limitations on the part of the phonological context. Consequently, D_1 should be regarded as the mapping dominative parameter of these phonemes, and the phonemes *r* and ʻ should relate to the class of consonantal phonemes. It is selfevident that only one of the consonantal dominative parameters of the phonemes *r* and *l* should be regarded as basic, but this question will not be taken up at this time.

Hence, from among the dominative parameters of a given phoneme one should select as basic that parameter in regard to which the phoneme possesses a minimal quantity of information; all remaining dominative parameters should be considered to be the mapping parameters of the given phoneme.

We see that the operation of mapping of classes by the relation of domination does in fact disclose the essential aspects of the inherent relationships among phonemes within the system of the phonological syllable.

Having examined the empirical purport of the rules of the basic component of the explantory generative model of the phonological syllable, of the relation of domination, and of the operation of the mapping of classes by the relation of domination we have covered the main aspects of this model which required a special analysis from the standpoint of their empirical substantiation. The empirical purport of the other aspects of this model, for instance the operation of substitution and the operation of application, is sufficiently selfevident, and so they do not require a special analysis from this standpoint.

5. RESULTS OF INVESTIGATION

The examination of the structure of the phonological syllable does not require the establishment of rules of correspondence since the phonological syllable constitutes a phonological construct whose connection with the level of observation is not direct, but is dependent on other phonological constructs, i.e. the phonemes which compose it. The phonological syllable can be considered as an elementary quantum of phonemic chain within whose framework there exist definite rules of phoneme combinations.

Within the framework of the two-level theory of phonology the patterning of the phonological syllable requires a preliminary splitting of the level of constructs into two planes: the descriptive plane and the immanent plane. At the descriptive plane we perceive the external relationships among phonemes, at the immanent plane their inherent relationships. Differentiation of these planes necessitates the construction of two generative models of the phonological syllable: the descriptive model and the explanatory model.

The descriptive generative model of the phonological syllable represents a phonological variant of the general-semiotic finite state model. By the same token, the explanatory model of the phonological syllable constitutes a phonological analogy of the phrase structure model fused with the transformational model of the grammar of language. The descriptive and the explanatory generative models of the phonological syllable are a closely related pair of models: the goal of the latter is the reduction of the external relationships among phonemes, revealed by the former model, to inherent relationships among the phonemes.

The explanatory model of the phonological syllable consists of two parts which need to be strictly differentiated; the two parts are the basic and the derivational part. Phonemic strings generated by the basic part of this model are subject to further transformation which is effected through four operations: the operation of mirror reflection, the operation of the mapping of classes by the relation of domination, the operation of substitution, and the operation of application. These four operations transform the basic phonemic strings into derivational phonemic strings. Together these operations enable us to generate from a finite number of basic syllabic phonemic strings and basic distributive phonemic classes an essentially infinite number of derivational syllabic phonemic strings and derivational distributive phonemic classes.

CONCLUSION

THE TWO-LEVEL THEORY OF PHONOLOGY AND THE PRINCIPLE OF COMPLEMENTARITY

Now that we have set forth the two-level theory of phonology and have considered within the framework of this theory the method of binary patterning of phonological oppositions as well as the method of patterning the phonological syllable, it will be useful to review this theory generally in a broad methodological context. We intend to relate the two-level theory of phonology to the principle of complementarity which is of considerable significance in the comprehension of certain fundamental epistemological situations which possess an analogous character although they arise in various, at the first glance unconnected, areas of knowledge.[1]

The discovery of the principle of complementarity is the achievement of the outstanding Danish physicist Niels Bohr. At the onset N. Bohr formulated the principle of complementarity as a purely physical principle; later, however, he extended its validity also to other areas of knowledge, above all to biology and psychology. At the present time the principle of complementarity is interpreted as a general methodological principle which characterizes a definite epistemological situation.

The essence of the principle of complementarity is described by N. Bohr as follows: "In order to characterize the relation between phenomena observed under different experimental conditions one has introduced the term complementarity to emphasize that such

[1] The possibility of regarding phonology from the standpoint of the principle of complementarity is examined in S. K. Schaumjan, "Der Gegenstand der Phonologie", *Zeitschrift für Phonetik und allgemeine Sprachwissenschaft,* 3 (1957).

phenomena together exhaust all definable information about the atomic objects. Far from containing any arbitrary renunciation of customary physical explanation, the notion of complementarity refers directly to our position as observers in a domain of experience where unambiguous application of the concept used in the description of phenomena depends essentially on the conditions of observation."[2] Elsewhere Bohr writes: "... in atomic physics, to characterize the relationship between experiences obtained by different experimental arrangements and visualizable only by mutually exclusive ideas, we may truly say that different human cultures are complementary to each other."[3]

In illustrating the principle of complementarity we can turn to the problem of the nature of light. Contemporary physics teaches that light has a double nature and, consequently, that diffusion of light cannot be described by a single theory. To describe it we must resort, writes the Polish physicist L. Infeld, to two theories, the corpuscular and the wave theory.[4]

The corpusculat theory and the wave theory cannot be reduced to one another. They are at once mutually exclusive and mutually complementary. This paradoxical epistemological situation where the examined phenomenon can be exhaustively described only by means of mutually exclusive and at the same time mutually complementary theories necessitates the creation of syncretic, dual concepts; in the given case such a dual concept is the concept of corpuscle-wave. Other examples of syncretic dual concepts are time-space and mass-energy.

If we revert from physics to phonology, the linguist who observes the sounds of language must inevitably admit that as an observer of the sound properties of language he is forced to utilize two kinds of experimental methods: on the one hand, the sounds of language can be subjected to experimental investigation in respect to their acoustic nature or to the physiological conditions of their forma-

[2] N. Bohr, *Atomic Physics and Human Knowledge* (New York, 1958), p. 99.
[3] N. Bohr, *op. cit.*, p. 30.
[4] L. Infeld, *Albert Einstein: his Work and its Influence on our World* (New York, 1950), p. 108.

tion and, on the other hand, it is possible to introduce different kinds of experiments with linguistic informants with view to the establishment of objective phonemic contrasts present in the given language.

These two kinds of experimental methods of investigation can be called the physical and the semiotic experimental method of investigation in phonology. The specific epistemological character of the semiotic and physical experimental methods of investigation in phonology consists in the fact that their results cannot be united into a single picture. Their results are mutually exclusive and, at the same time, mutually complementary. As a proof we can examine the problem of the identity of the sounds of language. For instance, investigation of the nasal vowel *ę* and the non-nasal vowel *e* in Polish by the physical experimental methods discloses an essential difference between these two vowels and relates them to two different classes of vowel sounds, to nasal and non-nasal vowels. However, investigation of the same vowels by the semiotic methods, i.e. by means of data of a linguistic informant concerning phonemic contrasts, leads to the conclusion that both vowels are identical. We see that the results of physical and semiotic methods of investigation of the Polish vowels *ę* and *e* cannot be united into a single picture. If we attempted to do that we could encounter an irreconcilable contradiction; we would have to admit that the vowels *ę* and *e* are mutually identical as well as non-identical. In order to avoid this contradiction, as well as other, analogous contradictions present in the observation of other sounds of natural languages, we have to admit that the picture of the identity of the language sounds obtained by physical experimental methods of investigation and the picture of the identity of the language sounds obtained by semiotic experimental methods of investigation are mutually exclusive and, at the same time, mutually complementary. Hence we encounter an epistemological situation which is analogous to epistemological situations encountered in physics and in other sciences. All such situations are embraced by the principle of complementarity.

The sounds of language possess a double nature as does light (on another plane, of course).

The phenomenon of the double nature of the sounds of language has been recognized implicitly by contemporary phonology. But because this phenomenon has been recognized by contemporary phonology only implicitly, there have not made, up to the present day, the necessary inferences.

As one of the necessary inferences based on this phenomenon we have introduced into phonology a number of basic syncretic, dual concepts which reflect mutually exclusive and, at the same time, mutually complementary results of physical and semiotic experimental methods of investigation in phonology. At the level of observation in the two-level theory of phonology there occur the following syncretic dual concepts:

(1) sound of language — phonemoid;
(2) acoustic property — differentoid;
(3) acoustic property — culminatoid.

The application of the physical experimental methods of investigation causes us to consider the sounds of language and acoustic properties as separate concepts. Phonemoids, differentoids, and culminatoids, as separate concepts, are the result of the application of the semiotic experimental methods of investigation. Since the results of the physical and the semiotic experimental methods of investigation are mutually exclusive but, at the same time, mutually complementary, the separate concepts are united into the aforementioned syncretic dual concepts: sound of language-phonemoid, acoustic property-differentoid, and acoustic property-culminatoid.

As was pointed out at the proper place, the concepts of phonemoid, differentoid, and culminatoid are correlated with corresponding constructs, the concept of phoneme, the concept of differentor, and the concept of culminator. Postulation of these constructs was dictated by the need to explain the results of the application of the semiotic experimental methods of investigation in phonology. If we approach the two-level theory of phonology from the standpoint of the principle of complementarity we can consider the demarcation of the two levels of phonological abstraction, the level of phonological observation and the level of phonological constructs, and the related pairs of corresponding concepts, phonemoid and phoneme, differentoid and differentor, culminatoid and culminator, as unavoidable consequences of the admission of the double nature of the sound aspect of language.

The above discussion leads to the assertion that within the framework of the two-level theory of phonology we can establish a mutual relationship between the methodological principle of two-levelness and the methodological principle of complementarity. Consequences of the phonological phenomena established in compliance with both these principles are mutually harmonious and effect a mutual reinforcement, shedding a new light on the foundation of the two-level theory of phonology, and ensuring a considerable degree of clarity and reliability.

INDEX OF NAMES